Palgrave's Critical Policing Studies

Series Editors
Elizabeth Aston
School of Applied Sciences
Edinburgh Napier University
Edinburgh, UK

Michael Rowe
Department of Social Sciences Newcastle City Campus
Northumbria University
Newcastle upon Tyne, UK

In a period where police and academics benefit from coproduction in research and education, the need for a critical perspective on key challenges is pressing. Palgrave's Critical Policing Studies is a series of high quality, research-based books which examine a range of cutting-edge challenges and developments to policing and their social and political contexts. They seek to provide evidence-based case studies and high quality research, combined with critique and theory, to address fundamental challenging questions about future directions in policing.

Through a range of formats including monographs, edited collections and short form Pivots, this series provides research at a variety of lengths to suit both academics and practitioners. The series brings together new topics at the forefront of policing scholarship but is also organised around who the contemporary police are, what they do, how they go about it, and the ever-changing external environments which bear upon their work.

The series will cover topics such as: the purpose of policing and public expectations, public health approaches to policing, policing of cybercrime, environmental policing, digital policing, social media, Artificial Intelligence and big data, accountability of complex networks of actors involved in policing, austerity, public scrutiny, technological and social changes, over-policing and marginalised groups, under-policing and corporate crime, institutional abuses, policing of climate change, ethics, workforce, education, evidence-based policing, and the pluralisation of policing.

More information about this series at
http://www.palgrave.com/gp/series/16586

James J. Nolan · Frank Crispino ·
Timothy Parsons
Editors

Policing in an Age of Reform

An Agenda for Research and Practice

palgrave
macmillan

Editors
James J. Nolan
Department of Sociology and Anthropology
West Virginia University
Morgantown, WV, USA

Frank Crispino
Department of Chemistry, Biochemistry
Université du Québec à Trois-Rivière
Québec, QC, Canada

Timothy Parsons
School of Justice Studies
Liverpool John Moores University
Liverpool, UK

ISSN 2730-535X ISSN 2730-5368 (electronic)
Palgrave's Critical Policing Studies
ISBN 978-3-030-56764-4 ISBN 978-3-030-56765-1 (eBook)
https://doi.org/10.1007/978-3-030-56765-1

Cover credit: Hal Bergman

This Palgrave Macmillan imprint is published by the registered company Springer Nature Switzerland AG
The registered company address is: Gewerbestrasse 11, 6330 Cham, Switzerland

Preface

In the first decade of the twenty-first century, a few short years following the 9/11 terror attacks in the United States, a group of police officials from North America and Europe met in Warsaw, Poland to discuss the problem of hate crime. The group was convened by the Organisation for Security and Co-operation in Europe's (OSCE) Office of Democratic Institutions and Human Rights (ODIHR) to develop training for law enforcement officers throughout Europe. Crimes motivated by bigotry were certainly familiar to most police officials, but the term "hate crime" was relatively new and still unfamiliar. Members of the group developed a series of hate crime seminars entitled the Law Enforcement Officers Programme for Combating Hate Crime (LEOP-CHC). They then delivered these trainings to a wide-ranging group of law enforcement officials from countries throughout Europe who convened in London, Paris, Warsaw, Sarajevo, Vienna, Budapest, Kiev, Cordoba, and Zagreb for these sessions. When our work with ODIHR was completed, many members of the initial LEOP group stayed in regular contact, letting each other know about professional progress and current projects mostly related to policing and police reform.

Having been police officers or members of national security forces in England, France, Canada, Hungary, Croatia, and the United States, we were all deeply invested in the profession. In the decade following our work with ODIHR, some of the group members went on to complete doctorates in various fields including education, social psychology, and forensic sciences and are now faculty members at major universities. In addition, two of the team members became senior officials at the national police academies in Croatia and Hungary and have been heavily involved in police training. In the decade following the ODIHR work, all of the team remained active in police training in Europe, North America, and the Middle East on a full array of topics relating to police operations and administration.

Then, in September 2018 as the second decade of the twenty-first century was coming to a close, four members of the original team met in Ontario, Canada for a LEOP reunion. We discovered during our discussions that we were prepared by our formal education, scholarly research, and practical experiences to consider writing a book together. This was an exciting prospect, but we took our time to consider the topics most relevant to policing in an age of reform. It took us about a year to prepare the proposal, getting commitments from just the right mix of authors to provide a rich body of work that is tailored for our rapidly changing times.

As we prepare to launch this book at the beginning of the third decade of the twenty-first century, there is so much uncertainty in the world, epitomized by the current worldwide covid-19 pandemic and widespread, international protests over police violence. Wars and world dice-reshuffling are raging in faraway places leaving millions of refugees looking for safe places to go. A general malaise is pervasive throughout the world, and many of the problems the police face locally are inextricably linked to crises occurring globally—and out of their direct control.

Policing in an Age of Reform provides many perspectives on policing in the current era. It is written for a wide and diverse audience, including academics, university students, policing scholars, police officers, forensic scientists, community members, and anyone who is interested in knowing about the field of policing and how it might be reformed. Here is a spoiler alert: Most of the authors were police officers and are now professors and researchers. They are also friends and respected colleagues. But, they do not always see things the same way. So, the reader will likely get a wide variety of viewpoints which we believe is a significant strength of this book.

Morgantown, USA — James J. Nolan
Trois-Rivières, Canada — Frank Crispino
Liverpool, UK — Timothy Parsons

Acknowledgments

The editors would like to thank all chapter authors for their willingness to contribute to this book. We acknowledge that we would not have worked together on this book without first meeting each other some 15 years ago. The Office of Democratic Institutions and Human Rights (ODIHR) organisers who initially brought us together to address hate crimes include Jo-Anne Bishop, Daniel Milo, Paul Goldenberg, Mark Genatempo, and John Howley. In addition to the editors, many of the book's chapters are authored or coauthored by members of the original ODIHR team, including James Brown, Zsolt Molnar, and Danijela Petković. We also appreciate the kind support we have received from Palgrave Macmillan publishers, especially Josephine Taylor and Liam Inscoe-Jones. The manuscript benefitted immensely from the thoughtful comments we received from three anonymous reviewers.

From James J. Nolan: Many good things converged in order to make this book possible. The most important was meeting my coeditors, Tim and Frank, who became great friends and valued colleagues. In addition, Chapters 5 and 12 were supported, in significant part, with funding from the United States Department of Justice, Office of Community Oriented Policing [Cooperative Agreement Number 2007-CK-WX-K009 to James Nolan]. I am grateful to the police departments in Wilmington, DE, Pittsburgh, PA, Wheeling, WV and Cleveland, OH for their support during this research. I also recognize the contributions of Norman Conti, Jack McDevitt, Susie Bennett, Ellen Rodrigues, Rachel Stein, Elizabeth Walling, Jeri Kirby, and students from West Virginia University who participated in various ways during this project. I also acknowledge the support I received from the Center for Drug and Health Studies at the University of Delaware and the Department of Sociology & Anthropology at West Virginia University. Many of the chapters in this volume were improved by the keen editing eyes of James Norton, an independent scholar/activist in West Virginia. I owe a special debt of gratitude to Brianna Squires, a bright criminology student who was instrumental in organizing the early neighborhood research. Tragically, Brianna died of a gunshot wound to the chest during a domestic argument with an off-duty Morgantown, WV police officer before the project ended. She was loved by many and her sudden death was a huge loss for us all. Finally, this project would not have been possible without the support of my family, especially my wife and closest friend Pamela Bopp Nolan.

From Frank Crispino: Although easily (and certainly rightly) labeled as a forensic scientist and academic, my involvement and thought on policing couldn't have been so relevant without the various positions I served for 25 years in my former Institution, the French Gendarmerie nationale, heartily dedicated to the French people security and safe being. I would like to express here my deep recognition to the various officers I met there, who enriched my vision and service as a criminal investigation, counterterrorist officer, and forensic manager. I regard my still current position as scientific collaborator at the Pole judiciaire de la gendarmerie nationale (merging the forensic Institut de recherche de la gendarmerie nationale and the Service central de renseignement criminel—Criminal intelligence center—) as a continuous and common trust extending to my academic career now. This second life gave me the opportunity to deepen my interest and so share my experience with students at my university (Université du Québec à Trois-Rivières, Canada) and researchers of the Centre international de criminologie comparée (https://www.

cicc-iccc.org/fr), the Laboratoire de recherche en criminalistique (www.uqtr.ca/LRC) and Universities of Lausanne (Switzerland) and Sydney (Australia), who continue to fuel my commitment for police science.

Last, but not least, the participation 15 years ago as French representative to the OSCE/ODIHR Hate Crime endeavour initiated a strong network with James, Jim, and Tim, that not only ended up with this edition adventure, but also a friendship of a lifetime. Nevertheless, nothing would have been possible, hence not this book, without the perennial support for these last 30 years of my wife, Nathalie, and my kids Corentin, Clothilde, and Clement who followed me worldwide, two of them up to our new country.

From Timothy Parsons: I am very much indebted to the assistance and support provided to me by Mehmood Naqshbandi. He has provided help and advice for more than a decade as my understanding of the issues covered in Chapter 7 evolved. This help included visits to numerous mosques and Islamic Centres in London and unlimited access to his own writing and research. Much help and support has also been provided by Dr. Robert Lambert, who over many years as an undercover police officer took enormous personal risks to protect the people of London. I would also like to thank former Assistant Commissioner Frank Armstrong QPM who actively encouraged and supported my participation in the LEOP project. My thanks also to my co-editors and great friends, Jim and Frank. Finally, I would like to thank Karon, my wife of 35 years and a former community police officer.

Contents

Notes on Contributors

Simon Baechler is head of forensic science and crime intelligence at the State Police of Neuchâtel, Switzerland. He is also a researcher and lecturer in forensic science and crime intelligence at the University of Lausanne, Switzerland, as well as an associate professor with the University of Québec in Trois-Rivières, Canada, and a collaborator of the International Centre for Comparative Criminology (ICCC). He conducted a Ph.D. related to forensic intelligence and the trafficking of fraudulent identity and travel documents. He has published several papers and chapters in various fields of forensic science, crime intelligence, and crime investigation. He is a member of the Joint Operational Team Document Fraud hosted by Europol.

James Brown is an adjunct professor at the University of Ontario, Institute of Technology. He has over 30 years of experience in policing at the municipal and international level. He has been seconded to work with Provincial and State agencies as well as with the OSCE. Brown's international experience included leading community consultations across Eastern Europe, leading police development missions to Russia, Ukraine, Poland, and Hungary, and leading Ministerial level negotiations focused on police training. During this time he led an international team of specialists in the design and delivery of the OSCE Law Enforcement Officers training program in responding to hate crimes in the OSCE Region. His Canadian police experience focused on major project management, designing and leading police reform and organisational change, business process mapping and analysis along with threat, risk, and vulnerability analysis. He has extensive experience in successfully building effective cross-functional teams; in successfully executing projects and in the management and operational application of new technologies.

Frank Crispino Director of the Forensic Science Research Group at the Université du Québec à Trois-Rivières (UQTR), regular researcher of the International Center for Comparative Criminology (CICC), Professor Crispino is author or coauthor of 2 books, 13 book chapters, more than 50 peer-reviewed articles, and more than 50 presentations worldwide.

Graduate from the French Air Force Academy and in Law, holding a Dental Identification degree, M.Phil. and Ph.D. in Forensic Science from Lausanne University, postgraduate from the French War College, Colonel Crispino joined the academy in 2012 after 25 years in the French Gendarmerie. His forensic career began in 1993, as the head of the newborn Forensic Anthropology Department at the Institut de recherche criminelle de la gendarmerie nationale (IRCGN), later of the Fingermarks and Shoemarks department.

He served for 3 years (1999–2002) as the forensic adviser of the EU Special Adviser's Office on Counterterrorism in the West Bank and the Gaza Strip.

Domestically, he was involved in various scientific investigations on serious crimes, organised crimes, and terrorism as head of two Criminal Investigation Departments in Bourges (2002–2003) and Bordeaux (2007–2011), and deputy head of the Anti-Terrorist Bureau at the General Headquarters of the French Gendarmerie in Paris (2004–2007).

He ended his military career as representative of the Division General in charge of the Pôle judiciaire de la gendarmerie nationale (PJGN), Forensic and Intelligence Hub, merging the IRCGN with the Criminal Intelligence Center.

His French and English CVs are available at www.uqtr.ca/Frankcris pino.

Olivier Delémont is a Professor in the School of Criminal Justice (Ecole des sciences criminelles) of the University of Lausanne, Switzerland. His research interests, rooted in the practice of forensic science, focus on the fields of crime scene investigation, fire and explosion investigation, and the contribution of traces for intelligence and investigative purposes. He has authored numerous peer-reviewed scientific publications, book chapters, and coauthored the Routledge International Handbook of Forensic Intelligence and Criminology. For almost 10 years, he shared his academic career with a position as a forensic scientist in the forensic brigade of a Swiss state police, where he worked in operational forensic activities. He lectures to students, law enforcement professionals and magistrates, and regularly conducts judicial expertise mandates in support of the police and judicial bodies.

Julie Delle Donne is a Ph.D. candidate in criminology at the Université de Montréal. She is interested in justice as well as private and public security. These interests have led her to enhance her expertise in criminology by completing a law degree and became a member of the Quebec Bar. Her current fields of research focus on the impact of new technologies on police organisations as well as on sexual delinquency against minors. She published a book that addresses the establishment in Québec of the police organisation called the Bureau des Enquêtes Indépendantes (BEI). She also conducted research on the adoption of social media by members of police organisations, the latter having led to several presentations and publications.

Francis Fortin is an assistant professor at the University of Montreal and researcher at the International Centre for Comparative Criminology of that university. His research focuses on cybercrime, criminal intelligence, data mining, and forensic analysis. He has published scientific papers, including one book on cyber-peadophiles and another on cybercrime. He also worked in the field of criminal investigations and intelligence for 15 years.

Joshua C. Hinkle is an Associate Professor in the Department of Criminal Justice and Criminology at Georgia State University and current editor of Criminal Justice Review. His research interests include evidence-based policing, crime and place, the disorder-crime nexus, and fear of crime. His work has been funded by the National Institute of Justice and the National Science Foundation and appears in journals such as *Criminology, Criminology & Public Policy*, the *Journal of Research in Crime and Delinquency* and the *Journal of Experimental Criminology*.

Justine Knop has spent five years studying criminology in four different countries. She completed a Bachelor of Arts in criminology from the University of Leicester in the United Kingdom, with a semester at California State University Long Beach. Her dissertation focused on the reaction of Parisians to the two terrorist attacks that occurred in Paris in 2015. She then graduated with a Masters of Science in criminology and criminalistics from the University of Montreal with a semester at the School of Criminal Sciences at the University of Lausanne in Switzerland. Her second dissertation analysed insulting tweets received by police forces across the United States and Canada. After some time working in the public sector, she is currently working as a fraud analyst for a bank app in France.

Robert Lambert, Ph.D., M.A., B.A. (Hons) served as a Metropolitan Police officer from 1977 to 2007. From 2008 to 2016 he was employed as a lecturer at the Centre for the Study of Terrorism and Political Violence (CSTPV), School of International Relations, University of St. Andrews and from 2012 to 2016 as a senior lecturer at the John Grieve Policing Centre, Faculty of Social Sciences and Humanities, London Metropolitan University. He is the author of *Countering Al-Qaeda in London: police and Muslims in partnership* (Hurst, 2011) and numerous peer-reviewed articles and book chapters on counterterrorism and community-based policing.

Zsolt Molnar is a diplomat for the Permanent Representation of Hungary to the European Union. He is a delegate to the Committee for Civilian Crisis Management (CivCom) and is working on the Common Security and Defence Policy of the EU. After graduating from the Hungarian Police College Dr. Molnár started his career in the police investigation department specialising in crimes against properties. He joined the United Nations Mission to Bosnia-Herzegovina (UN International Police Task Force: UNIPTF) in 1996. After completing his masters degree in law, he was assigned to head the Crime Prevention Academy and began to work on national and international academic courses, curriculum developments and other educational programs related to law enforcement and community development; tackling human trafficking and smuggling; strategising public security and safety and other subjects. Dr. Molnár has become a guest lecturer for the Budapest-based International Law Enforcement Academy (ILEA) and conducted training courses mainly in Europe, and in central/south Asia (Belorussia, Montenegro, Kirgizstan, Uzbekistan, Turkmenistan, and Afghanistan). He was a trainer in the OSCE/ODIHR sponsored law enforcement officers training programme against hate crime (LEOP), as well as a consultant of the Geneva Centre for Democratic Control over Armed Forces (DCAF) in their Indonesian mission, as well as in Ukraine and the Western Balkans. Mr. Molnár actively contributed to the training programme on integrity management for the public administration in Hungary (National University of Public Service).

Vincent Mousseau is a Ph.D. student (Vanier Scholar) in criminology at the School of Criminology of the University of Montreal and an associate researcher at the Forensic Research Group (LRC) of the University of Quebec in Trois-Rivieres. His main research interests sit at the intersection of sociology, criminology, and forensic science and include crime scene investigation and management and decision-making regarding the deployment of forensic resources by law enforcement agencies. His Ph.D. research aims to understand the decision-making and interpretative process underlying the prioritisation of the strategies used by crime scene examiners when searching for physical evidence. He is the author or coauthor of 3 book chapters, 3 research reports, 7 peer-reviewed articles, and more than 30 oral presentations given internationally. In parallel with his academic activities, he also works at the Laboratoire des Sciences judiciaires et de Medecine legale and at the Ecole Nationale de Police du Quebec.

James J. Nolan is a Professor and Chair of the Department of Sociology and Anthropology at West Virginia University. His research and teaching has focused on community policing, neighbourhood dynamics, police procedures, crime measurement, hate crimes, and equity and inclusion in higher education. He is the coauthor of "The Violence of Hate: Understanding Harmful Forms of Bias and Bigotry." His recent publications have appeared in the *Journal of Quantitative Criminology, Policing & Society, Criminal Justice Studies, Homicide Studies, Journal of Criminal Justice, The British Journal of Criminology,* and *The American Sociologist.* Dr. Nolan's professional career began as a police officer in Wilmington, Delaware, USA. In 13 years with that department, he worked in a variety of divisions, including patrol, community policing, organised crime and vice, and planning and research. He is a 1992 graduate of the FBI National Academy. Dr. Nolan earned a Ph.D. from Temple University where his graduate work focused on the study of group and social processes.

Victor Olisa is a Visiting Fellow at the London School of Economics and a Visiting Lecturer at the Universities of Portsmouth, Liverpool John Moores, and West London. Victor served as a police officer for 35 years. He joined Surrey Police in 1982 straight from university. He transferred to the City of London Police in 1990 and worked in various roles, including the Fraud Squad as Detective Inspector. In 2003 he was seconded to the Home Office to work on Stop and Search, which involved advising Ministers on policy and chief police officers on good practice. In 2005 he was awarded a Ph.D. in Criminology at the London School of Economics and Political Science (LSE). He transferred on promotion to the Metropolitan Police Service (MPS) in 2006 and in 2012 was promoted to Chief Superintendent and worked in Bexley and Haringey as Borough Commander. In 2016 he headed the MPS Diversity and Inclusion Unit. In 2017, he was awarded the Queen's Police Medal for distinguished police service. He joined the Board of Governors at NACRO in May 2020.

Timothy Parsons is a Visiting Lecturer in Police Studies at Liverpool John Moores University and an independent training consultant specialising in police education and reform programmes. Before taking up his current appointment he was a Senior Lecturer in Policing and Criminology at the John Grieve Centre for Policing and Community Safety, London Metropolitan University, a position held from 2010 to 2018. His research and teaching has focused on community policing, police reform, Islamism, and violent extremism. He has taught and lectured on these subjects in 25 countries advising both police forces and national governments. He has also led a number of research projects on policing for organisations including the OSCE, IOM, and OHCHR. Dr Parsons served for 30 years as a police officer with the City of London Police and has a doctorate in education from King's College London.

Danijela Petković is a Chief Police Advisor and a lecturer at the Police College/Police Academy of the Ministry of the Interior of the Republic of Croatia. She is a lawyer by profession and has been working at the Ministry for more than 30 years. As the Assistant Head of the Police Academy, she has been responsible for international and interinstitutional cooperation for many years, contributing to the establishment of the CEPOL National Unit, and still participating as a Voting member of the Management Board. Her main area of expertise is also protection and promotion of human rights. In that capacity she introduced the hate crime training for the police and worked closely with civil society organisations. She teaches Introduction into law and Constitutional law, and Social-communication skills practicum. She has published several articles and participated in different projects related to human rights and law enforcement training.

Olivier Ribaux is director of the School of Criminal Justice, University of Lausanne, Switzerland. After a 10-year career as a crime analyst in a Swiss cantonal police, he joined the university to conduct researches on the contribution of forensic science to intelligence-led policing (forensic intelligence). His interdisciplinary studies range from the expression of methods to the development of computerised tools, mostly for the monitoring and analysis of repetitive crimes. Much of his work is implemented in operational police environments in Switzerland. He is now developing a focus on digital transformations in forensic science and policing. He teaches crime analysis and forensic intelligence to university students, police officers, and magistrates.

Claude Roux is a Professor of Forensic Science and the founding Director of the Centre for Forensic Science at the University of Technology Sydney (UTS). His research activities cover a broad spectrum of forensic science, including microtraces and chemical criminalistics, documents, fingerprints, forensic intelligence, and the contribution of forensic science to policing and security. His professional motivation has been largely driven by his vision of forensic science as a distinctive academic and holistic research-based discipline. Claude has published more than 190 refereed papers and 26 book chapters. His research has been funded by the Australian Research Council, the Australian Defence Science and Technology Group, the US Combating Terrorism Technical Support Office and the US National Institute of Justice. Claude is a member of a number of expert and advisory groups in Australia and overseas. He is the current President of the International Association of Forensic Sciences (IAFS) and a Fellow of the Royal Society of New South Wales. He also serves on the Scientific Advisory Board of the International Criminal Court. He earned his undergraduate and Ph.D. degrees in forensic science and criminology from the University of Lausanne, Switzerland.

List of Figures

List of Tables

1

Introduction to Policing in an Age of Reform

Timothy Parsons, James J. Nolan, and Frank Crispino

Introduction

These are chaotic times marked by political, economic, and social upheavals that have resulted in war, genocide, mass refugee resettlement, and global and regional terrorism. Between the time of ideation of this book (2018) and its edition, international events seem to support our

T. Parsons
School of Justice Studies, Liverpool John Moores University, Liverpool, UK
e-mail: t.f.parsons@ljmu.ac.uk

J. J. Nolan (✉)
Department of Sociology and Anthropology, West Virginia University, Morgantown, WV, USA
e-mail: jim.nolan@mail.wvu.edu

F. Crispino
Department of Chemistry, Biochemistry, Université du Québec à Trois-rivière, Québec, QC, Canada
e-mail: frank.crispino@uqtr.ca

J. J. Nolan et al. (eds.), *Policing in an Age of Reform*, Palgrave's Critical Policing Studies,
https://doi.org/10.1007/978-3-030-56765-1_1

questioning about policing in an age of reform. As we begin this journey, we point out that simply living in an age of reform may or may not call for *police reform*. But, it does mean that the police institution is impacted by political, social, economic, and environmental turmoil in ways that impend over its stability. The French yellow vests ongoing protest could be seen as a first relevant incentive. As we wrote and collected colleagues' papers, a global pandemic killed thousands, and may threaten the long-term economic stability of the world. At the time we concluded this book, a "defund the police" trend was spreading in the United States following George Floyd's death, which also sparked worldwide a diffuse movement coalescing anti-racism, social inequality, and also various obvious political agendas. It only confirmed our stance that the police, as an institution, does not stand isolated from these events or from the many other institutions bearing the brunt of their combined force.

Later in this chapter, we describe varying perspectives on police reform. But first, the authors will briefly and broadly describe the conditions under which reform of the police is considered in Great Britain, the United States, and France.

Conditions for Reform in Great Britain

For people in Great Britain the impact of contemporary events has been profound. In March 2020, the British prime minister in a bold effort to combat the COVID-19 viral pandemic introduced what looked to many citizens very much like martial law (It is important to clarify that Britain was *not* under martial law, there were no troops on the street and the country was still fully under the control of a democratically elected government). Everyone in Britain was ordered to remain at home, to stay indoors and only to venture out to buy essential items such as food or medicine. The public was informed that these measures were mandatory not advisory and that the police had been given instructions to take enforcement action in the event of non-compliance. At the same time as these restrictions were being announced, very similar curtailments on citizens' lives were being implemented by governments across Europe, most notably in France, Italy, and Spain.

These sudden policy changes had major implications for policing in Britain. There is no national police force in Britain, policing continues to be delivered by a multiplicity of separate regional and provincial forces. Many are small, deploying only a thousand or so police officers. Police officers in Britain are still largely unarmed, an arrangement that most officers wish to continue. Unlike neighbouring countries in Europe, Britain's police forces are not backed up by a fully armed quasi-military force such as a gendarmerie, carabinieri, or civil guard. Police numbers in Britain have reduced by 20,000 over the period 2009–2016 (Disney & Simpson, 2017) and the country has a very small standing army. So, for police leaders in Britain as well as the British public the imposition of effective martial law by the government had some major implications. It quickly became clear that the police in Britain had neither the resources nor the intention of maintaining this martial law-lite by force or coercion. The aim was to use the well-honed policing techniques of politeness and persuasion, a markedly different approach to that being used in some countries in Europe where rigorous enforcement was the preferred tactic from the start. This approach had further relevance after the incidents of public disorder in London, Bristol and elsewhere in Britain that followed directly from the televised killing of George Floyd, a black man by police in Minnesota, USA on 25 May 2020. This highly controversial incident occurred while Britain was still under strict restrictions on public movement introduced to suppress the global pandemic. Nevertheless, crowds of disorderly and often violent protestors assembled in Central London where officers were violently attacked, property was damaged, and public monuments defaced. In the city of Bristol police officers stood by and watched as the mob toppled a statue and threw it into the nearby river Avon. Such lawlessness and inaction by the police was applauded by liberal news outlets and left-wing politicians. For many in Britain though these events provided an ugly portent of violence and political instability still to come. Under mob rule no one is safe and no property is secure.

It is too early to predict how these drastic changes may affect the longer-term relationship between the British public and their police. With falling numbers and shrinking budgets both police and the public have been forced to adapt to a shrinking police presence on the streets. That said, crime rates in Britain continue in the main to follow a downward trajectory (Crime in England & Wales, 2019). While there have been more recent upward trends in knife crime, firearms offences, and fraud, there are reasons to be optimistic about the ongoing police capability in reducing and suppressing crime. Where the system is quite clearly letting down the public is in the political prioritising of police resources. The introduction of elected Police and Crime Commissioners (PCC) in 2012 was an initiative by the government that intended to democratise policing and increase local accountability. In reality these positions have been quickly monopolised by placemen and women installed by the main political parties. These party hacks take their lead from national politicians and offer nothing but banal platitudes to voters. Inevitably this leads to an absence of local leadership and the entrenchment of a political structure that draws vital funds away from operational capabilities and funnels them into bureaucracy and partisan politicking. As the events briefly outlined above serve to illustrate, when police intervention is driven by political expediency rather than the criminal law, there are major ramifications for public safety in the future.

Sir Robert Peel's vision for a modern police service in Britain, the outline of which was set out nearly two centuries ago has all too often been misunderstood, misrepresented, and misquoted. British policymakers must seize the initiative and undertake a wide-ranging review of the Country's policing arrangements and introduce a comprehensive programme of structural reform, thereby creating an opportunity to preserve the most desirable aspects of the British policing tradition while facilitating the discontinuance of old, long-obsolete practices, processes, and procedures that cannot be adapted to fast-changing societal needs.

Conditions for Police Reform in the United States

In spring 2020, widespread rioting occurred in many US cities following the death of George Floyd, an unarmed African American man, who died while being taken into custody by the Minneapolis Police for a non-violent crime. Raw video footage showed four police officers placing Floyd face down on the ground in handcuffs while one of these officers had a knee on his neck. Floyd was seen on the video struggling in pain while telling officers "I can't breathe". He can be heard calling out for his mother with his dying breaths. This horrifying scene ignited international outrage. But, incidents like these, unarmed and non-violent African American men being killed by the police, have become commonplace in the United States. There was Eric Gardner in New York City, Tamir Rice in Cleveland, Freddy Gray in Baltimore, LaQuan McDonald in Chicago, Antwon Rose in East Pittsburgh, Michael Brown in Ferguson, Philando Castille in Minnesota, Walter Scott in South Carolina, and many more.

Decades of aggressive enforcement for minor crimes under programmes such as the "war on drugs" and "broken windows" policing, has all but destroyed trust in the police in many places, and has contributed to a violent code of the street in which gun violence threatens both the police and the community. Each year in America about 1000 people are shot and killed by the police. This is more than the number of US soldiers killed annually in Iraq during the most violent years of the war. Since late November 2014, when 12-year-old Tamir Rice was gunned down by police while playing with a toy pistol in a Cleveland city park, there have been 162 people with toy guns shot and killed by police. In 2019 in Fort Worth, Atatiana Jefferson was home playing video games with her nephew when the police, who were responding to a call of an open door, fired a shot through the window, killing her. This lethal gun violence—with nearly 300 unarmed people shot and killed by police during the last four years—is significant, but only a fraction of the total police violence at issue.

The Black Lives Matter (BLM) movement initially formed in 2013 in response to the acquittal of George Zimmerman, an armed member of a Florida neighbourhood watch group, in the shooting death of Trayvon Martin, an unarmed African American teen. BLM was the epicentre of protest following the police killing of Michael Brown in Ferguson and Eric Garner in New York City. It has helped organise street protests in these and many other US cities following the deaths of unarmed African American men at the hands of the police. The message from

BLM reformers easily connected to the chronic discontent many people felt about the police due to decades of aggressive enforcement in their local communities (Levin & Nolan, 2017).

The heavy emphasis on law enforcement outputs, such as arrests and the seizure of illegal guns and drugs, affects the disposition of officers in a way that puts them at odds with the community and increases their own risk for violence. About 100 police officers die in the line of duty each year, more than half of them intentionally murdered. Some of those murdered are selected randomly, but as revenge for particular acts of police violence. For example, in 2014 following the high profile police killings of unarmed African American men in Ferguson, Missouri and Staten Island, New York, a Baltimore man travelled by train to New York City seeking revenge. In Brooklyn, he walked up to a parked police car, opened the car door and shot officers Wenjian Liu and Rafael Ramos in the head and upper torso killing them both. Then, in 2016 five Dallas police officers were killed and nine injured as revenge for the police shootings of unarmed black men in Louisiana and Minnesota. Police reform in the United States is often discussed in the context of reducing violence by and against the police.

Conditions for an Age of Reform in France

The country of the Revolution and of Human rights, France has a long tradition of political public demonstrations, historically consecrated by the existence of permanent and professional anti-riot units in both police forces, the police nationale and the gendarmerie nationale, the officers of this last one serving under military status. As demonstrations are usually led by political parties or trade unions, identified as the political contact persons to solve the crisis, the political echelon has struggled to understand the dynamics of yellow vests appearing in October 2018. As a spontaneous social movement sparked by the increase of the internal consumption tax on energy products, it exposed the nakedness of the executive branch deprived of police intelligence to foresee the various weekly steps. Quickly, the demands widened to the social and political domains. Although demonstrations mainly took place on Saturdays, where several violent episodes occurred, notably on les Champs-Élysées, the protest also mobilised inhabitants of rural and peri-urban areas on week-long illegal blockades of roads and roundabouts.

The causes of this movement are certainly entrenched in a widespread and profound discomfort with perceived neoliberal world changes and government management in the French context (standard of living, taxation, feeling of neglect of certain territories, distrust of politicians and intermediary bodies, etc.). While acknowledging the inadmissible heavy casualties incurred by not only police and gendarmerie, but firefighting officers as well (about 2000 acknowledged by the Ministry of Interior as of October 2019), the French police have latterly been criticised in early 2020 for excessive use of violence by the very Minister, who defended it for months. Indeed, organisations such as Amnesty International criticised inappropriate policing, and institutions such as the United Nations and the Council of Europe have questioned the use of non-lethal weapons (Defence ball launchers and grenades), after a scientific article in the Lancet reported indiscriminate and heavy casualties on the demonstrators' side (Chauvin et al., 2019).

The still ongoing feedback from this unfinished period raises legitimate questions regarding interventions and the policing of demonstrations. It has created renewed tensions between both forces (police corporations have been reviving their request to demilitarise the gendarmerie and absorb it under police command, thereby avoiding the police corporation's own mismanagement issues, shifting responsibility instead to insufficient human resources). It also put to the front the lack of prior intelligence available beforehand to inform responses to the various episodes of this yellow vests saga, hence, addressing the nature of the relationships between the law enforcement forces and the French population. Indeed, this questioning could not be more relevant at a time when both forces were charged with enforcing what should have been a voluntary COVID-19 confinement, which has been obviously challenged in some suburbs that hosted three weeks of riots at the end of 2005, as a previously unknown in France Black Lives Matter movement following Floyd's death is reviving pending lethal cases of arraignment.

Where We Converge and Diverge on the Issues of Police Reform

As academics and practitioners, our views have coalesced around some central tenets. We firmly believe in the importance of democracy and democratic policing with all the checks, balances, and accountability mechanisms that are integral to such a model. We are also committed to a policing doctrine that has human rights as an under-pinning theme. Importantly, our imagining of human rights in policing does not include a system that provides exceptional privileges and protections for those who would do us harm, neither does it include a legal structure that would prevent severe and condign punishment for offenders who are guilty of grotesque acts of murder, torture, or genocide. It does, however, require an understanding of the human conditions that give rise to these atrocities and others and the limits of punishment alone as a tool for justice.

Where our views on the policy prescription for the future diverge, it is on the potential paths of future societal development. For some of our authors, the future is a liberal one. A future system of policing that seeks to evolve, reinforce, and expand the secular western political settlement. This approach envisions the continuity of rights-based individual freedoms with an internationalist attitude to cross-border cooperation and intergovernmental joint working on policy, protocols, and legal frameworks. A system that embraces and values multiculturalism, gender equality, the end of patriarchy, freedom of expression—within an acceptable liberal framework—and a more equitable distribution of wealth and opportunity for all people.

For others among our authors the future looks quite different. For them western liberalism has no future and has nothing to offer in an era of reform. This group of writers argue in favour of the nation state, the importance of national identity, shared history, culture, customs, and faith. In this future system of policing, individual rights are paramount and not to be tempered or mediated by an interventionist state. For these authors, rights come with responsibilities and a respect for nation for duty and sacrifice. This approach postulates a conservative route to reform, a return to fundamentals, a reconnection with the conventions, practices, and principles of the past. Of course, this dichotomist rift does allow for and embrace multiple shades of grey between both views. Regardless of where on this wide-reaching political spectrum our authors sit, they are agreed on the inherent nobility and essential goodness of the policing mission. This book is about doing the right thing. It readily acknowledges that not all police officers are good people, or that they consistently or even regularly do the right thing. It does regard as axiomatic the importance and desirability of police officers being good and virtuous people driven by a sense of vocation and enduring civic duty. Scruton (1998) captures this latter sentiment in the following passages:

Virtuous people have qualities which make them eminently useful to society. They sacrifice themselves for others; they stand up and are counted in the hour of need; they fight off enemies and succor friends; they administer impartial justice; and they are temperate in all their ways, so that long-term commitments come naturally to them. In short, they further the reproduction of society.

Here we confront an ancient paradox, as real for us as it was for the Greeks who first debated it. It seems that virtuous people are exposed to troubles that the weak-willed, the calculating and the vicious avoid. In battle it is the courageous person who takes the risks and the coward who comes home to tell the tale. It is the steadfast person who earns the abuse of the mob, and the weak-willed conformist who escapes their censure. It is the honest person who suffers when the villains call in the chips. (Scruton, R., 1998, *Do the Right Thing*, 52–53. Demos, London)

In a world where internet use has become ubiquitous and all-pervading, where the new opiate of the people has become social media, where anyone can, usually under the cloak of online anonymity, share with the world their innermost thoughts and feelings (which all too often turn out to be hate-filled, expletive-laden, incoherent, and ill-informed), the police must chart and conform to a new course, a refined mission, a new and evolving societal purpose.

Perspectives for Police Reform

At first, the term police reform could seem unambiguous with a common meaning, understood by all. However, this is not the case. For many, the police mandate is clear. The organisation of policing is aimed at preventing and controlling crime and arresting violators of the law, sometimes referred to as criminals. So, in the interest of professionalism and efficiency, police reform means improving the *methods* (or strategies) of the profession (Manning, 1978). Evidence-based policing is a popular version of this type of reform, as its various and competing claims about "what works" in policing must undergo rigorous testing to support these claims (Sherman, 2015). For example, a policing strategy known as Project Safe Neighbourhoods (PSN) was implemented in Chicago in the early 2000s. It had three broad goals (1) reduce demand among young gun offenders, (2) reduce the supply of guns by identifying and intervening in illegal gun markets, and (3) prevent the onset of gun violence. The tactics included increased federal prosecution for convicted felons carrying or using guns, lengthy sentences for federal prosecutions, increasing the rate of gun seizures via various policing strategies, social marketing of deterrence, and "social norms" messages at meetings with offenders which were designed to convey the serious consequences that would occur if they chose to use a gun or reoffend. The study used a quasi-experimental design to assess the effectiveness of this strategy. Treatment and control districts were selected non-randomly based on their rates of homicide and gun violence. The results showed that the districts where the treatment was used experienced a 37% drop in homicide rates during the observation period. It was noted by the authors of the study that the control group, and the entire city of Chicago, experienced declines in homicide during this period but were less pronounced than those in the treatment group (Papachristos, Meares, & Fagan, 2007). The Center for Evidence-Based Crime Policy in the Department of Criminology, Law, and Society at George Mason University provides the findings from more than a hundred studies in policing similar to the PSN study in Chicago. Along with results of the research, the Center provides recommendations for policy and practice (CEBCP, https://cebcp.org/).

An alternative type of police reform, albeit much less widely known or discussed, is one which seeks to reform the police *mandate* itself. Manning (1978) suggested that the mandate to prevent and control crime is actually impossible because the police cannot control the social processes that actually breed crime. These processes, he argues, emerge from values, norms, and social traditions in the larger society, and so the police are forced to deploy strategies aimed at managing appearances rather than preventing crime in any meaningful way. We think this point would be contested today. Over the past 20 years or so, sociological studies of crime have brought neighbourhood and community-level social processes more clearly into view (Sampson, Raudenbush, & Earls, 1997). We now see that the police mandate to prevent and control crime is not impossible due to lack of control of the social processes that breed crime, but because they fail to see their own contribution to them (Hinkle & Weisburd, 2008; Nolan, Conti, & McDevitt, 2004). From this point of view, the police mandate is part and parcel to the bundle of social conditions that maintain crime and criminality not reduce it.

Perhaps the reform of the police mandate is well beyond the power or scope of reformers inside police organisations, but it may be worthy of close consideration. Reforming the police mandate challenges basic assumptions about the nature of crime and criminality and our beliefs about the role of the police in contemporary society. Manning might suggest that the popular images of the police as warriors and crime fighters is better understood as managing impressions rather than actually suppressing crime.

With these two general types of reform in mind, i.e. those aimed at the *methods* of policing and those targeting the police *mandate*, we propose there are actually four general perspectives on police reform that relate to the body of work presented in this book. For clarity we labelled these perspectives (1) maintaining, (2) retrofitting, (3) co-opting, and (4) transforming in Fig. 1.1 and will describe them below.

Maintaining is a perspective on police reform that requires no change in police methods or mandate. It refers to reforming under-functioning police departments which are struggling to meet professional standards. In the United States organisations such as the Commission on Accreditation for Law Enforcement (CALEA) establish standards for

		***MANDATE*:** PREVENTION AND CONTROL OF CRIME AND ARREST OF CRIMINALS	
		SAME	CHANGE
	SAME	*(1) MAINTAINING*	*(3) COOPTING*
METHODS: POLICING STRATEGIES/ TECHNOLOGIES	CHANGE	*(2) RETROFITTING*	*(4) TRANSFORMING*

Fig. 1.1 Four perspectives on police reform: maintaining, retrofitting, co-opting, Transforming

professionalism in policing and they assist local and state agencies in meeting these standards (CALEA, https://www.calea.org/). *Maintaining* also reflects the perspective of those who see the police as a stabilising force in an age of reform where the world is tending towards chaotic fluctuations. The police should not change what they do, but rather stay the course of the mandate in ways that provide stability and security.

Retrofitting is a perspective that accepts the existing police mandate, but seeks to add new methods and technology to improve the functioning of the police within the boundaries of that mandate. New technologies such as Shot Spotter[1] for identifying the location of a gunshot, or real-time crime centres,[2] or new intelligence software[3] or sophisticated methods such as social network analysis[4] to track criminal offenders are considered police reform, because they are new tools that improve the efficiency and effectiveness of the stable and dependable law enforcement machine.

Co-opting is a perspective that aims at the police mandate itself, while accepting its tradition and methods. Reformers from this perspective challenge basic assumptions about crime and criminality and question the feasibility that the police alone can actually control crime.

[1] https://www.shotspotter.com/.

[2] https://www.cinemassive.com/solutions/public-safety/?mm_campaign=1D5234FC1CC4C6FE42B7C18C9B6747FD&mm_replace=true&utm_source=bing_desktop&utm_medium=ppc&utm_term=real%20time%20crime%20center&utm_campaign=law_enforcement.

[3] https://www.einvestigator.com/open-source-intelligence-tools/.

[4] https://www.policechiefmagazine.org/power-social-network-analysis/.

Police reform from this perspective starts by introducing new goals and outcome measures, such as social cohesion, trust in neighbours, the willingness to intervene for the common good, and trust in the police to do the right things. These reformers believe that methods of traditional policing, such as the enforcement of public order laws, joint task force operations, forensic investigations and intelligence gathering, and the use of surveillance technologies are well suited for the new mandate, but they must be used as tools with the new end in mind.

Finally, *Transforming* is a perspective on police reform that rejects both the methods and the mandate of traditional policing and seeks total reform of the profession. This is similar to the perspective *co-opting*, but it recognises that traditional methods will fall short in creating the kind of outcome imagined by the new mandate. In what Nolan, Conti, and McDevitt (2004) called situational policing, they show how a new mandate focused on strong, healthy community outcomes will need new strategies that are not currently employed or even considered presently in the law enforcement field. Getting community members mentally and physically engaged in ways that make places safe will take new skills and new metrics for success.

Throughout this book contributing authors approach the subject of reform in different ways and from a variety of perspectives. They show how the status quo in policing is *maintained* and reproduced (Chapter 2), how social change, scientific discoveries, and technological advances require *retrofitting* new methods to the old law enforcement machine (Chapters 4, 7, 8, 10, and 13), and how these retrofitted changes can create new problems and dilemmas (Chapters 3 and 6). Still others argue for police reforms that are transformative, starting with a new mandate and developing new metrics for success (Chapter 5). They also show how traditional police methods can be co-opted for use under a new mandate (Chapter 12). Moreover, a convincing argument is made to let technological advances lead police reforms rather than the other way around as is typically the case (Chapter 11). Whatever the intent of reform, one will need a plan and a way to assess behaviour towards a desired end (Chapter 9), and officers will need to know, specifically, what it means to do the right things (Chapter 14, 15). In the concluding chapter, we discuss why a consensus view of reform is probably not possible, or desirable, in a book about policing in an age of reform (Chapter 16).

Conclusions

Attempting to match the shape and pace of police reform to parallel evolutions in societal reform will always prove a challenge. Trying to predict with any level of confidence or hope of accuracy, the impending upheavals, cracks, fissures, disruptions, and realignments that may take place in our respective countries. Will nationalism and tribalism prevail over globalism and liberalism? Will the imagined conflict between *somewheres*, those who identify with nation, community, and cultural identity and *anywheres*, those who embrace the opportunities of globalism and a liberal new world order (Goodhart, 2017), become more bitter and intense or will it dissipate and disappear over time? Changing demographics in western countries may indeed have a transformative effect. The differing priorities of young urban cosmopolitan citizens may contrast starkly with those of older settled more conservative pensioners. Or it may be the case that the potential for intergenerational conflicts are over-stated and that culture, ethnicity, faith, and tradition prove to be more important dividing lines in our future societies. As White majorities in Europe recede and Black and Visible Ethnic Minority populations assert themselves, will there be a Balkanisation of our communities with different regions, cities, and provinces adopting different cultural norms, laws, and practices? This must surely be the undiscussed nightmare of western liberal politicians. And yet, it may transpire to be an arrangement that enjoys widespread popular support.

Whatever the future holds, the need for communities to feel safe, secure, and free from oppression, persecution, and crime will continue to concentrate the minds of citizens and policymakers alike. An ongoing process of police reform must be nurtured and encouraged through democratic discourse, argument, and debate. This book seeks to contribute to that discourse and to stimulate discussion, disagreement, criticism, and alternative critiques from students, practitioners, policymakers, commentators, and concerned citizens.

References

Chauvin, A., Bourges, J.-L., Korobelnik, J.-F., Paques, M., Lebranchu, P., Villeroy, F., ... Bodaghi, B. (2019). Ocular injuries caused by less-lethal weapons in France. *The Lancet, 394*(10209), 1616–1617. https://doi.org/10.1016/S0140-6736(19)31807-0.

Crime in England and Wales: year ending June 2019. Office for National Statistics.

Disney, R., & Simpson, P. (2017). *Police workforce and funding in England and Wales*. London: The Institute of Fiscal Studies.

Goodhart, D. (2017). *Road to somewhere: The populist revolt and the future of politics*. London: Hurst & Co.

Hinkle, J. C., & Weisburd, D. (2008). The irony of broken windows policing: A micro-place study of the relationship between disorder, focused police crackdowns and fear of crime. *Journal of Criminal Justice, 36,* 503–512.

Levin, J., & Nolan, J. (2017). *The violence of hate: Understanding harmful forms of bias and bigotry* (4th ed.). New York: Rowman & Littlefield.

Manning, P. K. (1978). The police mandate: Strategies and appearances. In P. K. Manning & J. Van Maanen (Eds.), *Policing: A view from the street*. New York: Random House.

Nolan, J., Conti, N., & McDevitt, J. (2004). Situational policing: Neighbourhood development and crime control. *Policing and Society, 14,* 99–117.

Sherman, L. W. (2015). A tipping point for "totally evidenced policing": Ten ideas for building an evidence-based police agency. *International Criminal Justice Review, 25,* 1–19.

Papachristos, A. V., Meares, T. L., & Fagan, J. (2007). Attention felons: Evaluation project safe neighborhoods in Chicago. *Journal of Empirical Legal Studies, 4,* 223–272.

Sampson, R. J., Raudenbush, S., & Earls, F. (1997). Neighborhoods and violent crime: A multilevel study of collective efficacy. *Science, 277,* 918–924.

Scruton, R. (1998). *Do the right thing* (pp. 52–53). London: Demos.

2

Changing the Game: A Sociological Perspective on Police Reform

James J. Nolan, Joshua C. Hinkle, and Zsolt Molnar

Introduction

From the rampant corruption and violent responses to riots between immigrant groups around the turn of the twentieth century, to violent police actions during the civil rights movement, to controversies around

J. J. Nolan (✉)
Department of Sociology and Anthropology, West Virginia University, Morgantown, WV, USA
e-mail: jim.nolan@mail.wvu.edu

J. C. Hinkle
Department of Criminal Justice and Criminology, Georgia State University, Atlanta, GA, USA
e-mail: jhinkle@gsu.edu

Z. Molnar
CivCom Delegate, Permanent Representation of Hungary to the European Union, Brussels, Belgium
e-mail: zsolt.molnar@mfa.gov.hu

J. J. Nolan et al. (eds.), *Policing in an Age of Reform*,
Palgrave's Critical Policing Studies,
https://doi.org/10.1007/978-3-030-56765-1_2

stop and frisk and other forms of aggressive policing, to the spat of highly publicised officer-involved shootings in recent years, there is a long history of conflict between the police and the public in America (Kraska, 2018). In the current national crisis in American policing, some suggest that a few 'bad apples' are responsible for damaged relations between the police and community (Morris, 2018). Others claim violence by the police is linked to individual and shared perceptions of legitimacy and procedural justice (Tyler, 2004). Still others point to implicit bias as the source of police violence and the deeply engrained hostilities between the police and many minority communities (Fridell, 2016; Price & Payton, 2017).

Although these explanations give us a way to understand contemporary problems in policing, they fail to provide the clarity needed for collective action toward real reform. In short, past work has paid far too little attention to the sociological roots of aggressive policing. In this time of strained police-community relations there is need to renew thinking about why there has been a tendency toward weak implementations of major reforms like community-oriented policing and problem-oriented policing that sought to shift the goals of policing and to expand their toolbox beyond law enforcement actions (Weisburd & Braga, 2006). Conversely, the reforms that have gained the most traction are things like hot spots policing (Braga, Turchan, Papachristos, & Hureau, 2019) and Compstat (Weisburd, Mastrofski, McNally, Greenspan, & Willis, 2003) which keep the police focus on making arrests and fit with the traditional mode of policing from the twentieth century, i.e. centralised police commands while carrying out 'one-fits-all' tactics citywide (Weisburd & Braga, 2006). This is troubling given what we know about the vast variation in crime, collective efficacy and social disorganisation, and police-community relationships from research on the criminology of place (Weisburd, Groff, & Yang, 2012). Work from that area strongly supports the notion that different places will need different policing strategies if crime is to be controlled, collective efficacy enhanced and police-community relationships repaired.

To add clarity to the issue of police reform, we draw on insights from Pierre Bourdieu (1977/2013) to explain how the structured field of policing, with its rules, resources, and rewards, promotes aggressive law enforcement and undermines police legitimacy and the collective support of citizens that is necessary to make places safe (Chan, 2007). In a case example from Wilmington, Delaware in the United States, we show the futility of change efforts aimed at police dispositions and biases, and how the 'game' of law enforcement, itself, gives rise to a logic of practice and a police disposition that works against reform.

A Sociological Perspective

When we hear reports of excessive violence by the police or against them, it is often difficult to know exactly where to focus our attention. Should we look first at the larger social structures that give rise to inequality and violence and create dangerous situations for the police and public? Or, should we fix our gaze on the human actors—police and citizens—who are committing the violent acts, presumably with some measure of reason and forethought (Morris, 2018)? Social scientists make competing claims about the preeminence of social structure over human agency, and vice versa, in explaining human behaviour (Clifton, Repper, Banks, & Remnant, 2013; Rigby, Woulfin, & Marz, 2016; Sewell, 1992). Stated broadly, social structure refers to rules, resources, and underlying principles that *determine* patterns of interactions and individual behaviours (Sewell, 1992). The notion that we are products of our environment is an example of this view. Human agency, on the other hand, is the capacity of people to reason and exercise control over their lives (Bandura, 2001). The belief that we are able to rise above our circumstances to achieve great things fits this agentic perspective. Rather than picking a side and arguing for the primacy of structure or human agency, sociologist Pierre Bourdieu provides an integrated framework that links four interdependent concepts: field, habitus, capital, and doxa (Bourdieu, 1977/2013). According to Bourdieu, *social practice* is the outcome of the 'ontological complicity' of these concepts (Bourdieu & Wacquant, 1992, p. 128). Let us explain.

The concept 'field' refers to something like a sports field with rules of engagement, boundaries, positions of power and prestige, and a logic that everyone knows, i.e. something like a football field. Individually and collectively, the players understand what others expected of them. They know how to score points for the team and how to gain status as individuals. Success on the field requires players to internalise the logic of the game. Bourdieu refers to this as 'habitus' (Bourdieu & Wacquant, 1992, p. 115). The habitus is a socialised *disposition* and *worldview* that helps players adapt to contingencies on the field. Habitus enables individual actors to develop a 'sense of the game' in order to reason quickly and effectively (Bourdieu & Wacquant, 1992, p. 128).

Bourdieu used the term *capital* to mean the variety of ways human agents on the social field are recognised and rewarded for doing the *right* things. Generally, there are two broad types of capital: economic and symbolic. Economic capital refers to things like wages and profits that reflect power and status on the field, whether it be in an organisation, profession, or community. Symbolic capital, too, denotes status, albeit not directly related to mercantile exchange but, nonetheless, having exchange value. For example, being recognised favourably as having special knowledge or skills (cultural capital), or having close connections to people in power (social capital), may affect a person's position on the field and the logic of his or her specific behaviours (Moore, 2008).

The term *doxa* is used in Bourdieu's sociological framework to refer to a condition where the objective structures (field) and subjective structures (habitus) are so closely aligned that the arbitrariness of the *status quo* goes unnoticed. In other words, the way things are in practice is misrecognised as the natural way they should be. Therefore, the question of legitimacy of the social order is never questioned. This holds true even when the outcomes of the social order appear paradoxical, i.e. they go against doxic assumptions. For example, the assumptions underlying gun rights in the U.S. Constitution are never seriously questioned by anybody even though there are hundreds of mass shootings with multiple deaths each year.[1] Gun rights—as constructed in the U.S. Constitution—appear to citizens as natural rights rather than something arbitrary that can be changed.

[1] See the Gun Violence Archive at https://www.gunviolencearchive.org/.

The Logic of Practice

For Bourdieu, behaviour emerges from the *logic of practice*. In any type of game on a field of play there are multiple ways to make good plays and bad plays, and there are corresponding rewards and sanctions that accompany these actions. Individuals with interest in success on the social field are likely to develop a disposition or way of seeing the world that conforms to the logic of the game. The value or morality of behaviour, then, is assessed in accord with this logic. For example, a violent tackle on the field of American football is celebrated with spontaneous cheering. But that same play on the field of international football (soccer) is likely to get the player a red card, ejection from the game, and vigorous booing. Similarly, although we generally accept the morality of telling the truth, even when it hurts, the logic of a card game or criminal trial makes it a *good* play to conceal the truth within the established rules and logic of the field. Those who master the games on particular *fields* are those whose *habitus* (socially produced dispositions and mental habits) align with the structure of the game (see Fig. 2.1).

The triangle in Fig. 2.1 is a symbol representing the structure of the field. It stands for the rules of engagement, policies, practices, and positions of status and power attained through the accumulation of various forms of capital. Presented here, it is simply a symbol that stands for *the way things are*. The triangle on the forehead of the person represents the internalised structure—or *habitus*—, which influences the decisions and actions of individuals, engaged with each other on the field. The structured field determines—and is determined by—the actions of human agents. In Fig. 2.1 the arrow pointing in both directions depicts this

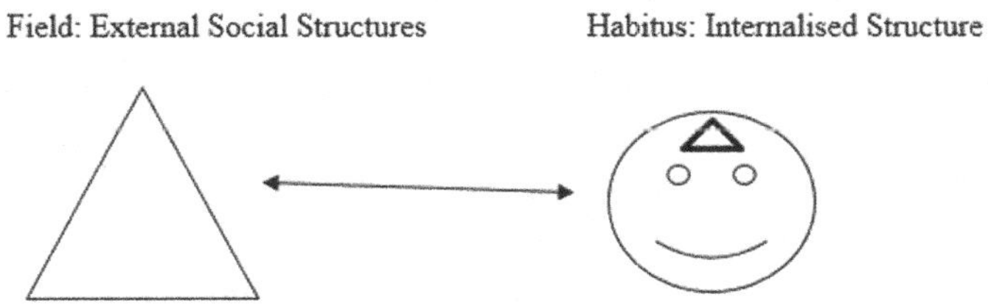

Fig. 2.1 Bourdieu's concepts 'field' and 'habitus'

bidirectional interaction between the structured field and habitus. When internal structures (habitus) align with external structures (field), participants on the field act intuitively and decisively in accord with the *common sense* of the field. As we have described earlier, the term *doxa* describes the taken-for-granted aspects of our social world that result from the close alignment of field and habitus. Like a 'fish in water', social actors on the field develop an intuitive feel for the game and never question the game itself (Maton, 2008, p. 59). Doing the 'right thing' is less about a general moral reasoning or rational calculation and more about how closely the observed behaviour aligns with the logic of the field. As Bourdieu would say: The 'logic of practice is logical up to the point where to be logical would cease to be practical' (Bourdieu & Wacquant, 1992, pp. 22–23).

This perspective is particularly useful for understanding how organisations and institutions like the police reproduce themselves even when they become ineffective and harmful (Chan, 1997). Those with the power to transform the field are likely to mistake the status quo for the *natural* way things should be and work hard to maintain and reproduce it (Weisburd et al., 2003). Below, we demonstrate the interaction of field, habitus, capital, and doxa in a case study from Wilmington, Delaware USA.

The Logic of Police Practice: An Example from Wilmington, Delaware

From August 2013 through August 2014, the first author conducted a year-long study of police practices in Wilmington, Delaware. Using a variety of methods, including surveys, interviews, and structured observations, he clearly established that the 'game' being played at the Wilmington Police Department was street-level law enforcement (Nolan, 2016). Status and power in the department (forms of capital) were tied closely to street arrests and gun and drug seizures. Officers often spoke enthusiastically of the heroics of 'running and gunning', a phrase meaning to chase down armed criminal suspects. Inside the department, the idea of providing service to a community meant 'locking people up'. For example, when robberies and burglaries increased in particular neighbourhoods, a team of police officers would be dispatched into the community to enforce laws. The team of officers, known officially as Operation Disrupt, would not attempt to help the residents being plagued by crime or to actually solve the robberies and burglaries and arrest the perpetrators. Instead, the team would focus on enforcing minor violations of the law such as possessing open containers of alcohol or loitering. The game of policing, as it was being played in Wilmington, created a habitus (disposition and worldview) in officers that made them 'hyper vigilant of danger, fixated on sorting the good people from bad and uninterested in the long-term harms to individuals and communities that result from their law enforcement efforts' (Nolan, 2016).

While crime rates nationwide declined and remained lower from the mid-1990s into recent years, Wilmington experienced large increases in crime. In fact, according to the FBI, the violent crime rate in Wilmington is more than three times higher than the violent crime rate for the state of Delaware and more than four times higher than that of the United States as a whole.[2] It is in places like Wilmington that many of the controversies about policing practices are taking place. In these places, due in part to a current trend of aggressive street-level enforcement, the police are often viewed as occupying forces by the people who live there. The broken relationships between the police and community can have deep implications for public safety. For example, between 2010 and 2015 there were about 150 homicides in Wilmington and about 6000 burglaries.[3] During this time, the Wilmington Police Department (WPD) solved 33% of the murders and 9% of the burglaries, both well below the national average. WPD officers claimed that 'stop snitching' campaigns, resident apathy, and lack of trust in the criminal justice system were responsible for these low clearance rates. Although WPD made relatively few arrests for the serious crimes that were occurring, officers were very busy enforcing the law. The most frequent charge for people arrested by WPD during this time was 'resisting arrest'

[2] *Source* Federal Bureau of Investigation, UCR Datatool [Online]. Accessed at https://ucrdatatool.gov/.

[3] *Source* State of Delaware, City of Wilmington incident-level reports 2010–2015.

(2002 incidents), next was 'loitering' (1921 incidents), and 'offensive touching' (1811 incidents). Other high arrest counts were observed for the crimes 'possession of an open container of alcohol' (888 incidents) and 'disorderly conduct' (909 incidents).

Modeling the 'broken windows' tactics of cities like New York and Toronto in the 1990s, the aggressive enforcement of relatively low-level offences has become the *raison d'etre* of many departments, including WPD (Bratton & Knobler, 1998; DeKeseredy, Alvi, Schwartz, & Tomaszewski, 2003; Giuliani & Kurson, 2002; Wilson & Kelling, 1982). On the policing field, progress is assessed almost solely on police outputs, such as the number of arrests or the quantity of drugs and guns seized, rather than community outcomes. In many ways, policing is still plagued by the same 'means over ends' problem Herman Goldstein (1979) lamented over in developing problem-oriented policing. Based on Bourdieu's ideas reviewed above, this is unsurprising. The term *police* is now used interchangeably with the term *law enforcement*. This is particularly evident in police management innovations such as Compstat, data-driven deployment of officers, and real time crime centres that reward and reinforce traditional law enforcement tactics as the main ways to earn praise, promotion, and status in the eyes of peers (Weisburd et al., 2003).

The law enforcement game has rendered the police helpless in mobilising sustained support from residents in preventing and solving serious crimes. Indeed, some have argued that aggressive enforcement, especially for low-level offences, may undermine police legitimacy as residents begin to feel like targets rather than partners of the police (Rosenbaum, 2006). Moreover, aggressive law enforcement practices aimed at low-level offences have been found to generate negative consequences in communities. For instance, one study found that despite reducing disorder, aggressive policing in Jersey City, NJ actually made people more fearful and isolated thus likely preventing them from being engaged in collaborative activities to prevent or solve crimes (Hinkle & Weisburd, 2008).

In an essay for the online publication *The Conversation*, Nolan (2016) described how the current policing field produces a logic of practice and disposition in officers that is counterproductive. He wrote the following:

> In this hardcore version of the law enforcement game, well-intentioned and highly competent officers seemed blind to the consequences of their actions and indifferent to harm it caused. It didn't seem to matter to them whether a neighbourhood was ultimately safer following police action, or whether convictions were won in court. It also didn't seem to matter whether serious crimes like robbery or burglary were ever solved, or whether families and communities would suffer from widespread police sweeps and the disruption of mass arrests. Worse, nobody worried that the broken trust in the police would contribute indirectly to more killings. These things were not part of the logic. The only thing that mattered was that 'lockups' were made and that guns and drugs were seized. 'Community policing' meant placating the community with a few friendly faces so that real police work – arresting criminals – could go on unimpeded. (Nolan, 2016)

The sociological argument here is that the practice of policing is a function of the interplay of field, habitus, capital, and doxa. On the field of play, officers are engaged in a game of 'law enforcement' where citizen/residents are viewed as objects (criminals or potential criminals) that can be converted to capital via arrest. It is an exciting contest of good versus evil, in which stories of heroism abound and the model police officer is an aggressive, no-nonsense law enforcer. Status and positions of power (i.e. capital) in the police organisation and 'law enforcement' profession are aligned with the expectations of the game. Promotions, desirable assignments, titles, and awards are given for heroism and aggressive law enforcement. This game, along with forms of capital for playing a certain way, produces a logic that becomes the 'common sense' of policing. It also fosters in officers a worldview and disposition (habitus) that keeps them at war. The battle lines are the boundary lines they draw between good and evil, order and disorder, us and them. In this environment, relationships between the police and community have become extremely strained, especially in places like Wilmington where crime and violence thrive. The assumptions underlying law enforcement practice as a means to keep neighbourhoods safe are never seriously examined because law enforcement as the mission and purpose of policing is accepted as natural rather than arbitrary and changeable.

Bourdieu's framework helps us see the value and limitations of doxa created by the close alignment of field and habitus. On one hand the policing field presents a logic for collaborative action. By internalising this logic and embracing a disposition (habitus) that promises success on the field, police officials develop a 'feel for the game' that guides decisions and coordinates activities in helpful and efficient ways (Maton, 2008, p. 54). On the other hand, doxa creates the false view that the police field (i.e. the law enforcement mandate) is the natural way it should be rather than socially constructed, arbitrary, and changeable. This keeps the social field exempt from serious inquiry, and all but guarantees it will continue *as is* into the future. Doxa keeps the false underlying beliefs of the status quo sacred and unquestioned.

Our use of the word *sacred* extends beyond the world of religion to include secular laws, institutions, and customs that are considered worthy of reverence and respect. Many of the things we consider sacred are linked to doxa because they appear natural and beyond question. Challenging the sacred has always been a dangerous thing to do. In the Sixteenth-Century Copernicus and Galileo were shunned or persecuted for challenging the doxa of the church and holy scriptures by placing the sun, rather than the Earth, at the centre of the universe (Leveillee, 2011). It may be less risky today in the physical sciences to challenge the authority of the Bible on things like the age of the Earth, the origins of the universe, and the evolution of humans from the sea (Glanz, 1999). But, it is still taboo in many places to question the existence of God, the reality of heaven and hell, or the essence of a soul.

The problems in challenging sacred institutions are even more dangerous today in the social sciences than it is in the physical sciences. Social facts often have ramifications that touch the interests of groups and individuals whose very existence is rooted in a world that diverges from these facts (Wirth, 1936). For this reason, the *truth* of an idea is often determined by the degree to which it corresponds with one's own world view and interests. Ideas that challenge the sacred are viewed as 'dangerous thought'. According to Wirth (1936) the things that are dangerous to think about may differ from society to society and from age to age, but what makes them dangerous is that they challenge the beliefs held most sacred in society. A thought can be dangerous and subversive,

Wirth writes '(f)or thought is a catalytic agent that is capable of unsettling routines, disorganizing habits, breaking up customs, undermining faiths, and generating skepticism' (p. xvii).

Thought as a Struggle for Power

It may be true that individuals are the only ones who can formulate a thought, but, it is wrong to think that individuals alone are the originators of that thought (Mannheim, 1936). We inherit ideas in the same way we inherit language. Beliefs and ideas are embedded in a social context. They are also a product of the times and the social circumstances of the person doing the thinking. A thought may be triggered by an observation that appears to an observer as objective reality. But, this is actually a subjective interpretation based on unconscious forces rooted in a particular social context. Individuals in a society see things differently which alone may not be an insurmountable problem. Because we can communicate with others through language, our divergent thoughts can be pulled together into a unified view, a more truthful view. Getting the whole picture from divergent views is complicated because of special interests. This is why sociologists like Karl Mannheim and Pierre Bourdieu have considered the search for knowledge not as a cooperative endeavour to find truth and share power, but as the struggle for power on a battlefield of special interests. The police too are a special interest group on this battlefield for distinction and power and where it is more important to be 'in the right', legally, politically, and in alignment with the interests of the group, than it is to be right (Wirth, 1936, p. xxvi).

The terms ideology and utopia relate to the socially situated roots of thought and the struggle for distinction and power described briefly above. Ideological thinking is most likely to occur in the group whose interests are most served by the status quo. Their thoughts tend to block or ignore facts that might undermine their power or destabilise the current conditions. In our four perspective model of police reform (Chapter 1) ideological thinking would align with the perspectives 'maintaining' or 'retrofitting' because *if* anything needs to be reformed it is only the methods and *not* the police mandate. On the other hand, utopian thinking generally pertains to the thoughts of those seeking power or redistribution of power. They tend to focus too narrowly on the conditions that negate the status quo because their aim is to transform it. The utopian mentality tends to block or ignore facts that support the existing order because their focus is primarily fixed on its destruction and transformation. Utopian thinking is most closely aligned with the 'transforming' and 'coopting' perspectives on police reform because their aim is to change the police mandate (Chapter 1).

It is important to note that *both* ideological and utopian thinking are equally problematic for reformers looking for solutions, albeit in different ways. Each offers important insights about the true nature of social problems but blocks others. Recognising this fact and opening oneself to the ideas and concerns of the other side is necessary for successful police reform to become possible.

Summary and Conclusion

In this chapter we began by looking at the *status quo* and the mechanisms by which it is continually reproduced even when it produces harmful outcomes. By using the conceptual tools of Pierre Bourdieu, we show the interplay of field, habitus, capital, and doxa and how they work together to ensure the status quo remains intact. On the field of policing there is a game being played, one that every police officer knows. It is a game that gives priority to law enforcement outputs over the more complex and ambiguous community outcomes. To the police, the causes of crime and violence may appear to be out of their control. Officers surely recognise the impact of poverty, unemployment, and drug abuse as key contributors to crime. But, they rarely question the assumptions behind law enforcement as a solution to crime or recognise that what the police are doing actually makes things worse in many places. The game on the field shapes the outlook and disposition of officers. They know what to do without much rational calculation because the rules of the game have been internalised. The logic of the game becomes 'common sense' to officers, which enables them to act quickly and decisively to *do the right* things in the myriad of chaotic situations they face each day.

This close relation between the objective field of policing and the subjective habitus of officers creates doxa, a condition in which the game of policing appears natural and unquestionable. The logic of the game and the assumptions about crime and community safety are never questioned. They simply never come up, because no one thinks to bring them up. This is why many reformers only aim at the methods of policing, but not the mandate.

There is one example in recent years of a national police agency rethinking its mandate in the throes of chaos following the terror attacks of 11 September 2001. At this time the Hungarian Crime Prevention Academy was established. Its police mission was to combat terrorism by building strong communities (Conti, Nolan, & Molnar, 2011). At a time when the Department of Homeland Security in the United States was being instituted to protect citizens from terrorism, the opposite was happening in Hungary. The Ministry of the Interior was attempting to promote a '…crime prevention attitude in the daily activity and way of thinking of state organisations, local authorities, civilian organisations, businesses and private individuals' (p. 17). Because the focus was to create a 'prevention mindset' in everyone, the Academy's strategies included employing wide circles of participation from community groups throughout the country. Once the game shifted from 'a few protecting the many' to building relationships so that the 'many could protect each other', a different logic emerged. The new game required officers to think about sharing power and responsibility with local residents. A total shift in thinking about the purpose of policing is necessary before transformational change can take place. In later chapters we describe in some detail how this can be accomplished.

Policing in this age of reform will require collaboration from many individuals and groups who have competing views. Placing the roots of our thoughts in social contexts and special interests, we are better able to see the limits of ideological and utopian thinking. When they are in direct opposition to each other, as in the battlefield metaphor, each serves equally to preserve the war for power and distinction. But, in the end, this does not need to be the case. The battlefield is a metaphor and not a natural law, even though it appears that way. A construction metaphor, in which many diverse views and skills are brought together to design and erect a new building, may be more appropriate.

References

Bandura, A. (2001). Social cognitive theory: An agentic perspective. *Annual Review of Psychology, 52,* 1–26.

Bourdieu, P. (1977/2013). *Outline of a theory of practice*. Cambridge, UK: Cambridge University Press.

Bourdieu, P., & Wacquant, L. J. D. (1992). *An invitation to reflexive sociology*. Chicago, IL: University of Chicago Press.

Braga, A. A., Turchan, B., Papachristos, A. V., & Hureau, D. M. (2019). Hot spots policing of small geographic areas effects on crime. *Campbell Systematic Reviews,* 15(3). https://doi.org/10.1002/cl2.1046.

Bratton, W. J., & Knobler, P. (1998). *Turnaround: How America's top cop reversed the crime epidemic*. New York: Random House.

Chan, J. (1997). *Changing police culture: Policing in a multicultural society*. Cambridge, UK: Cambridge University Press.

Chan, J. (2007). Making sense of police reforms. *Theoretical Criminology, 11,* 323–345.

Clifton, A., Repper, J., Banks, D., & Remnant, J. (2013). Co-producing social inclusion: The structure/agency conundrum. *Journal of Psychiatric and Mental Health Nursing, 20,* 514–524.

Conti, N., Nolan, J., & Molnar, Z. (2011). Global law enforcement and the cosmopolitan police response: The role of situational policing in transnational crime rrevention—An example from Hungary. In J. Albrecht & D. Das (Eds.), *Effective crime reduction strategies: International perspectives*. New York: CRC Press.

DeKeseredy, W. S., Alvi, S., Schwartz, M. D., & Tomaszewski, A. (2003). *Under siege: Poverty and crime in a public housing community*. Boston: Lexington.

Fridell, L. (2016, August 1). Can better training solve cops' implicit biases? *Democracy*. Retrieved at https://democracyjournal.org/arguments/can-better-training-solve-cops-implicit-biases/.

Giuliani, R. W., & Kurson, K. (2002). *Leadership*. Westport, CT: Hyperion.

Glanz, J. (1999, October 10). Science vs. the Bible: Debate Moves to the Cosmos. *The New York Times*. Retrieved from https://www.nytimes.com/1999/10/10/us/science-vs-the-bible-debate-moves-to-the-cosmos.html?searchResultPosition=1.

Goldstein, H. (1979). Improving policing: A problem-oriented approach. *Crime and Delinquency, 25,* 236–258.

Hinkle, J. C., & Weisburd, D. (2008). The irony of broken windows policing: A micro-place study of the relationship between disorder, focused police crackdowns and fear of crime. *Journal of Criminal Justice, 36,* 503–512.
Kraska, P. B. (2018). Militarizing American police: An overview. In W. S. DeKeseredy & M. Dragiewicz (Eds.), *Routledge handbook of critical criminology* (2nd ed.). New York, NY: Routledge.
Leveillee, N. P. (2011). Conernicus, Galileo, and the church: Science in the religious world. *Inquires: Social Sciences, Arts & Humanities, 3*(5) 1–2. Retrieved from http://www.inquiriesjournal.com/articles/1675/copernicus-galileo-and-the-church-science-in-a-religious-world.
Mannheim, K. (1936). *Ideology and Utopia.* New York: Harcourt, Brace & World.
Maton, K. (2008). Habitus. In M. Grenfell (Ed.), *Pierre Bourdieu: Key concepts.* Acumen: Durham, UK.
Moore, R. (2008). Capital. In M. Grenfell (Ed.), *Pierre Bourdieu: Key concepts.* Acumen: Durham, UK.
Morris, D. (2018, February 17). Bad apples have spoiled the Baltimore police barrel. *The Baltimore Sun.* Retrieved from http://www.baltimoresun.com/news/opinion/oped/bs-ed-op-0218-bad-apples-20180215-story.html.
Nolan, J. (2016). How American policing fails neighborhoods—And cops. *The Conversation.* Retrieved from https://theconversation.com/how-american-policing-fails-neighborhoods-and-cops-63302.
Price, J., & Payton, E. (2017). Implicit bias and police use of lethal force: Justifiable homicide or potential discrimination? *Journal of African American Studies, 21,* 674–683.
Rigby, J. G., Woulfin, S. L., & Marz, V. (2016). Understanding how structure and agency influence education policy implementation and organisational change. *American Journal of Education, 122,* 295–302.
Rosenbaum, D. P. (2006). The limits of hot spots policing. In D. Weisburd & A. A. Braga (Eds.), *Police innovation: Contrasting perspectives.* Cambridge, UK: Cambridge University Press.
Sewell, W. H. (1992). The theory of structure: Duality, agency, and transformation. *American Journal of Sociology, 98,* 1–29.
Tyler, T. R. (2004). Enhancing police legitimacy. *The Annals of the American Academy of Political and Social Science, 593,* 84–99.
Weisburd, D., & Braga, A. A. (2006). *Police innovation: Contrasting perspectives.* Cambridge, UK: Cambridge University Press.

Weisburd, D., Groff, E. R., & Yang, S. M. (2012). *The criminology of place: Street segments and our understanding of the crime problem.* Oxford, UK: Oxford University Press.

Weisburd, D., Mastrofski, S. D., McNally, A. M., Greenspan, R., & Willis, J. J. (2003). Reforming to preserve: Compstat and strategic problem-solving in American policing. *Criminology & Public Policy, 2,* 421–456.

Wilson, J. Q., & Kelling, G. L. (1982). Broken windows: The police and neighborhood safety. *Atlantic Monthly, 211,* 29–38.

Wirth, L. (1936). *Preface to Karl Manheim's Ideology and Utopia.* New York: Harvest.

3

Community Policing: Often Advocated, Rarely Practiced

Timothy Parsons

Ask a citizen out on the street about community policing and they are likely to show some recognition of the term. It may strike them as oddly familiar, a term they have heard before, an established phrase that arises periodically in public discourse. Enquire of them further about the actual meaning of the term community policing and they may well begin to struggle. In that, they will not be alone, as many experienced police officers would probably also struggle to define what community policing is. This should not surprise anyone as there is no universally accepted definition of community policing or what the term actually means. Of course, there are many scholars and policymakers who have offered their own interpretations but there is variation in how the term is understood and what it describes.

T. Parsons (✉)
School of Justice Studies,
Liverpool John Moores University, Liverpool, UK
e-mail: T.F.Parsons@ljmu.ac.uk

J. J. Nolan et al. (eds.), *Policing in an Age of Reform*,
Palgrave's Critical Policing Studies,
https://doi.org/10.1007/978-3-030-56765-1_3

For some it is simply a policing approach that includes some form of consultation or partnership between the public and the police. For others it provides a wide-ranging and sophisticated vehicle for major police reform. From Australia to Armenia police services have committed themselves to introducing community policing programmes and practices and permanently embedding them within the organisational outputs of their respective services. There is clear evidence that the language and terminology of community policing has for many years now become enshrined in the international policing lexicon. Casey (2010, p. 11) points to what in effect is an often loosely defined concept, influencing wider discussions of policing approaches and becoming a form of "ideological cult with more slogans than substance and more followers than leaders". The pervasive influence of the community policing debate can even be detected in countries with tyrannical and despotic governments such as China and Zimbabwe, which also claim to have community policing at the core of a state-wide policing philosophy.

A series of similar but slightly different definitions of community policing can cause still further confusion in the minds of practitioner and citizen alike. Variously described as community-based, community-oriented or even neighbourhood policing, a lack of clarity in defining such terms can lead to a wide variety of strategic approaches and varying degrees of success in operational implementation. The OSCE (2008, p. 5) has defined community policing thus:

"A philosophy and organisational strategy that promotes a partnership-based, collaborative effort between the police and the community to more effectively and efficiently identify, prevent and solve problems of crime, the fear of crime, physical and social disorder, and neighbourhood decay in order to improve the quality of life for everyone".

Whilst Fielding (2005, p. 460) describes community policing as: "an iconic style of policing in which the police are close to the public, know their concerns from regular everyday contacts, and act on them in accord with the community's wishes".

Although these definitions are helpful in describing the philosophical approach to community policing as well as a vision for what it might deliver, it is useful to consider a more detailed analysis of the core components of a successful community policing programme. A wide-ranging study of approaches to community policing conducted by Mackenzie and Henry (2009) for the Government of Scotland analysed some 420 articles, books and research reports on the subject drawn from three major databases. The researchers distilled down the data looking both for similarities and differences across recently implemented community policing strategies in a number of different jurisdictions. From this they identified five key features common to successful community policing initiatives (1) Decentralisation—officers on the ground need to be able to respond to public concerns and make things happen at a local level. Centralised command structures slow down decision making with key decisions being made by senior officers remote from the context and location of any emerging problem. (2) Partnership—with other agencies, so police can act as an intermediary or facilitator when the public demand action on issues outside the immediate remit of law enforcement. (This may include local government, schools, youth workers, voluntary sector organisations or local businesses.) (3) Community Engagement—communities need to have a real voice that can be fed into police priorities and practices where appropriate. (4) Proactive and Problem-Solving—community policing marks a shift away from reactive "fire brigade" policing, this connects it with problem-oriented (POP) and intelligence-led (ILP) approaches to policing. This requires action to be initiated and directed by the engagement process, not shaped by existing, unreflective police definitions of local problems. (The problem-oriented model of policing was originally developed by Goldstein [1979] and comprised a system through which police officers develop effective strategies to prevent and reduce crime by a process of in-depth analysis of community crime problems, the crafting of a targeted response, followed by an assessment of the impact of the police intervention on the original problem.) (5) Philosophy—community policing heralds a changed understanding of real police work akin to peace officers embedded in the networks of their communities rather than as reactive law officers, although law enforcement remains important and should not be neglected.

A separate review conducted on behalf of the New Zealand Police, Coquilhat (2008) at around the same time and which also included a review of international literature reached, unsurprisingly, almost identical conclusions. This review identified partnerships, decentralisation and problem-solving as key components in any successful community policing strategy, adding flexibility and accountability as being equally important considerations.

Oversight and Accountability

Other studies of community policing, particularly as part of a wider police reform process in emerging democracies, have highlighted the requirement for a series of further supporting structures if community policing programmes are to endure and deliver positive results. Groenewald and Peake (2004, p. 10) suggested that these include structures for national and local oversight that encompass mechanisms with real and not just symbolic power and the authority to address problems. They go on to argue that there should also be clear roles and division of responsibilities with civilian participation in conducting oversight activities. In addition to appropriate oversight structures, a transparent process of police accountability should also be put in place. Accountability structures should provide a clear system of police accountability to government, parliament and the public (p. 18). Included in this system should be methods of direct communication with the public, including the introduction of hotlines and anonymous reporting mechanisms for complaints against the police. To be effective the public must have easy access to any complaints procedure.

To ensure successful implementation of new community policing programmes or the revision and refinement of existing programmes the role of the citizen is central. For community policing to work police organisations need to inform their public of any new strategy, raising awareness and enlisting the participation of the local community in making the initiative work. Murray (2005, p. 10). This should include raising people's awareness of their legal and human rights as well as their civic responsibilities. If required the police can assist local community groups to organise and mobilise public support.

Organisational Levels of Community Policing

Williams (2003), argues that delivering an effective and sustainable community policing strategy requires some major internal reform and re-organisation in the police service itself. At the central command level a major organisational change programme has to be initiated to realign internal departmental structures and resources to best support the implementation of a community policing approach at local level. Management structures must also be reformed with decision-making devolved down to neighbourhood level; empowering first and second line supervisors to respond quickly to locally identified problems and concerns by designing and delivering solutions using a problem-solving approach. Traditional and often long-established management approaches based upon military hierarchies would need to be changed, with a shift of emphasis away from discipline and compliance and towards leadership and empowerment. Mechanisms for providing reward, recognition and promotion for officers would ideally be aligned to qualitative measures (public satisfaction, letters of appreciation, increased community participation) and not crude quantitative measures of performance such as the numbers of arrests and stops and searches carried out in any given period. Finally budgeting and finance would have to be re-organised to support community policing with control over local policing budgets being devolved down to local commanders circumventing the need for central budget and spending authorisations.

Converting strategic objectives into tactical successes can present some significant challenges. And hovering above this theoretical corpus rests a fundamental question that has to be answered: if the essential components of a successful community policing strategy have been clearly identified, comprehensively described and widely circulated, why does the encounter with community policing in practice so often prove to be elusive? The first point to make here is that successful and recognisable community policing can only occur in a democratic space. That is to say that community policing can only be established and maintained in a constitutional environment inhabited by democratic government. Why is this distinction so important? Simply put, countries with no democracy, no rule of law no fundamental rights and freedoms, are unable to provide a system of policing that could remotely resemble community policing. It is an observable fact that in countries where autocratic regimes hold power there are present in the streets and other public spaces large numbers of men and women wearing uniforms with the word police written on them, but in reality these state officials are not engaged in policing. They are there to suppress dissent, to deny people their human rights and to use physical force to protect an undemocratic and unaccountable regime. That is not police work. Democratic policing, which must include a community policing approach to win public trust; cannot flourish in a vacuum, indeed it cannot exist at all unless it can be situated within a wider constitutional landscape. To be both effective and durable, a community policing programme will depend on a number of essential supporting pillars being in place. These would include; political oversight but not direct control, an independent judiciary, a free and independent press, strong civil society, public scrutiny and accountability, the rule of law and commitments to human rights and an independent body to investigate complaints of police malpractice. It is immediately obvious that none of these supporting pillars are likely to be present in a dictatorial or autocratic regime. But what might be the barriers to effective implementation and durability of community policing in a democratic country? Here the essential pillars of support outlined above are almost certainly going to be present and well-established.

One of the explanations put forward to explain the lack of success in establishing effective long-term community policing programmes is that the nature of police culture militates against it. This point is raised specifically in Coquilhat's paper as a likely barrier to implementation and acceptance. Concerns about the corrosive nature of police culture, sometimes referred to as canteen culture, have been raised on many occasions. In the UK the issue of a perceived malign police sub-culture came to prominence after incidents of violent disorder occurred in cities across Britain in 1981. The catalyst for these was a breakdown in relations between the Metropolitan Police and Black communities in Brixton and other areas of London. These events prompted the Home Secretary of the day to establish a judge-led inquiry into the causes of the trouble chaired by Lord Scarman (1986). Although complimentary about the efforts of the police in confronting and stemming the violence, Scarman also reflected on the need for the police to maintain the consent and support of the community. He also advised that officers should be trained in the problems of policing a multicultural society. These recommendations were accepted by the government, Belstead (1981) and yet four years later, following a raid on a premises in Broadwater Farm estate in Tottenham where a black woman Cynthia Jarrett collapsed and died following a police raid on her house to conduct a search for evidence against her son, a violent mob surrounded and murdered an unarmed community police officer, PC Keith Blakelock. Blakelock was slashed and stabbed by thirteen different weapons (and therefore presumably that number of assailants), with efforts made to decapitate him. To date no one has been brought to justice for his murder. These two events were significant, not just because of the public concern that they generated about the state of British policing, but because they also fueled a compelling narrative about a racist, aggressive and misogynist sub-culture that emanated from a white, largely male, working-class police workforce. Waddington (1999, p. 289), sought to analyse and untangle this narrative as thoroughly as possible. As a former senior police officer he had had the opportunity to observe this phenomenon at first hand. But taking a methodical approach and reviewing a considerable body of associated literature he concluded that "there is little relationship between the privately expressed views of police officers and their actual; behaviour on the streets, it appears that the concept of a police sub-culture contributes little to the explanation of policing".

On the issue of alleged misogyny among the police workforce Waddington concluded that the sexist attitudes of male police officers, which he didn't deny existed, was straightforwardly a manifestation of patriarchal beliefs abroad in wider society. An entirely plausible explanation. Writing at around the same time, Hall (1999, p. 189) was dismissive of suggestions that police attitudes largely reflected those of the population that they were recruited from. For Hall such arguments were "cynical and constitutionally unacceptable", he believed that they "could not be legitimately advanced". And yet, to hold a group of low-paid, poorly-trained and relatively low-ranking public servants to a higher standard of probity and ethical conduct than that found in wider society seems risible. Particularly in light of so many well-publicised cases of parliamentarians, members of the judiciary, hospital consultants and senior officers in HM armed forces being prosecuted and convicted of a wide range of criminal offences, ranging from fraud, to paedophilia. Hall and many like him; wrote with confidence and authority about an institution and organisational culture about which he knew nothing. Waddington rather sourly observed that the literature on police sub-culture "tells us more about the peculiarities of academic life than it does about the distinctiveness of the police". But Hall was confident of his own thesis that racism and bigotry were part of the organisational culture of policing and that discriminatory practices were an "indestructible part of the institutional habitus". Harnessing a term brought to prominence by the French sociologist Pierre Bourdieu.

Bourdieu's (1996, p. 10) societal critique is relevant here, although perhaps not in the way that Hall envisaged. Bourdieu's conception of habitus describes a social space that a person occupies. It refers to a person's tastes, habits, interests and opinions. Here lies the seed of another substantial barrier to community policing being both effective and enduring. Over the last thirty years in Britain at least, the shape and character of the police workforce has changed markedly. What was once a largely if not exclusively proletarian occupation employing white working-class men and women in a blue-collar job that required only basic levels of literacy and numeracy as requirements for entry, has metamorphasised into a profession: now into an all-graduate profession. This puts social distance between the police officer and the community being policed. But the process of distancing does not end there. Bourdieu also reflects on the meaning of space, of physical space and social space.

"Social space is an invisible set of relationships which tends to retranslate itself, in a more or less direct manner, into physical space in the form of a definite distributional arrangement of agents and properties". It is significant that as the police population transformed from working-class to middle-class, so too did the physical distribution of those officers change. From the mid-1990s onward changes to police housing allowance and the provision of police flats and houses for officers to live in, underwent wide-ranging reform. Allowances were reduced and police flats and houses sold off, thereby reducing the likelihood that officers, certainly in London, would continue to live close to the area where they worked. In a research report published by a UK think tank Gaskath (2016, p. 8), revealed that of the 18,179 officers assigned to local borough policing only 8896 lived in Central London and only 1261 lived in the borough that they policed. Some London police officers lived as far away as Cornwall or the South of France. This matters because it serves to undermine the fundamentals of community policing doctrine. With physical detachment comes emotional detachment and the crime and security problems of the area being policed can easily be forgotten on the journey home from work. This is unlikely to happen if the officer lives in the neighbourhood that he or she polices. In that circumstance local crime problems become personal; because they also affect the officer concerned and the officer's family. So with police officers being in some sense distant from the community they police the likelihood of them developing a close and trusting relationship with the citizens they are responsible for is quickly diminished.

So what conceivably can be done to address the structural weaknesses of current approaches to establishing long-term community policing programmes, as well as some of the cultural barriers articulated above? A recent study by Walton and Falkner (2019, p. 29), seeks to address these very points. The study is given greater gravitas by the fact that one of the authors Richard Walton is a recently retired commander in the Metropolitan Police with important insider perspectives on how present problems have evolved and the sort of measures that might be taken to ameliorate them.

Walton and Falkner postulate that there are five key challenges facing UK policing at present: increasing crime levels, linked to greater demand and reduced budgets, neighbourhood decline, national security threats a disempowered workforce and a policing model that is outpaced by technology. In a classic defence of the community policing approach and with a gently muted echo of Bourdieu they state "The presence of dedicated officers in a local "place" allows them to build up their knowledge of an area and gather better intelligence of local issues and individuals most likely to be involved in crime, either as perpetrators or victims". The authors argue for a new community policing strategy to be rolled-out nationwide. Specifically, they call for "high-impact community policing re-invigorated with a stronger focus". They acknowledge the problem outlined above of community police officers having to commute into the areas that they work in, rather than being domiciled in the local area itself. Their solution is to use the power of local government to ensure that some houses in new developments are allocated to local police officers and that interest-free loans are made available to officers to assist them to offset or defer some of the costs associated with moving home. Importantly, Walton & Falkner also call for a new national policing infrastructure with a service that is "nationally led, regionally co-ordinated" but still "responsive to local communities". The authors recommend the retention of the 43 territorial police forces in England and Wales (the eight police forces in Scotland were amalgamated into a single force, Police Scotland, by the Scottish Government in 2013), and acknowledge the importance of the National Crime Agency in tackling the threat from organised crime.

The Way Forward

It is undoubtedly true that the societal environment in which policing operates is changing. A consequence of globalisation and the combined effects of conflict, political instability and climate change in some parts of the world means that people are on the move and populations are changing. Technological change, the evolution and near universal adoption of internet services including social media platforms has led to new opportunities for organised crime groups and terrorists to operate and expand their influence across multiple jurisdictions. For politicians and policymakers these changes have acted as a catalyst for new thinking about the function, role and structure of modern police services. In the UK there is a move towards an all-graduate service with a need for a better-educated, more technologically proficient class of officer being required, located in a far more professionalised working environment than was the case only a few decades ago. Explaining the rationale behind this new approach the College of Policing notes that[1]:

"Police officers make difficult decisions which impact the public every day. They face complex problems, often in dangerous situations, with growing demands from digital investigation and vulnerable people.

The existing recruit training programme for officers at the start of their career wasn't designed with these demands in mind. The new programme recognises constables operate at a level where they take personal responsibility for decisions in complex, unpredictable environments".

All of this may be true, but it is also the case that the fundamentals of policing have not changed and that much, if not the majority of police work is low-tech, if not no-tech and requires the same skills now from police officers that were required fifty years ago. Officers routinely deal with people who are drunk, drugged or mentally ill (often a combination of these three factors are in play). Similarly, officers have to respond to incidents of domestic abuse and sexual violence, child exploitation and in some communities, ongoing problems with anti-social behaviour. None of these problems are new or particularly enabled by developing technology. To address these problems effectively officers require, patience, empathy, communication skills and personal integrity. None of these vital attributes are confined to or necessarily associated with degree-level learning. By instigating these policy changes linked to recruitment, police leaders are effectively excluding from participation in the service the very demographic that has provided the bulk of officers for the past 180 years. That is to say, white working-class men and women and diversity targets notwithstanding, working-class individuals from other ethnic groups. For recruits drawn from the working class the police service has historically provided a career that could be accessed with the minimum of educational requirements and which provided opportunities for development and professional advancement.

Thirty years ago, the majority of UK Chief Constables would not have had degrees, nor indeed would they have had experience of any higher-level education. And yet those men (and they were at the time all men), were in the main, charismatic and effective leaders; police officers who

[1] www.college.police.uk "what we do".

had worked their way up through the ranks gaining knowledge, experience and professional expertise as they went. To deny future access to the service for people such as this seems short-sighted, pernicious and counter-productive. For community policing to work the community police officers need to understand and experience the life led by the citizens that they are there to protect and support. If community police officers are socially, professionally and for much of the time physically distant from the people they serve, or occupy an entirely separate habitus as Bourdieu would put it, then the whole enterprise risks becoming some grim sociological experiment where well-educated professionals travel in each day to examine, analyse and categorise the threats, risks and challenges confronting the local residents. Where is the human component in this?

Walton and Falkner are right to call for changes to the national policing infrastructure and the College of Policing is right to identify that policing occurs in a complex and unpredictable environment. But rather than simply establishing better structures or co-ordinating bodies to respond to evolving change across the national (and international) landscape, a more radical reform to structure and organisation might be called for. A new National Constabulary (perhaps a Royal Constabulary), could be established to provide a stronger and more effective enforcement arm to compliment and support the crucial and expanding workload of the National Crime Agency (NCA).

Providing a national force would solve some of the cross-border confusion and dissipated effort that inevitably results from having so many separate and autonomous police forces. This new force would be permanently armed thereby addressing the obvious vulnerability to mass-casualty terrorist attacks that a country with a largely unarmed police service is exposed to. Assuming responsibility for firearms operations, public order policing, roads policing, much of the counter-terrorism policing effort and border security the new force would, to all intents and purposes resemble a UK gendarmerie or civil guard. Of course such an innovation would be anathema to many police leaders and politicians who would argue with some justification that it would completely change the established UK policing model. But if the most valued and valuable aspects of that model are to survive, radical changes must be made. A major structural change such as this would allow for the continuation of the 43 force structure with local and community policing remaining in the hands of provincial forces with local governance and accountability and importantly, locally focused recruitment.

A more flexible and pragmatic approach could be taken to how community police officers are selected trained and qualified. The days of the police generalist must surely be at an end. In the not so distant past, police officers could join the service undertake some rather rudimentary basic training and then with experience and support from above move into more specialised areas of policing, whether into criminal investigation, forensics, economic crime, public order, firearms or many other discrete specialisms within the service. Such a system is no longer viable for reasons of cost and efficiency as well increased specialisation, which requires an officer to take much longer to build up and develop the requisite skills. So in an era of specialisation it must be both appropriate and desirable to categorise the community officer as a "specialist". These officers should be ring-fenced and not placed in a flexible pool of non-specialist officers who can be called upon at short notice to deploy to other areas wherever a short-term staffing shortage is identified. Efforts to protect the status of community officers have been made before, to ensure compliance it should be enshrined in legislation thereby giving status and protection to the vitally important community police officer as well as communicating to the communities that they serve, the importance with which the role is regarded by officialdom, by Police and Crime Commissioners, Chief Constables and Government ministers. Through such a reform can both police and public confidence be restored in the role and function of community policing.

Conclusion

To conclude, it is obvious that a community policing strategy of any description can only exist in a democratic country with the rule of law and the necessary supporting pillars in place that are described above. There are barriers to the successful introduction, implementation and durability of community policing strategies. Whilst organisational culture, or rather sub-culture may have presented a malign influence in the past its relevance was almost certainly over-stated and its very presence remains a contested area of debate. With changes to wider society have come changes to the demographics of the police workforce. There is a greater representation of women, gay officers and a multiplicity of different ethnicities, nationalities and religious beliefs now being represented within the ranks of the modern police service. These changes have occurred organically and gradually with little influence from policymakers. However, changes to educational requirements for entry, multiple points of entry into the service allowing for the effective introduction of an officer class into what has always historically been a proletarian occupation has occurred as a consequence of deliberate political intervention. The results of these changes are still being played out and it is too soon to assess their impact with confidence.

Structural changes to the police organisation, the formation of a national force with nationwide powers and officers deployed across the regions would seem to present a rational, effective response to changes in crime patterns and the increased threat from cross-border organised crime and terrorism. Enshrining both the role and presence of experienced and dedicated community police officers in communities through changes to legislation and public duties placed upon elected Police and Crime Commissioners would provide a permanence and sustainability to community policing that has been absent up till now. A professionalised, all-graduate service may deliver some benefits at the technical edge of modern crime-fighting but it also threatens to undermine and neutralise the accrued benefits of close police-community interaction, co-operation and inter-dependence.

References

Belstead, L. (1981). *House of Lords debate on the Scarman inquiry* (Hansard vol. 425, CC 769–787). Retrieved from https://api.parliament.uk/historic-hansard/lords/1981/nov/25/the-scarman-report.

Bourdieu, P. (1996). *Physical space, social space & habitus: Rapport 10:1996*. Oslo: Institute for Sociology and Human Geography, University of Oslo, 11–20. Retrieved from https://archives.library.illinois.edu/erec/University%20Archives/2401001/Production_website/pages/StewardingExcellence/Physical%20Space,%20Social%20Space%20and%20Habitus.pdf.

Casey, J. (2010). Implementing community policing in different countries and cultures. *Pakistan Journal of Criminology, 2*(4), 55–75. College of Policing website https://www.college.police.uk/What-we-do/Learning/Policing-Education-Qualifications-Framework/Entry-routes-for-police-constables/Pages/Entry-routes-for-police-constables.aspx.

Coquilhat, J. (2008). *Community policing: An international literature review*. New Zealand: Evaluation Team, Organisational Assurance, New Zealand Police.

Fielding, N. G. (2005). Concepts & theory in community policing. *The Howard Journal, 44*(5), 460–472.

Gaskath, G. (2016). *Commuter cops: Helping our police to live in the city they serve*. London: Policy Exchange, Capital City Foundation.

Goldstein, H. (1979). Improving policing: A problem-oriented approach. *Crime & Delinquency, 25*(2), 236–258.

Groenewald, H., & Peake, G. (2004). *Police reform through community-based policing: Philosophy and guidelines for implementation*. New York, NY: International Peace Academy, pp. 15–20.

Hall, S. (1999). From Scarman to Stephen Lawrence. *History Workshop Journal, 48*(1), 187–197.

Mackenzie, S., & Henry, A. (2009). *Community policing: A review of the evidence*. Edinburgh: Scottish Government Social Research.

Murray, J. (2005). Policing terrorism: A threat to community policing or just a shift in priorities? *Police Practice & Research, 6*(4), 347–361.

Scarman, L. S. (1986). *The Scarman report* (Report of an inquiry). England: Penguin.

Senior Police Adviser to the OSCE Secretary General. (2008). *Good practices in building police-public partnerships*. Vienna: OSCE. Retrieved from https://www.osce.org/secretariat/32547?download=true.

Waddington, P. A. J. (1999). Police (canteen) sub-culture: An appreciation. *British Journal of Criminology, 39*(2), 286–308.

Walton, R., & Falkner, S. (2019). *Rekindling British policing: A 10-point plan*. London: Policy Exchange, 25–46.

Williams, E. J. (2003). Structuring in community policing: Institutionalizing innovative change. *Police Practice and Research, l4*(2), 119–129.

4

Policing in an Age of Reform—An Overview of the United Kingdom Community-Centred Police Model

Victor Olisa

The public's expectation is that the police should be ever-present to deal with any situation where there is uncertainty. Which, in a way, is also the same expectation as operational police officers, the world over. Take the example of an activation of the ubiquitous burglar alarm on a high-value property. Regardless of the fact that operational experience and statistics show that most activations are false alarms, nonetheless, officers—both experienced and inexperienced, will rush to attend an activated alarm and will do so in numbers. Bitner's (1990, p. 249) description of the police mission neatly captures the vagueness and ambiguity that is the inevitable consequence of a vast multiplicity of tasks that are routinely undertaken by patrolling police officers. Many of those tasks such as safeguarding the mentally ill and other vulnerable groups are not always undertaken willingly or with the application of much expertise. Historically police officers have evolved as quintessential generalists collecting

V. Olisa (✉)
VP Olissa Associates, Godalming, UK
e-mail: Infor@vp.olisaassociateslimited.com

J. J. Nolan et al. (eds.), *Policing in an Age of Reform*,
Palgrave's Critical Policing Studies,
https://doi.org/10.1007/978-3-030-56765-1_4

tasks and responsibilities that they are often ill-equipped to undertake but which are nevertheless discharged with the support and consent of the citizenry.

In the United Kingdom, this policing by consent style is exemplified by the nine Principles supposedly advocated by Sir Robert Peel.[1] The police service is a powerful social institution that carries out the activities of policing remarkably similarly regardless of which democratic country those activities are taking place in. This chapter seeks to explain that one of the reasons for this is because of the core characteristics of police culture. Bourdieu (1977) refers to a mindset—*habitus*—that ensures that regardless of the environment and circumstances—*field*—in which policing is being delivered, police officers have the unerring ability to interpret their local rules, regulations and processes in a way that creates a police milieu; bring a group of officers together from different parts of the globe and within a short time they will develop a shared understanding of how they should carry out their work and behave (Klockars, Kutnjak, Ivkovic, & Haberfield, 2004). So, although their original *field* of operation may be different, the concept of the 'policeman's working personality' (Skolnick, p. 19) could help explain why they are swift and adept at establishing a common *habitus*.

Policing by Consent and How It Is Applied

The concept of 'policing by consent' although not the cornerstone of policing in the United Kingdom, does have considerable relevance in the strategic direction pursued by all British police organisations. This concept is the basis of a model of policing that seeks the support or at least the acquiescence of most of the populace. To achieve this, the police have developed strategies to steer their operational activities towards closer working with their local public, coupled with more

[1]The precise origins of the Peelite principles are a contested area of debate. It is most unlikely that they originated with Peel or with the first commissioners of the Metropolitan Police, Rowan and Mayne. The most credible explanation is that they were drawn up by a police historian called Charles Reith in the 1940s. (See: Emsley, C. (2013) "Peel's Principles" in J. Brown (ed) The Future of Policing, London. Routledge.)

frequent dialogue with communities at local levels. Variations of this model can be discerned in other police organisations across the globe and coupled with differences in the *fields* in other countries one would have expected some differences in the *habitus*. In the last decade, there has been uncertainty in the UK *fields* (and elsewhere), caused by the implementation of austerity measures that resulted in reduction in budgets, reduction in recruitment that led to reduction in police officer numbers, reduction in training, increases in certain crimes, such as cybercrime (fraud, child abuse and exploitation) that pulled officers away from 'front line' public space activities and consequently led to reduced visibility and accessibility to many communities. Additionally, there has been increased public knowledge and awareness of police organisations as a consequence of increased media coverage, published research studies and publicly available results of scrutiny efforts by different regulatory bodies, such as Her Majesty's Inspectorate of Constabulary and Fire & Rescue Services (formerly Her Majesty's Inspectorate of Constabulary), the Independent Office for Police Conduct (formerly Independent Police Complaints Commission) and Independent Inquiries (Flanagan, 2008; Lammy, 2017; Macpherson, 1999). These significant changes in the *field* of policing have had some effect on the structure and style of policing in Britain and one would have expected this to manifest itself differently in the *habitus* in the different police organisations.

Neighbourhood Policing

The model for delivering community-centred policing in the United Kingdom is Safer Neighbourhood Policing, which was launched in 2004 in London. In a Home Office strategy document titled *Building Communities, Beating Crime: a better police service for the 21st century* the government of the day set out its vision for the future of neighbourhood policing in England and Wales. The document noted that 'People and in particular victims and witnesses, will only engage with their local police if they have confidence that when they make contact they will be treated well and that their concerns will be listened to and acted on effectively' (p. 7). A clear and ambitious vision was set out for every district to have a dedicated neighbourhood policing team. And yet, as all too often happens the political ambition fell some way short of the experienced reality for citizens. In a report conducted on behalf of the UK Government cabinet office in 2008 titled *Engaging Communities in Fighting Crime* respondents to a focus group observed.

> The experience for most residents is, we call the police, they tell us it is not a policing issue, it is a housing issue. You go to housing and they will tell you that you need to go to social services, they will tell you that you need to go to environmental health. The residents have given up hope of having some of these things resolved. (p. 36)

It is inevitable that public confidence in the police and policing will be significantly undermined if a continuous stream of pledges are made with detailed descriptions of the service that will be provided but the lived experience, the street-level reality for residents is something entirely different from the vision of life that has been promised to them by politicians.

A Summary of Some of the Public Disturbances and Concerns

In 2009 after significant public disorder occurred on the streets of London following a controversial meeting of the G20 group of nations aimed at resolving the global financial crisis, Her Majesty's Inspectors of Constabulary (HMIC) published a review of public order policing tactics, *Adapting to Protest: Nurturing the British Policing Model* in which the inspectors noted the following:

> The original British model of policing—is designed to be adaptable to ensure the safety of the public and the preservation of the peace within a tolerant, plural society. This is what makes the British model attractive to so many abroad as well as at home. There is no convincing evidence that a radical change—whether of individual components or of the entire British policing model—would yield better results for the public and any

> proposed change would require a carefully considered assessment of the impact on British heritage, politics, law and police operations. (p. 12)

Such complacency bordering on hubris was sure to rebound on the report's authors and so it was to be. In 2011, following the entirely lawful shooting of a suspect by armed police in London, towns and cities across England became the scene of widespread rioting, looting, and disorder. The police struggled to cope. After five years of theorising about the root cause of the riots in England in 2011, Hallsworth (2016) offered a new perspective that was different from either the government's hard line on the involvement of gangs or the left's view of the looting as an anti-capitalist protest. He explained, in his article title 'What the 2011 Summer Riots Were Really About'; published in the online version of VICE,

> It's been five years, and the question still remains of how we make sense of the English riots of 2011. Riots that saw more than 14,000 people take to the streets across England for three days. Events that saw buildings destroyed, neighbourhoods wrecked, shops looted and five lives lost. There can be no doubt that it was a social event of some magnitude—but quite what it meant and represented is still open to debate. For the government and tabloid media, it was, from the beginning, all about gangs and "mindless criminality". And even when it became clear that gangs didn't cause the riots and that, arguably, a more sophisticated understanding was needed to explain the worst outbreak of disorder the UK had witnessed in the post-World War era, gang suppression was still trotted out as the dominant government response to riots not caused by gangs. So much for evidence-based policy. (para. 2)

For academics Hall and Winlow (2014), the riots simply expressed the situation of the urban poor in a post-political present.

> Vaguely pissed off about their situation but lacking any capacity to articulate their opposition to the system that marginalised them, in rioting they blindly acted out their discontent. There may be a different interpretation; one that considers the riots less from the perspective of what people said about them after they happened, but attends more closely to

> the acts the rioters were actually engaged in. By looking more closely at what people did as opposed to what they retrospectively said they were doing, a different interpretation of the riots emerges. (ibid., para .4)

The precise cause or causes of such widespread rioting and disorder will remain a contested area of debate, the fact was that the police response was inadequate and once again citizens were put in danger and much property was damaged. The Inspectors of Constabulary published another review of public order policing, *Policing Public Order* (2011). In this report the authors noted that 'The inescapable fact is that adaptability and preparedness come at a cost – a significant cost potentially in these straitened times' but 'The police must prevail in these circumstances to keep the peace' (p. 5).

In an environment of social and political change, police leaders and policy makers are confronted with the task of reflecting upon the strengths, weaknesses, vulnerabilities and legacy of a long-established policing system whilst simultaneously attempting to frame a new approach suitable for twenty first century Britain. The political rhetoric, the narrative of success, the endless commitments to reform and improved service simply do not materialise. A fact most graphically illustrated by comments made in 2013 by Sir Peter Fahy, the then Chief Constable of greater Manchester Police, one of England's largest forces. He claimed that six out of ten crimes were not investigated by police with officers concentrating on the 40% of most serious crimes with the rest being effectively shelved (Chorley, 2013). Fahy spoke with commendable frankness but his disclosure sits in stark contrast to those pledges contained in the *Building Communities, Beating Crime* strategy published nine years previously. It would be pleasing to think that in recent times the situation had improved, that the propinquity between police officer and citizen, between police leader and police minister had somehow drawn closer with all focused on a central mission of police reform. And yet evidence points to the opposite being true. Following the death of a black man, George Floyd, at the hands of a white police officer in Minnesota in May of this year (2020), widespread violence and disorder broke out across the United Kingdom and police officers struggled to respond. But, the difference in attitude to these events by political leaders couldn't have been more stark. Diane Abbot a black Labour MP and Shadow Home Secretary from 2016–2020, had this to say, as reported in her local newspaper:

> "Tory MPs are saying people shouldn't go out and demonstrate for safety reasons but police violence is a threat to the safety of black people, particularly black men, internationally. It's right to demonstrate against that." (Hackney Gazette)

These comments contrast with the tone struck by the current Conservative Home Secretary Priti Patel, an MP of British Indian descent, after police officers were attacked in South London. Patel described violence shown towards police officers as 'utterly vile' (Braddick, 2020). Earlier Patel had clashed in Parliament with black Labour MPs who condemned the government for not taking attacks on black and visible ethnic minorities seriously. Patel took exception to this describing her own experiences of racism and discrimination (McGuiness, 2020). With such partisan divisions apparent in the UK parliament and the vexed issue of police reform being constantly viewed through the prism of race, the path towards enlightened consensus appears strewn with obstacles.

Culture and Service Delivery

In his study of *Organisational Culture and Leadership,* Schein (2004) explains that 'culture can be analysed at several different levels, with the term *level* meaning the degree to which the cultural phenomenon is *visible* to the observer' (p. 25). At the level of personal observation there are artifacts. These include '...all the phenomenon that one sees, hears and feels when one encounters a new group with an unfamiliar culture' (p. 26). Artifacts include the products of an organisation, profession or group that include symbols, rituals and ceremonies. This model of culture helps us explain how different *fields* of policing produce very similar *habitus* in officers: The values of each police organisation are very similar, despite the fact that they are operating in different environments and the model for delivering community-centred policing is different across the globe. It can be persuasively argued that the stated values of each organisation do not correspond to the activities of a policing service provided to communities made up of people from minority ethnic backgrounds. Indeed the current crisis in UK policing is in large measure a consequence of the inability of policy makers and police leaders to offer a prescription for police reform that effectively side lines obsolete practices and procedures whilst at the same time responding to demands for greater sensitivity and understanding of the fast-changing demographics in Britain, a country with a highly complex and extremely diverse population encompassing a multitude of different nationalities, cultures, religions, ethnicities and backgrounds. Alarmingly, under constant assault from politicians and mainstream media outlets the police service in Britain begins to resemble a frightened rabbit caught in the spotlight of public scrutiny and lacking sufficient internal momentum to move forward in any given direction. When headlines in national newspapers begin to appear such as this:

> Britain's woke police forces have lost their way. In their desperation to be loved and not seen as racist, officers are failing to keep order in response to hooliganism and violence, (Murray, 2020)

And this: 'Our police are a bigger threat to your freedom than Putin. Reform the police now or regret it forever' (Hitchens, 2019). It becomes painfully clear that confidence and trust in police organisations and the police mission itself is fast becoming eroded. The brief examination of public disturbances and concerns with the way that force has been used by police officers, all show a level of distrust of the police by people from minority ethnic backgrounds because of the negative way the police treat them, and yet as we see in the headlines reproduced above that perspective is not shared by all. It becomes increasingly apparent that despite promises by those in authority and positions of power that there would be improvements in the social conditions and police contact with these groups of people, things have not improved. One often expressed explanation by minority communities was that the authorities did not care about them. These people are marginalised and stigmatised, often stereotyped as criminogenic and under such circumstances it is not surprising that one of the solutions to the challenges that officers face in dealing with these groups that has worked, is treating people from that group as 'police property' (Reiner, 2000, p. 93). Reiner explains it in the following way:

> ...a category becomes police property when the dominant powers of society (in the economy, polity, etc.) leave the problems of social control of that category to the police. They are low-status, powerless groups whom the dominant majority see as problematic or distasteful. The majority are prepared to let the police deal with their 'property' and turn a blind eye to the manner in which this is done....The concerns with 'police property' is not so much to enforce the law as to maintain order using the law as one resource among others. (ibid., p. 93)

Whilst this might have been a viable tactic in the past, the days of such an approach being either effective or accepted, are long gone. Today people from across communities in the United Kingdom are looking for a more responsive, more flexible, more proactive stance from all of the nation's different police organisations. There is clearly an absence of both leadership and vision in the upper echelons of the service which is why the police find themselves being buffeted by current events rather than charting a sustained and viable path to reorganisation and reform.

Conclusion

Policing is a complex social activity because people want and expect different things from the police and consequently people's judgement of the effectiveness of the police will also be different. These two factors alone have the potential of making any judgement of police effectiveness and fairness on an objective basis very difficult. Nonetheless, there is consistency in the policing styles, informed by a similar mindset of officers—the *habitus*—of certain groups by most policing organisations despite the differences in the geographical areas—their *field*. The way police officers view their milieu is a powerful factor that shapes the core components of police culture. The one component of that culture that influences their power difference with some sections of communities and consequently their disproportionate policing rather than service provision, is their view of who are 'police property'. But powerful voices have spoken against this approach and the clash of ethnic minority voices within the UK parliament itself is a testimony to the new power and influence of a previously discriminated against and often voiceless minority. Nevertheless the endless over-promising and under-delivering of successive governments in the arena of policing and community safety, serves to gradually drain away the confidence and trust of all communities in the ability of the police to consistently and reliably provide safe streets, secure property and access to justice. One challenge for police leaders and leadership in the future is their ability and desire to harness all the positive aspects of police culture to ensure that the *habitus* of officers is informed by evidence that leads to provision of policing services that is fair and equitable and consistent with the *field* in which the service is delivered. Enabling a police service that is fastidiously non-political, non-sectarian, impartial and transparent in its dealings with the public is, paradoxically a very political undertaking. Government must create both the means and the momentum for change. The United Kingdom is a diverse and multicultural society, to succeed and flourish the police service too must reflect that diversity and array of different cultures. That is a difficult task to deliver, it requires bold leadership from both police leaders and politicians, people of vision and character who can negotiate their way past the short term and often inflammatory rhetoric of press and social media, entrenching a new and equitable approach to policing around which all communities may congregate with confidence and trust.

References

Ascoli, D. (1979). *The queen's peace: The origins and development of the metropolitan police 1829–1979*. London: Hamish Hamilton.

Bitner, E. (1990). *Aspects of police work*. Boston: Northeastern University Press.

Bourdieu, P. (1977). *Outline of a theory of practice*. Cambridge, UK: Cambridge University Press.

Braddick, I. (2020). *Home secretary Priti Patel has condemned the "utterly vile" violence at a street party in South London*. https://www.standard.co.uk/news/crime/brixton-street-party-priti-patel-reaction-a4479736.html (Accessed 30/6/20).

Chorley, M. (2013). *Six in ten crimes never investigated admits Manchester's police chief*. https://www.dailymail.co.uk/news/article-2411191/Manchester-police-chief-Six-10-crimes-investigated.html.

Critchley, T. A. (1978). *A history of police in England and Wales*. London: Constable.

Flanagan, R. (2008). *The review of policing: Final report*. https://www.justiceinspectorates.gov.uk/hmicfrs/media/flanagan-review-of-policing-20080201.pdf.

Hall, S., & Winlow, S. (2014). The English riots of 2011: Misreading the signs on the road to the society of enemies. In F. Pakes & D. Pritchard (Eds.), *Riot: Unrest and protest on the global stage*. Basingstoke: Palgrave Macmillan.

Hallsworth, S. (2016). What the 2011 Summer riots were really about. *VICE online magazine*. 6th August. https://www.vice.com/en_uk/article/kwkbde/england-riots-2011-five-years-later-analysis (Accessed 29/6/20).

Hitchens, P. (2019). *Our police are a bigger threat to your freedom than Putin*. https://www.dailymail.co.uk/debate/article-7318515/PETER-HITCHENS-police-bigger-threat-freedom-Putin.html (Accessed 30/6/20).

HMIC. (2011). *Policing public order: An overview and review of progress against the recommendations of adapting to protest and nurturing the British policing model*. https://www.justiceinspectorates.gov.uk/hmicfrs/media/policing-public-order-20110208.pdf (Accessed 29/6/20).

Klockars, C. B., Kutnjak, Ivkovic, S., & Haberfeld, M. R (2004). *The contours of police integrity*. London: Sage.

Lammy, D. (2017). *An independent review into the treatment of, and outcomes for black, Asian and minority ethnic individuals in the criminal justice system*. https://www.gov.uk/government/publications/lammy-review-final-report (Accessed 29/6/20).

Macpherson, W. (1999). *The Stephen Lawrence inquiry report*. https://www.gov.uk/government/publications/the-stephen-lawrence-inquiry (Accessed 29/6/20).

McGuiness, A. (2020). *Priti Patel says she will not be silenced.* https://news.sky.com/story/labour-mps-accuse-priti-patel-of-using-her-experiences-of-racism-to-gaslight-other-minority-communities-12004894 (Accessed 30/6/20).

Murray, D. (2020). *Britain's woke police forces have lost their way.* https://www.telegraph.co.uk/news/2020/06/30/britains-woke-police-forces-have-lost-way/ (Accessed 30/6/20).

Reiner, R. (2000). *The politics of the police.* Oxford: Oxford University Press.

Schein, E. H. (2004). *Organisational culture and leadership* (3rd ed.). San Francisco, CA: Jossey Bass.

Skolnick, J. H. (1966). *Justice without trial: Law enforcement in democratic society.* New York: Wiley.

Storch, R. D. (1975). "The plague of blue locusts": Police reform and popular resistance in Northern England 1840–1857. *International Review of Social History, 20,* 61–90.

Van Maanen, J. (1978). The asshole. In J. Van Maanen & P. Manning (Eds.), *Policing: A view from the streets* (pp. 302–328). New York: Random House.

5

Community Dynamics, Collective Efficacy, and Police Reform

James J. Nolan and Joshua C. Hinkle

Introduction

> The task is to produce, if not a "new person," then at least a "new gaze," a sociological eye. And this cannot be done without a genuine conversion, a *metanoia*, a mental revolution, a transformation of one's whole vision of the social world. (Bourdieu & Wacquant, 1992, p. 251)

J. J. Nolan (✉)
Department of Sociology and Anthropology, West Virginia University, Morgantown, WV, USA
e-mail: jim.nolan@mail.wvu.edu

J. C. Hinkle
Department of Criminal Justice and Criminology, Georgia State University, Atlanta, GA, USA
e-mail: jhinkle@gsu.edu

J. J. Nolan et al. (eds.), *Policing in an Age of Reform*,
Palgrave's Critical Policing Studies,
https://doi.org/10.1007/978-3-030-56765-1_5

In this chapter, we shift our focus from what the police do—and think they *should* do—to what the research says about community safety. In particular, we draw from the literature on place-based *social mechanisms* and crime (Donnermeyer & DeKeseredy, 2014; Sampson, 2013). Collective efficacy has been defined by sociologists as "cohesion among residents combined with shared expectations for social control in public space" (Sampson & Raudenbush, 1999, p. 603). Studies conducted in diverse places such as Chicago, Miami-Dade, and Stockholm, Sweden, have found that among neighbourhoods with similar characteristics those with higher levels of collective efficacy had significantly lower rates of crime (Sampson, 2013; Sampson & Raudenbush, 1999; Uchida, Swatt, Solomon, & Varano, 2014). It is difficult to overstate the recent interest in collective efficacy as a focus of study in criminology and sociology. Nearly 1500 research articles focusing on collective efficacy and crime were published in top sociology journals between 1999 and 2018.[1] Notably, in his 2012 Presidential address to the American Society of Criminology, Robert Sampson, a leading figure in the study of collective efficacy and crime, asked the question "…what role can the police play in building collective efficacy?" (Sampson, 2013, p. 22).

From our perspective this is a good question. We presume that neighbourhoods with low levels of collective efficacy are places where crimes are likely to occur and where the police will spend much of their time. Given this, we wondered what conditions existed in places where collective efficacy was low. We imagined a neighbourhood as a container—like a cup or bowl—that contained only a little collective efficacy. So we asked, what would the remainder of the neighbourhood cup be filled with? Our search for the answer to this question has led to our key concept of *neighbourhood atmosphere*, which we will explain in some detail below. First, however, we must explain the connection between modes of human agency and their related forms of efficacy beliefs.

---

[1]The JSTOR search was conducted by the first author on March 16, 2018, and it included only the 148 sociology journals indexed in the database. A search for terms 'collective efficacy' and 'crime' revealed a sixfold increase in published research in sociology journals (from 243 to 1499) in the 20-year period 1999–2018 compared with the period 1969–1988.

Human Agency and Efficacy Beliefs

Human agency is the capacity of individuals and groups to intentionally exercise control over the nature and quality of their lives. Efficacy beliefs provide the motivation to act and the perseverance needed for human agents to struggle and succeed (Bandura, 2001). In Bandura's social cognitive theory, there are three modes of human agency—personal, proxy, and collective—each with their own particular form of efficacy beliefs. Personal agency refers to the ways in which individuals, on their own, can influence events that affect their lives. Self-efficacy beliefs provide the motive force for personal agency. It affects the ways in which the individual views his or her chances of success, the choices he/she makes to continue or abandon certain activities or to modify them. High levels of self-efficacy beliefs predict success as individuals struggle to achieve personal aims. Proxy agency, on the other hand, refers to intentional efforts of individuals to get others to act on their behalf to achieve a particular outcome. Hiring a plumber or electrician to make home repairs, calling on legislators to advocate for certain laws on behalf of the community, or asking the police to reduce crime for a community are examples of proxy agency. Proxy (or social) efficacy beliefs are related to proxy agency in that they reflect the expectation one might have for success in enlisting competent help in achieving some desired end.

Finally, collective agency refers to intentional acts by groups of people to accomplish something together. Collective efficacy, then, refers specifically to the shared belief among members in the ability of the group to produce its desired results. Collective efficacy is an emergent group-level property and not the sum of its members' self-efficacy beliefs (Bandura, 2001). In neighbourhood research collective efficacy has typically been conceptualized on a linear scale from low to high. But, this conceptualization conceals the richer—and arguably more useful—dynamic processes that lead to or away from high levels of collective efficacy. In the following sections we explain this more fully beginning with the concept of neighbourhood.

The Concept of Neighbourhood

In the practice of policing and in police research the term neighbourhood is frequently used; however, there is little agreement on the best way to define neighbourhoods for research purposes and competing definitions can often be confusing. Sometimes neighbourhoods are small units of geography such as the face block or street segment (Suttles, 1972; Weisburd, Groff, & Yang, 2012). At other times, neighbourhoods are defined by commercial or government interests, such as the statistical reporting of social characteristics or the assignment of city resources, including the police (Sampson & Raudenbush, 1999; Suttles, 1972). Larger formulations of neighbourhood include what Suttles (1972) called "expanded community of limited liability", which might include places such as the South Side of Chicago or the East Side of St. Louis.

Since we are interested in exploring the dynamic properties of the neighbourhood-as-a-whole, our focus is the small "home areas" within corporate or government-defined neighbourhoods, perhaps a "5 to 10-minute walk from one's home" (Kearns & Parkinson, 2001, p. 2103). Milgram (1977) identified these smaller areas as having psychological boundaries associated with a comfortable familiarity rather than well-defined geographic lines. Similarly, thoughts on psychological definitions of neighbourhoods can be found in Hipp and Boessen's (2013) work on Egohoods. Following these ideas, and given our focus on the dynamic properties of the neighbourhood-as-a-whole (discussed below), we define these neighbourhood "home areas" as "the area closest to one's home where residents are likely to meet face-to-face and share mutual public safety problems and concerns". In a city or town this may be the block where one lives or a two- to three-block area around the home (Nolan, Conti, & McDevitt, 2004). In a city neighbourhood with a corporate identity such as Hedgeville in Wilmington, Delaware or Mount Pleasant in Cleveland, Ohio there would be many smaller "home areas" where dynamic processes were taking place.

Neighbourhoods as Groups

In order to assert that neighbourhoods have collective properties such as efficacy beliefs, and that group-level phenomena do occur there, we must first be able to argue that neighbourhoods—or at least the home areas within neighbourhoods—*are* groups. Early sociologists such as Cooley (1909/1965) considered neighbourhoods as "primary groups" like families because they involved face-to-face interaction and cooperation. Decades later, group theorists classified groups according to the interdependence (Cartwright & Zander, 1968; Lewin, 1948), core sentiments of its members (Homans, 1950), frequent patterns of interaction and the recognition of who belongs and who does not (Merton, 1957), and common goals (Deutsch, 1949). Our conceptualization of the neighbourhood group follows the guidance of these early theorists. The home areas within neighbourhoods have collective properties like efficacy beliefs and undergo psychodynamic processes because of the interdependence of members, i.e. what happens to one member is likely to directly affect other members. In these home areas residents generally know who belongs and who does not. Moreover, they participate in regular patterns of interaction, such as a wave or a nod, or where residents intentionally try to avoid each other. Most importantly, we recognize—as did Sampson and Raudenbush (1999)—the implicit common goal of residents living near each other to live in safe environment free of crime and disorder.

Neighbourhood Dynamics, Neighbourhood Atmosphere, and Collective Efficacy

Neighbourhood dynamics are created by the mere fact of people living near each other and desiring a safe place to live. As it pertains to crime and neighbourhood policing, the dynamic process begins with the *expectations* the police and community have of each other. Either they believe the police are primarily responsible for crime control in the neighbourhood (proxy agency) or that they (residents) are co-responsible for creating safe conditions in the community (collective agency). This is shown in the first column of Fig. 5.1. If residents and the police both believe that the police alone (i.e., as crime fighters) are primarily responsible for protecting communities (i.e., proxy agents), then the success of the police in this endeavor—or lack thereof—will influence either low or high levels of proxy efficacy beliefs (the second column of Fig. 5.1. When proxy efficacy is high, the neighbourhood atmosphere—a shared emotion—is experienced as a *dependence* on the police for protection (the third column of Fig. 5.1). On the other hand, when proxy efficacy beliefs are low, the neighbourhood atmosphere might reflect high levels of frustration and conflict between the police and community which we denote as *conflict/frustration.*

Similarly, when the community and police share the expectation that they are co-responsible for crime control and community safety, a different type of efficacy belief becomes possible, i.e., collective efficacy. When the community is satisfied both with the way fellow residents and the police interact together to keep the community safe, collective efficacy beliefs are high. When residents or police fail to live up to the expectations of collective responsibility then collective efficacy beliefs are low. High levels of collective efficacy are related to the neighbourhood

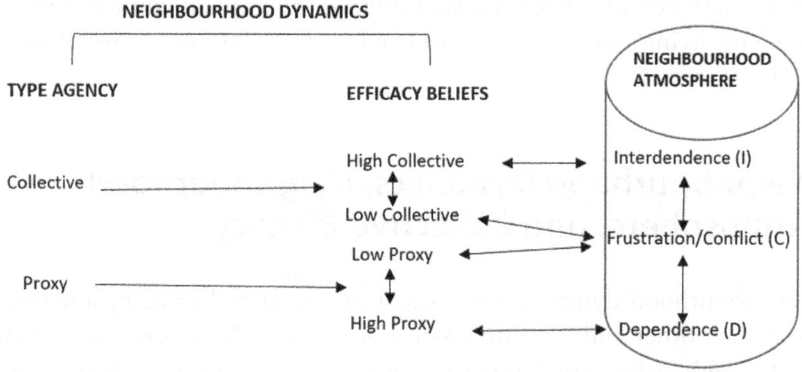

Fig. 5.1 Neighbourhood dynamics and the neighbourhood atmosphere

atmosphere we call *interdependence.* When collective efficacy is low, residents and the police may experience frustration and conflict (denoted as the neighbourhood atmosphere *conflict/frustration* in Fig. 5.1).

In sum, we are arguing that we can better understand place-based collective efficacy and its relationship to crime, community safety, and police reform by not simply categorising it as "high" or "low". Instead, by conceptualising *neighbourhood atmosphere*, we provide a richer and arguably more accurate picture of the dynamic processes in local places that are inherent in the interplay of efficacy beliefs with forms of human agency (collective and proxy). In the sections below we demonstrate why we believe neighbourhood atmosphere is important to police reform efforts using findings from the study of neighbourhoods in two cities.

Data and Methods

The data for this analysis come from a study funded by the U.S. DOJ Office of Community Oriented Policing Services (COPS). It involved survey data collection in 16 neighbourhoods in 4 cities: Pittsburgh, Pennsylvania, Cleveland, Ohio, Wilmington, Delaware, and Wheeling, West Virginia (Nolan, 2013). Police officials in all four cities agreed to cooperate with researchers in identifying neighbourhoods for the project. The ones they provided were all struggling with crime and other social problems. Police officials also introduced the research team to community members who could help guide student survey researchers through the neighbourhoods on a door-to-door canvas. The research team included the lead author, two graduate research assistants, two senior faculty consultants, and approximately 15 upper-level undergraduate students who had registered for an independent study course in survey research methods. This semester-long course was offered several times over three years (2008–2010) as the research team moved from one city to the next.

Initially, a sampling strategy involving the random selection of face blocks was employed. But, after several attempts at this, the research team found it more productive to go door-to-door on every block in order to obtain a sufficient number of completed surveys. We tested for selection bias by comparing known neighbourhood demographic parameters, such as percent white or black or Hispanic and percent renters versus home owners with estimates we obtained from the survey. The research team also facilitated discussions of the study's findings and their implications for police-community relations at several community-based forums involving residents and the police.

Although the neighbourhood dynamics survey items were modified at various stages throughout the multi-year study, the Cleveland and Wilmington versions of the survey instrument were identical. These surveys were administered in 7 neighbourhoods (5 in Cleveland and 2 in Wilmington, $n = 544$), so we pooled them into a single data file for analysis. The survey items began with the statement "Generally speaking, the people in my neighbourhood…" and were completed by a list of items such as "…want more police protection" and "…are willing to help one another". Respondents were asked to respond to the neighbourhood dynamics items on a scale of 1 to 9, where 1 is very strongly disagree and 9 is very strongly agree (see Table 5.1 for the full list of neighbourhood dynamics items).

In addition, the survey included collective efficacy items to find out whether respondents thought their neighbours would intervene in relatively minor but potentially dangerous situations such as kids skipping school. These items also included more serious situations such as a fight in the street in front of their house, or someone in the neighbourhood threatening suicide. The choices for type of intervention included 0 = would not intervene, 1 = would call the police (a formal intervention) or 3 = would interrupt the situation personally either alone or with others (an informal intervention). In addition, a survey item was added that asked whether respondents thought their neighbours would be likely to help a person returning to the neighbourhood from prison. The choices ranged from very unlikely = 1 to very likely = 4 (see Table 5.2).

Table 5.1 Neighbourhood atmosphere items from Cleveland and Wilmington neighbourhoods

Neighbourhood atmosphere question: Generally speaking, the people in my neighbourhood or community ...	*N*	Mean	Standard deviation
...want more police protection	514	7.33	2.30
...don't get along with one another	503	4.40	2.55
...know how to deal with minor community problems	505	4.89	2.47
...are willing to help one another	511	5.46	2.70
...watch out for each other's property	505	5.68	2.78
... feel frustrated with each other	497	4.27	2.53
...tell each other what is going on	498	5.50	2.75
...do not work well together on community problems	506	4.62	2.77
...trust each other	502	4.43	2.62
...rely heavily on each other	506	3.95	2.55
...are frustrated with the police	517	5.24	2.77
...call the police for most community problems	509	5.79	2.62
...think the police don't seem to care	514	5.65	2.75
...think the police do very little to prevent crime	514	5.52	2.72
...trust the police to do the right things	517	5.50	2.71
...assume the police know what is going on	511	5.50	2.69
...rely heavily on the police	510	5.02	2.76
...think the police are ineffective	510	5.26	2.59
...have confidence that the police alone are capable of preventing crime	517	4.94	2.77

Table 5.2 "Expectations for intervention and prevention" and support for someone returning to the neighbourhood from prison: Cleveland and Wilmington neighbourhoods

Expectation for intervention and prevention question: If the following situations were to occur in your neighbourhood, how likely is it that your neighbours would intervene?	Valid responses	% likely to "do nothing"	Percentage likely to "call police"	Percentage likely to respond "alone or with others"
Kids skipping school	513	37.2	36.6	26.1
Fight in street near your house	496	15.1	70.0	14.9
Neighbour threatening suicide	489	13.1	52.6	34.4
Expectations for intervention for someone returning from prison (N= 403)	Very unlikely	Unlikely	Likely	Very likely
Suppose that a person returned to your neighbourhood from prison. How likely is it that your neighbours would help out?	141 34.99%	138 34.24%	82 20.35%	42 10.42%

Analytic Strategy

First, we used factor analyses to see if the component parts of neighbourhood atmosphere outlined above are supported empirically. Then, we examined whether the relationship between neighbourhood atmosphere and collective efficacy follows expectations—i.e. that collective efficacy is lowest in conflict neighbourhoods and highest in areas of interdependence.

We conducted a factor analysis (with Varimax rotation) of the 18 neighbourhood dynamics survey items. The Cleveland/Wilmington neighbourhood atmosphere variables loaded on four factors with eigenvalues greater than 1. We forced the Cleveland/Wilmington responses into three factors by raising our clustering criteria to eigenvalues over 1.3. We did this because the four-factor model presented a separate factor for each source of conflict/frustration—the one that comes from collective agency with low collective efficacy beliefs, and the one that comes from proxy agency with low efficacy beliefs (see Fig. 5.1). Although the difference in the source of conflict/frustration may be important, we have found that the impact of these two forms of conflict/frustration are so similar that we reduced it to one factor for analysis.

Table 5.3 presents the results of the three-factor analysis from Cleveland and Wilmington neighbourhoods. The factor loadings shown in these tables are very consistent with the three types of neighbourhood atmosphere we introduced above: dependence, conflict/frustration, and interdependence. For instance, dependence emerges from proxy agency with high efficacy beliefs (Fig. 5.1) and is characterised by items such as people "assume the police know what is going on" and people "rely heavily on the police". On the other hand, conflict/frustration emerges from either collective or proxy agency, but in either case efficacy belief (collective or proxy) is low. It is characterized by items such as people "don't get along with one another" and people "are frustrated with the police". Finally, interdependence is rooted in collective agency and where efficacy beliefs are high (i.e., collective efficacy). It is expressed by high scores on survey items like people in my neighbourhood or community "know how to deal with minor community problems' and people "trust each other".

Table 5.3 Results of neighbourhood atmosphere factor analysis in Cleveland and Wilmington surveys

Generally speaking, the people in my neighbourhood, or community ...	Factor 1—interdependence	Factor 2—conflict	Factor 3—dependence
...want more police protection	.008	.395	.371
...don't get along with one another	−.316	**.382**	.208
...know how to deal with minor community problems	**.662**	−.164	.142
...are willing to help one another	**.813**	−.145	.104
...watch out for each other's property	**.808**	−.137	.111
... feel frustrated with each other	−.327	**.397**	.070
...tell each other what is going on	**.752**	−.042	.050
...do not work well together on community problems	−.388	**.414**	−.072
...trust each other	**.719**	−.104	−.090
...rely heavily on each other	**.711**	−.038	.145
...are frustrated with the police	−.034	**.739**	−.199
...call the police for most community problems	.131	.189	**.535**
...think the police don't seem to care	−.049	**.770**	−.139
...think the police do very little to prevent crime	−.111	**.736**	−.008
...trust the police to do the right things	.135	−.223	**.724**

(continued)

Table 5.3 (continued)

Generally speaking, the people in my neighbourhood, or community ...	Factor 1—interdependence	Factor 2—conflict	Factor 3—dependence
...assume the police know what is going on	−.011	.018	**.626**
...rely heavily on the police	.121	−.026	**.756**
...think the police are ineffective	−.170	**.689**	−.069
...have confidence that the police alone are capable of preventing crime	.111	−.296	**.696**

KMO measure of sampling adequacy = .840
Cumulative variance explained with three factors—49.6%

Findings

Table 5.4 presents the results of a series multinomial and binomial logistic regression analyses examining the relationship between neighbourhood atmosphere and collective efficacy. The collective efficacy items (see Table 5.2) presented respondents with a series of hypothetical public safety situations and asked how they thought their neighbours would respond. Respondents could choose "do nothing", "call the police" (a formal intervention), or "intervene directly either alone or with someone else" (an informal intervention). The neighbourhood atmosphere scores are the pasted factor scores calculated as variables for each respondent via a regression method. The odds ratios from the multinomial logistic regressions reflect the change in odds for 0 (do nothing) to 1 (call the police) in the columns marked "formal" and the change in odds from 0 to 2 (intervened directly either alone or with others) in the columns marked "informal". The final column of Table 5.4 presents the results of a binomial logistic regression that examines the relationship between neighbourhood atmosphere and neighbours' willingness to support a person returning to the neighbourhood from prison (0 = unlikely to help, 1 = likely to help). The control variable for

Table 5.4 Multinomial and binomial logistic regression estimates of neighbourhood atmosphere and collective efficacy

	Skipping school (Formal)		Skipping school (Informal)		Fight in front of house (Formal)		Fight in front of house (Informal)		Neighbour threatening suicide (Formal)		Neighbour threatening suicide (Informal)		Support someone returning from prison[a]	
	B	Odds ratio	B	Odds ratio	B	Odds ratio	B	Odds ratio	B	Odds ratio	B	Odds ratio	B	Odds ratio
Interdependence factor	.860**	2.364	1.292**	3.641	1.003**	2.727	1.289**	3.628	1.013**	2.754	1.372**	2.567	.877**	2.404
Conflict/frustration factor	−.522**	.593	−.604**	.547	−.453**	.636	−.552**	.576	−.378*	.685	−.284	.753	−.281*	.755
Dependence factor	.072	1.074	−.048	.953	.387*	1.472	.016	1.016	.411*	1.509	.156	1.169	−.204	.816
Cleveland N1	−.339	.712	−.297	.743	−1.188*	.305	−.496	.609	−.474	.622	.160	1.174	.155	1.167
Cleveland N2	−.057	.994	−.619	.538	−.438	.645	.284	1.328	−1.266*	.282	−.397	.672	−.405	.667
Cleveland N3	−1.104	.331	−.632	.532	.016	.984	−.089	.9151	−.602	.548	−.255	.775	−.161	.852
Cleveland N4	−.329	.720	−.289	.749	.050	.952	.921	2.512	−.086	.918	−.086	.918	.797	2.220
Cleveland N5	.093	1.098	−.244	.784	−.390	.677	−.385	.434	.904	.2.470	.904	2.470	−.306	.736
Wilmington N6	−.905	.405	−.728*	.483	−.297	.743	−.415	.661	−.264	.768	−.146	.864	.029	1.029
Wilmington N7 (reference)	0	–	–	–	–	–	–	–						
Intercept	.494		.030		2.417**		.338		2.406**		1.501*		−.937*	

[a]Binomial logistic regression. 0 = unlikely to help and 1 = likely to help
$*p <= .05$
$**p <= .01$

these analyses is neighbourhood, a categorical variable with Wilmington neighbourhood 7 as the reference group.

In the first scenario, "kids skipping school", we compared the odds that neighbours would "do nothing" with the odds they would intervene formally by calling the police or informally either alone or with others. We found that a one standard deviation increase in the neighbourhood atmosphere *interdependence* was associated with 2.3 times higher odds of calling the police and 3.6 times higher odds of responding informally either alone or with others compared with doing nothing. The reverse was true for the neighbourhood atmosphere *conflict/frustration.* As conflict/frustration increased the odds that respondents would say their neighbours would intervene rather than do nothing decreased significantly (49% lower odds for calling the police and 45% lower odds for responding informally). The neighbourhood atmosphere *dependence* had no significant impact on the expectations of neighbours for kids skipping school.

In the second scenario, a fight in the street in front of the respondent's house, *interdependence* was significantly related to increased odds of reporting to the police (2.7 times higher than doing nothing) and responding informally to break it up (3.6 times higher than doing nothing). As expected the reverse was true for *conflict/frustration* which recorded significantly lower odds for calling the police (−36%) or intervening informally (−42%) compared with doing nothing. As *dependence* increased by one standard deviation the odds of calling the police increased by 47%, but there was no significant change in the odds of an informal response.

In the third scenario, a neighbourhood resident threatening suicide, increases in *interdependence* were similarly associated with increased odds of calling the police (2.7 times more likely) or responding informally (2.6 times more likely) compared with the odds of doing nothing. Increases in *conflict/frustration* were associated with lower odds of calling the police (−31%) compared with the odds of doing nothing. The relationship between *conflict/frustration* and an informal response to a resident threatening suicide was not significant. Finally, increases in *dependence* were associated with 50% higher odds for calling the police, but the relationship to an informal response to a resident threatening suicide was not significant.

In the final column of Table 5.4 the responses were recoded for analysis as 0 = unlikely to help and 1 = likely to help. Increases in interdependence were associated with 2.4 times higher odds for supporting those returning to the neighbourhood from prison. The reverse was true for increases in *conflict/frustration* which resulted in 25% lower odds for support. The impact of dependence on support for a person returning to the neighbourhood from prison was not significant.

As depicted in Fig. 5.1, we conceived of the neighbourhood (or home area) as being a full container of "atmosphere", albeit with varying levels of interdependence, conflict/frustration, and dependence. With the results of the binomial logistic regression analysis presented in Table 5.4, we constructed three neighbourhood types via Eq. 5.1, where a is the intercept, b_1 is the dependence slope, b_2 is the conflict slope, and b_3 is the interdependence slope. The x values reflect factor analysis regression scores and follow a z score distribution with a mean of zero and standard deviation of 1.

$$Y = e^{a+(b_1x_1)+(b_2x_2)+(b_3x_3)} \tag{5.1}$$

The three constructed neighbourhoods depicted in Fig. 5.2 are meant to represent scenarios in which the x value for the primary atmosphere (either interdependence, conflict, or dependence) is set at +3 while the other two categories are set at −3. An x score of +3 indicates 3 standard deviations above the mean of 0. An x score of −3 indicates 3 standard deviations below the mean. For each of the constructed neighbourhood types, we calculated the probabilities for each of the collective efficacy items via Eq. 5.2.

$$\rho = \frac{e^{a+(b_1x_1)+(b_2x_2)+(b_3x_3)}}{1 + e^{a+(b_1x_1)+(b_2x_2)+(b_3x_3)}} \tag{5.2}$$

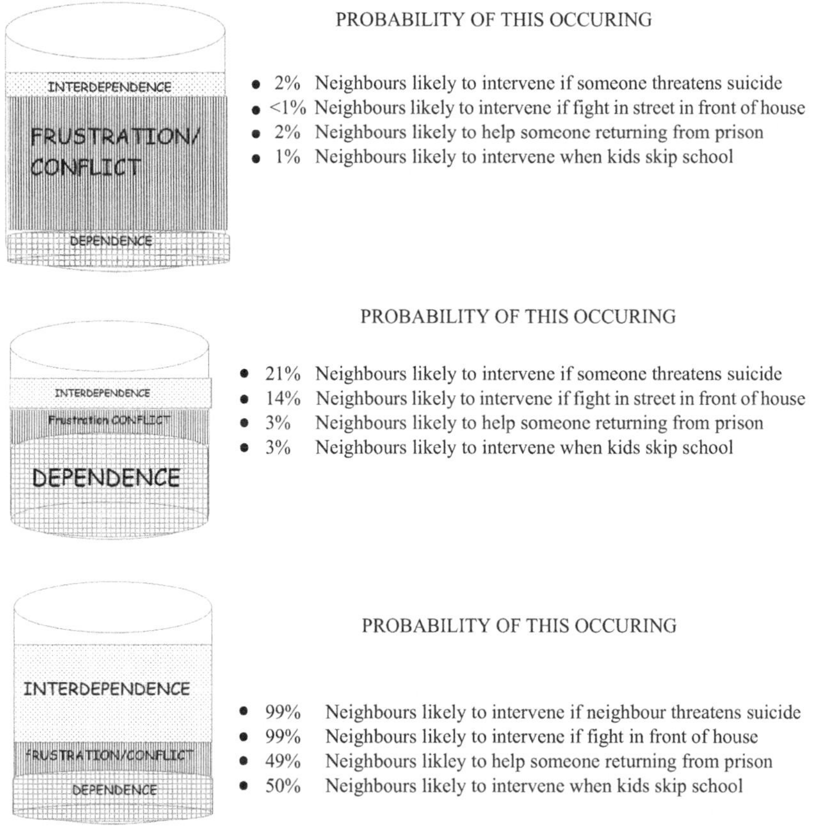

Fig. 5.2 Collective efficacy and community dynamics in three constructed neighbourhoods

Figure 5.2 presents the three constructed neighbourhoods types along the risks they represent. The first community type with high levels of interdependence and low levels of conflict/frustration and dependence seem to have the highest levels of collective efficacy. In this type of place, we computed a 99% probability that residents would expect neighbours to intervene if a neighbour threatened suicide or if a fight broke out in front of their house. In these places, there was about a 50% probability that residents would expect their neighbours to assist someone returning from prison or if they saw kids skipping school. This is in stark contrast to the community type with high levels of conflict/frustration and low levels of interdependence and dependence. In this type of place, the probability of that a respondent would expect his or her neighbourhood to intervene in any of the listed situations was less than 2%. Lastly, the community type with high levels of dependence and low levels of conflict/frustration and interdependence appears safer than the conflict/frustration community, but significantly more dangerous than the interdependent community. There is less than 20% chance that residents would expect neighbours to intervene if someone was threatening suicide or if there was a fight in front of their house. In these type of places, there is less than 3% chance respondents would indicate their neighbours would help someone returning from prison or intervene if they saw a child skipping school.

Discussion

Our goal in this chapter was to imagine a policing field (its mandate, objectives, structure, measures of success) that aligns with contemporary research on neighbourhoods safety. Instead of asking "what works in policing?"—a perennial police reform question—we asked "what works to keep neighbourhoods and communities safe and strong?" This led us first to the concept of collective efficacy and then to further develop and operationalise the concepts neighbourhood dynamics and neighbourhood atmosphere. Levels of collective efficacy, a group-level property, had been typically evaluated on a linear scale from low to high (Sampson & Raudenbush, 1999; Uchida et al., 2014). But, in this conceptualisation it was not entirely clear what low collective efficacy was like and how it might be experienced by the police. We argued that small "home areas" within corporate or government-defined neighbourhoods and communities are subject to the same dynamic processes as small groups. These group processes are a product of the expectations members have of each other and the authorities relative to an explicit or implicit common goal, such as living in a safe place (Bennis & Shepard, 1956; Bion, 1959; Wheelan, 1994). Through this conceptualisation we exposed the multifaceted nature of low collective efficacy. On one hand low collective efficacy is, as the term implies, low efficacy beliefs among the collective. This type of efficacy belief is only possible when it is grounded in expectations of collective agency. However, when residents hand over their role for community safety to the police as proxy agents, then low collective efficacy may appear as high (or low) efficacy beliefs in the police.

We termed the interplay of agency expectations (collective and proxy) and efficacy beliefs "neighbourhood dynamics" (see Fig. 5.1). We then showed how these (psycho)dynamic processes in the neighbourhood group created three types of neighbourhood atmosphere: *interdependence*, *conflict/frustration*, and *dependence*. Interdependence emerges from expectations of collective agency with high collective efficacy beliefs. Conflict/frustration results from low efficacy beliefs in neighbours or low efficacy beliefs in the police. Dependence results from high efficacy beliefs in the police.

In the Cleveland and Wilmington study we showed how neighbourhood atmosphere relates to expectations for formal and informal control. Through a series of public safety situations, respondents were asked what they expected their neighbours to do. As expected, interdependence was positively related to expectations that neighbours would intervene in minor or serious situations such as kids skipping school, a fight in the street, threats of suicide, and support for a person returning to the neighbourhood from prison. The reverse was true for conflict/frustration. As this type of neighbourhood atmosphere increased, respondents were significantly less likely to intervene by calling the police or responding informally. Finally, dependence on the police is positively related to the expectations that neighbours would intervene by calling the police in serious situations such as a fight in the street and when a neighbour was threatening suicide. Otherwise dependence had no effect on respondents' expectations for neighbourhood intervention or support for a person returning from prison.

To depict this under ideal circumstances we constructed three hypothetical neighbourhoods (via Eq. 5.1): (1) High interdependence, low conflict/frustration and low dependence, (2) high conflict/frustration, low dependence and low interdependence, and (3) high dependence, low interdependence and low conflict/frustration. We then applied our actual survey results to the three neighbourhood conditions. The high interdependence, low conflict/frustration and low dependence places were the most secure. The areas with least protection were those experiencing high conflict and frustration while interdependence and dependence were low. Places with high levels of dependence and low conflict/frustration and low interdependence also appear to be unsafe and unwelcoming to those returning from prison.

In sum, this study shows how collective efficacy is related to neighbourhood dynamics. The logic of the current law enforcement game discussed in Chapter 2 of this book is that the police are protectors and that residents can depend on them to rid the neighbourhood of crime. This is problematic from our view as the law enforcement game aims at dependence rather than interdependence and almost certainly results in a neighbourhood atmosphere of frustration and conflict (Hinkle & Weisburd, 2008) and loss of perceived legitimacy (Tyler, 1990, 2004). Thus, it is important to consider how the current results can help guide transformative reforms in policing which empower police and residents to work together to build stronger and safer neighbourhoods.

Conclusion

In Chapter 2 we showed that the logic of the current law enforcement game casts the police as protectors of the public assuming primary responsibility for crime and public safety. In this chapter we demonstrated why this is a problem. The law enforcement game is likely to foster dependence if it is successful; it is likely to result in conflict/frustration if it is not (Hinkle & Weisburd, 2008; Manning, 1978). Either way, it does not aim at creating and maintaining interdependence—the neighbourhood atmosphere that really keeps places safe and strong. Interdependence is not possible until residents and the police recognise they are co-responsible for crime control and work together to achieve it.

The findings presented here suggest the need for transformational police reform that focuses primarily on neighbourhood dynamics and creating interdependent places. Such a change would shift the focus of policing away from police officer outputs (enforcing the law) to safe, interdependent community outcomes (Markovic, 2009; Nolan, Conti, & McDevitt, 2004). This change would likely impact what citizens thought of as legitimate police practices or as procedural justice (Tyler, 1990, 2004). Changes to the policing field that prioritise neighbourhood dynamics might also generate new research questions and inform the evaluation of evidence-based policing (Sherman, 2015). None of this is to suggest that the police would no longer enforce the law. Rather, it means that law enforcement activities may be most appropriate if they are used as one of many tools in the furtherance of a new police mandate aimed at building safe interdependent places. Bourdieu might argue that a "new game" such as this would produce a new logic and common sense that necessitates a new police disposition, one that values relationship building and problem solving and has a greater appreciation for diversity (Conti & Nolan, 2005). Later, in Chapter 12 we introduce concepts, tools, and methods for the type of police reform that actually changes its purpose from law enforcement outputs to strong, interdependent community outcomes.

References

Bandura, A. (2001). Social cognitive theory: An agentic perspective. *Annual Review of Psychology, 52,* 1–26.

Bennis, W. G., & Shepard, H. A. (1956). A theory of group development. *Human Relations, 9,* 415–437.

Bion, W. R. (1959). *Experiences in groups.* New York: Basic Books.

Bourdieu, P., & Wacquant, L. J. D. (1992). *An invitation to reflexive sociology.* Chicago, IL: University of Chicago Press.

Cartwright, D., & Zander, A. (Eds.). (1968). *Group dynamics: Research and theory* (3rd ed.). New York: Harper & Row.

Conti, N., & Nolan, J. (2005). Policing the platonic cave: Ethics and efficacy in police training. *Policing and Society, 15,* 166–186.

Cooley, C. (1909/1965). Primary groups. In A. P. Hare, E. F. Borgatta, & R. F. Bales (Eds.), *Small groups: Studies in social interaction* (Rev. ed.). New York: Alfred A. Knopf.

Deutsch, M. (1949). A theory of cooperation and competition. *Human Relations, 2,* 129–152.

Donnermeyer, J. F., & DeKeseredy, W. S. (2014). *Rural criminology*. New York: Routledge.

Hinkle, J. C., & Weisburd, D. (2008). The irony of broken windows policing: A micro-place study of the relationship between disorder, focused police crackdowns and fear of crime. *Journal of Criminal Justice, 36,* 503–512.

Hipp, J. R., & Boessen, A. (2013). Egohoods as waves washing across the city: A new measure of "neighborhoods". *Criminology, 51,* 287–327.

Homans, G. (1950). *The human group*. New York: Harcourt, Brace & World.

Kearns, A., & Parkinson, M. (2001). The significance of neighbourhood. *Urban Studies, 38*(12), 2103–2110.

Lewin, K. (1948). *Resolving social conflicts*. New York: Harper.

Manning, P. K. (1978). The police mandate: Strategies and appearances. In P. K. Manning & J. Van Maanen (Eds.), *Policing: A view from the street*. New York: Random House.

Markovic, J. (2009). Neighborhoods matter: A situational policing perspective. *Geography and Public Safety, 2*(2), 10–12. Retrieved from https://www.nij.gov/topics/technology/maps/Documents/gps-bulletin-v2i2.pdf?Redirected=true.

Merton, R. K. (1957). *Social theory and social structure* (Rev. ed.). Glencoe, IL: Free Press.

Milgram, S. (1977). *The individual in a social world: Essays and experiments.* Reading, MA: Addison-Wesley.

Nolan, J. (2013). *Situational policing*. An unpublished technical report to the U.S. Department of Justice, Community Policing Services. Available upon request.

Nolan, J. (2016). How American policing fails neighborhoods—And cops. *The Conversation.* Retrieved from https://theconversation.com/how-american-policing-fails-neighborhoods-and-cops-63302.

Nolan, J., Conti, N., & McDevitt, J. (2004). Situational policing: Neighbourhood development and crime control. *Policing and Society, 14,* 99–117.

Sampson, R. J. (2013). The place of context: A theory and strategy for criminology's hard problems. *Criminology, 51,* 1–31.

Sampson, R. J., & Raudenbush, S. W. (1999). Systematic social observation of public spaces: A new look at disorder in urban neighborhoods. *American Journal of Sociology, 105*(3), 603–651.

Sampson, R. J., Raudenbush, S., & Earls, F. (1997). Neighborhoods and violent crime: A multilevel study of collective efficacy. *Science, 277*, 918–924.

Sherman, L. W. (2015). A tipping point for "totally evidenced policing": Ten ideas for building an evidence-based police agency. *International Criminal Justice Review, 25*, 1–19.

Suttles, G. D. (1972). *The social construction of communities*. Chicago, IL: University of Chicago Press.

Tyler, T. R. (1990). *Why people obey the law*. New Haven, CT: Yale University Press.

Tyler, T. R. (2004). Enhancing police legitimacy. *The Annals of the American Academy of Political and Social Science, 593*, 84–99.

Uchida, C. D., Swatt, M. L., Solomon, S. E., & Varano, S. (2014). *Neighbourhoods and crime: Collective efficacy and social cohesion in Miami-Dade County*. Washington, DC: National Institute of Justice. Retrieved from https://www.ncjrs.gov/pdffiles1/nij/grants/245407.pdf.

Weisburd, D., Groff, E. R., & Yang, S. M. (2012). *The criminology of place: Street segments and our understanding of the crime problem*. Oxford, UK: Oxford University Press.

Wheelan, S. A. (1994). *Group processes: A developmental perspective*. Boston, MA: Allyn & Bacon.

6

Policing Hate Crime: Dilemmas in Policy and Practice

Robert Lambert

In this book on policing in an era of reform, it is important to draw lessons from recent reform efforts. The case of hate crime policing in the UK is an example. This chapter identifies and illustrates three dilemmas in the policy and practice of policing hate crime. Before identifying the three dilemmas it will help to introduce the subject matter—hate crime. Essentially, the term *hate crime* denotes experiences for particular categories or groups of victims, specifically victims targeted by virtue of their race, religion, disability, sexual orientation or transgender status (College of Policing, 2014, p. 2). Broadly speaking, this understanding of the term follows academic definitions of hate crime that have established hatred (or more properly prejudice) as being necessarily directed towards 'stigmatised and marginalised groups' (Perry, 2001, p. 10).

In practice, two types of criminal offence have arisen in consequence. The first is an aggravated version of existing offences such as an assault

R. Lambert (✉)
London, UK
e-mail: T.F.Parsons@ljmu.ac.uk

J. J. Nolan et al. (eds.), *Policing in an Age of Reform*,
Palgrave's Critical Policing Studies,
https://doi.org/10.1007/978-3-030-56765-1_6

causing actual bodily harm (as per section 47, Offences Against the Person Act, 1861) or uttering insulting or abusive remarks or using insulting or abusive behaviour within the hearing or sight of a person 'likely to be caused harassment, alarm or distress' (as per section 5, Public Order Act, 1986). In this type of offence, the additional presence of a hate crime will allow the court to impose a harsher sentence. The second type of offence is wholly novel and is focused on abusive or insulting words that may occur outside of a public order scenario and thereby outside the parameters of the Public Order Act and the remit of public order policing. Thus, for the first time, words that may be either oral or written, public or private and either spoken in person or 'online' (see for example, section 1, Racial and Religious Hatred Act 2006) have become subject to police investigation and prosecution.

In the last decade of the 20th and the first two decades of the twenty-first-century policing hate crime established itself as an important, high profile area of work undertaken by police services in the UK. Previously, from the inception of modern policing in London in the third decade of the nineteenth century onwards, policing was conducted without any reference to the concept of hate crime at all—quite simply, because the concept or category did not exist. Not least because it has passed largely unremarked, it should be stressed that the adoption of hate crime policing marked a fundamental and significant change across three centuries of modern policing. Essentially, the change in policy and practice has two elements: firstly, police constables became required to report some (but not all) allegations of insulting and abusive language that they were previously not required to; and concomitantly, when determining if and when this new duty fell to be applied police constables were required to have regard to the identity of the person making the allegation.

Whereas, previously, police constables were trained to interrogate the authenticity and credibility of accounts from a complainant, victim or witness impartially and without regard to the person's identity, they were now being instructed to afford a kind of de facto credence to one person's account and not to another's. Significantly, policy makers and police chiefs appear never to have considered the extent to which this change to a police constable's duties might infringe upon the notion of policing by consent. That such a risk needs to be considered arises from the way in which hate crime policy rejects the long-held notion of a standard police response dispensed equally to all members of the public.

It is also important to note that the term 'police constables' is used to describe (i) police officers of the rank of police constable and (ii) all other police officers of all ranks who retain the 'office' of police constable in respect of their powers. Moreover, police officers are 'not employees, they are not agents of the police force, police authority or government', rather 'those who hold the Office of Constable are servants of the Crown' (Police Federation, 2018).

Given that police constables would be attending the same range and types of incidents as they did before the advent of hate crime policing it was axiomatic that they were being required to review and re-interpret what they witnessed and what was reported to them and then, depending on their assessment, to respond in a new way to familiar situations. This might be described as being akin to a scenario in which nurses in an accident and emergency department at a hospital are required to implement a new policy towards patients that fundamentally countermands long established procedures. The comparison is especially germane in respect of cases of violent crime where police constables, ambulance crews, paramedics and nurses in accident and emergency departments combine their skills to prevent loss of life, administer first aid and treat injuries. Suffice to say, nothing in hate crime policing policy inhibits the policing duty to treat all injured parties with equal care, but it does impose new policing duties in regard to other less urgent aspects of cases of violent crime. Such a major policy change inevitably required a new training programme for police constables and in London by the beginning of the twenty-first century all members of the 30,000 strong Metropolitan Police Service had undergone a three-day diversity training course that introduced the new policy in respect of black and minority ethnic communities (Rowe & Garland, 2007, pp. 43–65). Subsequent training would guide constables when policing hate crimes committed against members of other minority communities.

In the circumstances, for a hitherto hidebound institution, it is to be expected that such a new and innovative policing initiative would give rise to dilemmas in policy and practice. Although the three identified dilemmas are overlapping they are discussed in sequence. The first dilemma emerges from the fundamental policy of affording enhanced credibility to individuals reporting allegations of hate crime to police. The second dilemma revolves around the inclusion and exclusion of individuals, groups and issues that come under the rubric of hate crime. The third dilemma is perhaps the most intractable and focuses on those hate crimes that do not involve physical violence or harm. While the chapter has a UK focus it also has resonance with the experience of policing hate crime in the US (where the notion or concept of hate crime was born), Canada, Australia and New Zealand. Significantly, because policing hate crime is community focused, the chapter dovetails with closely related issues discussed by Tim Parsons in Chapters 3 and 7.

Notwithstanding a growth in occupational health and safety policies and practice, police chiefs generally relish a reputation for having a 'can-do' attitude. Almost a default policing position, a 'can-do' approach, certainly helps to explain a willing and eager response by police chiefs to embrace the new task of policing hate crimes in the latter half of the 1990s. Not that the introduction of hate crime policing signalled a new kind of criminal behaviour in the UK. Rather, focused as it then was, principally on racist behaviour it denoted an urgent response to a finding of institutional racism against the Metropolitan Police in the influential Macpherson Report at the conclusion of the watershed Stephen Lawrence Inquiry (Hall, 2014; Macpherson, 1999; Souhami, 2007). Moreover, given the extent to which the finding of institutional racism was endorsed by all sections of the political establishment, and most especially Prime Minister Tony Blair's recently elected 'New Labour' government it was unsurprising that police chiefs enthusiastically embraced the notion of hate crime policing without reflecting too deeply on the foreseeable dilemmas it might give rise to.

In fact, it became the key plank in a wide ranging policy designed to rebuild trust and confidence in the police amongst black and minority ethnic communities (Grieve & French, 2002). In due course, police chiefs displayed the same enthusiasm when other marginalised minority groups were added to the hate crime cannon. Laudable and arguably long overdue as this approach was, it might also be fair to say that the police chiefs involved failed to anticipate the full impact of the dilemmas that it would necessarily give rise to.

First Dilemma: Granting Enhanced Credibility to Individuals Reporting Hate Crimes

Central to policy and practice of policing hate crimes is the granting of enhanced credibility to individuals reporting a hate crime. This fundamental feature was intended to ensure a discredited police service took such allegations seriously and thereby begin to repair fragile confidence in black and minority ethnic communities. Paradoxically, it ended what had become known as 'blind policing', a practice hitherto intended by police to demonstrate equality and neutrality and thereby allay community concerns that some citizens might be treated more favourably than others. This was an approach that had its roots in the founding principle of policing by consent. As Sir Richard Mayne noted in *Principles of Policing* at the founding of the Metropolitan Police in 1829, 'the power of the police to fulfil their functions and duties is dependent on public approval of their existence, actions and behaviour and on their ability to secure and maintain public respect' (Quoted in Reiner, 1985, p. 49; discussed in Lambert, 2011, p. 18). Crucially, as Parsons and the present author note, Mayne 'did not suggest that public approval was confined to one particular community in London but rather that the principle of policing by consent was the bedrock of the relationship between the police, who were drawn from the citizens of London, and all their fellow citizens'. 'For sure', they observe, 'either London's wealthiest or its most vocal and well organised citizens have often had the greatest influence on policing policy in London but it is when the principle of policing by consent has been seen to also take account of the city's poorest and least vocal citizens that it has served the capital best' (Lambert & Parsons, 2017, p. 1057).

Instead, as the Macpherson Report made explicit, such long established '*colour blind* policing must be outlawed', and, 'the police must deliver a service which recognises the different experiences, perceptions and needs of a diverse society' (Macpherson, 1999). The manifest police failings in the Stephen Lawrence murder case certainly warranted Macpherson's recommendation for a police service that recognised the different experiences, perceptions and needs of a diverse society but it did not by any means follow that a founding principle of policing by consent needed to be jettisoned. That said, the pressure for an improved police service for black and minority ethnic citizens was real and urgent and the dilemmas that have subsequently arisen as a result of affording enhanced credibility to individuals reporting allegations of hate crime to police should be seen as an unintended consequence of a well-intended and expedient response to a major crisis of confidence in policing. To contextualise the dilemma associated with the policy of affording enhanced credibility to complainants in hate crime cases it will be helpful to review the inception and definition of hate crime.

Significantly, in adopting the policy and practice of hate crime policing, police chiefs engaged to an unprecedented extent with academic researchers (Grieve & French, 2002; Hall, 2014). There was a very good reason for this collaboration: hate crime was essentially an academic construction (Hall, 2005; Perry, 2001) and there was an evident need for police participation in its implementation. The extent of this collaboration became evident in 2005 when the Association of Chief Police Officers (ACPO) published a two-part definition in which a *hate crime* is understood in relation to a *hate incident*. (For the record, following the recommendations of the Parker Review, ACPO was disbanded in 2015 and superseded by the National Police Chiefs' Council [NPCC]). First, a hate incident is defined as 'any incident, which may or may not constitute a criminal offence, which is perceived by the victim or any other person, as being motivated by *prejudice or hate*' (emphasis added in italics). From this, a hate crime is defined as 'any hate incident, which constitutes a criminal offence, perceived by the victim or any other person, as being motivated by *prejudice or hate*' (ACPO, 2005, p. 9).

At first sight this appears very wide ranging but in fact the vast majority of experiences of incidents—whether they be crimes or not—that involve some element of prejudice or hate are excluded from consideration. For example, incidents in which hatred is directed towards a victim of violence by virtue of personal animosity or by virtue of a drunken (or sober) disagreement are excluded from consideration. To be clear, however surprising it might seem to newcomers to the topic, *hate* per se is not really a key ingredient of a hate crime at all (Chakraborti & Garland, 2009, p. 4). The weakness of *hate* as an explanatory term can probably be discerned in a small but significant change to the police definition of hate crime from *prejudice or hate* in the 2005 version to *hostility or prejudice* a decade later (College of Policing, 2014, p. 3).

Notwithstanding this odd definitional weakness, Chakraborti and Garland acknowledge the fact that *hate crime* has proved to be a striking label that has helped to achieve the purpose of promoting crimes that have otherwise been in danger of being neglected. It follows, they suggest, that 'the various types of victimisation associated with this label [*hate crime*] are now widely accepted as significant social problems and are prioritised within research and policy agendas to a much greater extent than ever before' (2009, p. 2). Hall, for example, highlights the crucial importance of the 'legacy of Stephen Lawrence' (Macpherson, 1999) in helping hate crime investigations change so as to 'better meet the needs of diverse communities'. This improvement is vital, he suggests, because hate crime victims often experience repeated offences, 'often expect their victimisation to continue' or 'are otherwise fearful of attacks in the future'. Hall also explains that 'hate crimes can have a greater emotional impact on the victim than comparable non-hate crimes, and can cause increased levels of fear and anxiety that can also permeate through wider communities' (Hall, 2014). Hall's perceptive observations lead neatly to the second dilemma.

Second Dilemma: Inclusion Within, and Exclusion from, Hate Crime Status

The second dilemma revolves around the expansion of groups and issues that are included under the rubric of hate crime—and those groups and issues that are excluded. As such, hate crime policing policy and practice expanded to become concerned with the experiences of victims targeted by virtue of their race, religion, disability, sexual orientation or transgender status and these types of crimes were designated as *monitored* hate crimes by police (College of Policing, 2014, p. 2). This was not intended to exclude all other categories of victim from consideration, but it was—according to a comprehensive and detailed police report—to recognise that the victim must fulfil the basic requirement of being a representative of a targeted, marginalised, minority group (2014, pp. 2–7).

Here, Sophie Lancaster, murdered for being a *Goth*—a member of a youth movement; a sub-culture—is offered as an example of a case that has achieved hate crime status by virtue of its particular circumstances (2014, p. 8). Police guidance also highlights the potential for caste crimes and crimes against sex workers to achieve the necessary criteria to be recorded and treated as hate crimes in the future (ibid., pp. 8–9). In respect of caste crimes it is useful to note that the College of Policing report explains that 'some communities have a historical culture of caste definition where some sections of communities are considered to be less worthy than others'. 'This can', the report continues, 'lead to isolation of subgroups within broader communities and discrimination in relation to employment and relationships, but can, on occasions, lead to hostility and crime' (2014, p. 8).

Traditionally seen as conservative, defending the social status quo, by embracing hate crime policing, police leaders might now be seen to be more enlightened and aligned to what is known as progressive politics. Broadly speaking, this a political perspective adopted by the vast majority of academics practicing criminology and the social sciences more generally. However welcome this might be, it can lead to dilemmas that may not always be foreseen by police leaders or their collaborators in criminology. For example, police leaders appeared not to anticipate that by adding transgender status to the list of marginalised groups coming under the protection of hate crime policy and practice that they might be creating tension with other protected groups. This is simply to acknowledge that policing policy and practice will sometimes find itself in an increasingly complex and conflicted position when supporting the transgender community while simultaneously looking to support (some) gay and feminist campaigners at ideological odds with (some) transgender activists. It may take a decade for this debate to be resolved and it might have been wiser for police leaders to await its outcome before stepping into such a contested arena.

Where both police and academic discussions tend to be unforthcoming is in explaining the kinds of victim that are excluded. Nevertheless, it is reasonable to speculate that any suggestion of power or privilege on the part of a victim would be sufficient to warrant exclusion from *hate crime* status. For example, while perpetrators, victims, witnesses and police responders to incidents of abuse, threats, spitting and assaults carried out by anarchist Class War *Bash the Rich* demonstrators against participants at the Henley regatta in 1985 (Bone, 2006) might be clear about the level of hate and prejudice involved, their victim's status as *the rich* would seem to be sufficient to exclude them. Much the same applied thirty years later when the 2015 incarnation of Class War led a noisy and angry demonstration in London that involved protesters causing criminal damage to a hipster café and an estate agent office in affluent, gentrified Shoreditch. In fact, according to one report, 'hundreds of protesters attacked a cereal cafe in east London on Saturday night, daubing the word 'scum' on the shop window and setting fire to an effigy of a police officer'. In response, riot police were called in to defend the café after it was targeted 'by a large crowd of anti-gentrification activists carrying pigs' heads and torches'. In the morning after the violence, the owners of the cafe, were reported as saying 'that the attack left customers including children "terrified for their lives"' (*Guardian*, 2015).

Equally, it seems safe to assume that victims of violence and harm who were members or supporters of the now defunct English Defence League (EDL) would be excluded—which is particularly instructive given that they would be certain to be included if they were perpetrators rather than victims of violence or harm. This is to recognise that a group linked—by some if not all academics and commentators (see for example, Busher, 2016; Copsey, 2010)—to the far right are traditionally seen as being the persecutors of vulnerable, minority communities. That such a group perceives itself to be a beleaguered minority itself is unlikely to cut any ice with academics and policy makers concerned with establishing and managing the categories of hate crime victims. For police, however, such cases require a careful balancing of fundamental responsibilities. On the one hand, taking action to ensure that all groups and individuals have the opportunity to exercise their right to demonstrate and express their views—however popular or unpopular they may be—safely and responsibly. On the other hand, taking action to ensure that demonstrators are not allowed to inflame or incite violence or to commit any crimes involving violence and harm.

In addition, it is worth noting that demonstrations of any kind are designated by police as public order events and therefore policed according to a different set of protocols and resources than applies to incidents of violence and harm that arise in most other scenarios. In consequence a riot trained police officer belonging to the Metropolitan Police Territorial Support Group will spend a typical weekend policing public order events with a view to keeping the peace, if necessary by recourse to tactics of crowd control that rest on extensive and regular training. This removes them from the role of community focused policing where there is more scope to build a rapport with the public and acknowledge and report hate crimes. This fact helps explain why a victim of violence and harm sustained in a public order context may sometimes necessarily receive a less sensitive police response than a victim of the same type and level of violence and harm sustained in an everyday setting.

Third Dilemma: Policing Hate Crimes That Do Not Involve Physical Violence or Harm

A third dilemma arises when policing hate crimes that do not involve violence or harm. Prior to the implementation of hate crime policing the circumstances in which police constables might investigate and exercise powers of arrest for abusive or insulting speech or gestures were extremely limited. Broadly speaking, police action would previously be restricted to cases that occurred in a public order context or in cases where the speech or gestures were ancillary to acts of violence or harm. With the advent of hate crime policing, however, a police constable was required for the first time to take action in respect of incidents that consisted purely of abusive or insulting speech or gestures out with a public order context and neither being ancillary to acts of violence or harm. This represented a fundamental change to the way a police constable was required to perform his or her duties. To be sure, the sense of a dramatic change would be most keenly felt by long serving police constables who had become familiar with the limits of their powers and responsibilities. By the same token, less experienced police constables would doubtless adapt to the change more readily.

To put the change into context it is worth recalling that police constables were previously trained to regard the criminal law as grading violence and harm as steps in severity that culminate in murder. So, for example, the gradations of assault from common assault, to actual bodily harm, to grievous bodily harm, to manslaughter and finally to murder, under the Offences against the Person Act 1861 (sections 42, 47, 5 and 1 respectively). Similar gradations of seriousness are also reflected in the Criminal Damage Act 1971 whereby 'a person who without lawful excuse, destroys or damages any property belonging to another intending to destroy or damage any such property or being reckless as to whether any such property would be destroyed or damaged shall be guilty of an offence' (section 1(1)). Greater severity (of crime and punishment) is reflected in the case of arson (section 1 (3)) and where there is an intention 'by the destruction or damage to endanger the life of another or being reckless as to whether the life of another would be thereby endangered shall be guilty of an offence' (section 1(2)). Separated by over a century both pieces of legislation provided the staple resource for police constables dealing with incidents of violence and harm in public places.

Before focusing on cases without violence and harm (as conceived by legislators in 1861 and 1971) it will be helpful to illustrate those cases of violence and harm that have the capacity to aggravate, alter or subvert the gradations of seriousness that otherwise apply in criminal law. There are many examples of this capacity and two may suffice. Firstly, if during the course of a fight between two schoolchildren in a public place one is heard to shout racist abuse at the other then the incident is more likely to be reported and investigated by police than a similar incident (in terms of levels of violence) without racist abuse being uttered. Secondly, when a far right group is suspected of carrying out an arson attack on a mosque it is likely to give rise to a specialist police response that may be more resource intensive than a police response to a similar attack on a mosque suspected of being carried out by a disgruntled member of the mosque management committee. The point being that seriousness in our field of inquiry is determined as much by motivation or the identity of the victim as by levels of violence and harm—a feature that was not anticipated by the legislators of either the Offences Against the Persons Act 1861 or the Criminal Damage Act 1971—probably the two pieces of legislation that have provided charges and convictions for more cases of violence, damage and harm in the UK than any other.

Outside of public order settings, police officers responding to incidents of violence and harm are very often likely to establish circumstances that will result in the incident being recorded and investigated as a hate crime. Indeed, in research conducted by experienced hate crime scholar Nathan Hall, police officers in London have tended to err towards recording too many incidents as hate crimes, rather than too few (Hall, 2014, p. 200). This research finding dates from the period when hate crimes were a new feature in the repertoire of police duties and is likely to have lessened over time. When recorded accurately as a hate crime, this will entail an incident that might not otherwise be investigated pro-actively—for example incidents involving abuse, threats and minor violence or damage—instead receiving investigative attention more normally reserved for incidents in which more serious violence and harm has been inflicted. In such cases the police officers' actions reflect what Hall explains in a foreword to the College of Policing's *Hate Crime Operational Guidance* booklet: that hate crime involves a level of victimisation that sets the experience apart from the experience of victims of comparable crimes. This in turn explains, as Hall puts it, 'why all victims should not be treated the same' (Hall, 2014, p. 1). A key part of the explanation for this priority attention lies in the identity of all individuals afforded the status of hate crime victims: they are perceived to have been targeted by virtue of the group they belong to. However, not all individuals who are targeted by virtue of the group they belong to will be afforded this status—and the premier police service that is intended to accompany it.

Particularly when dealing with hate crimes that consist of written or spoken words, police officers may find that they are required to mediate between two competing claims to 'victim' status. For example, citizen A alleges that citizen B uttered an abusive word during the course of an otherwise courteous dispute about citizen B's reprimand that citizen A had jumped the queue at a bus stop. In response, citizen B denies the allegation and instead alleges that citizen A uttered an abusive word. Of itself, this is hardly a novel situation for police officers to negotiate. However, it may easily pose a dilemma for police officers if their handling of the situation is seen to be guided favourably towards the claim of either citizen A or citizen B by virtue of their identity rather than based on an assessment of their counter claims. In fact, however trivial it may seem, the mundane example serves to highlight the risk of police action alienating members of one section of a community while actively nurturing support from members of another.

Dealing with Dilemmas

To be sure, dilemmas are intrinsic to all aspects of policing policy and practice. What sets the three dilemmas identified in this chapter apart is the fact that policing hate crime is of a truly pioneering nature. The granting of enhanced credibility to individuals reporting hate crimes; the inclusion of some groups or categories of victims within, and the exclusion of others from, hate crime status; and the policing of hate crimes that do not involve physical violence or harm each raise significant dilemmas that might have been anticipated at inception but seemingly were not. Instead, the dilemmas have emerged as they have been encountered as the new policy has unfolded in practice. In these circumstances, it will be important for police leaders to be seen to understand the dilemmas and to be concerned to balance the competing demands they often make on police policy and practice.

In striking such a balance, due regard should be paid to the fundamental and defining role of the police constable who seeks the support of all sections of the community. The necessary imperative to restore the support of those sections of the community where confidence in the police has been eroded is usefully addressed by the adoption of hate crime policing. However, the exclusion or alienation of sections of the community from hate crime status or hate crime policing would be an unintended and negative consequence of a well-intentioned and worthwhile initiative.

References

Association of Chief Police Officers (ACPO). (2005). *Hate crime: Delivering a quality service: Good practice and tactical guidance*. London: Home Office Police Standards Unit.

BBC News. (2015, June 5). *Met acknowledges 'some justification' to claims the force is 'racist'*. Retrieved from http://www.bbc.co.uk/news/uk-england-london-33025853.

Bone, I. (2006). *True life confessions of an anarchist in the UK*. London: Naked Guides.

Brodeur, J. P. (1983). High policing and low policing: Remarks about the policing of political activities. *Social Problems, 30*(5), 507–520.

Busher, J. (2016). *The making of anti-Muslim protest: Grassroots activism in the English Defence League*. London: Routledge.

Chakraborti, N., & Garland, J. (2009). *Hate crime: Impact, causes and responses.* London: Sage.

Chakraborti, N., & Garland, J. (2015). *Hate crime: Impact, causes and responses* (2nd ed.). London: Sage.

College of Policing. (2014). *Hate crime: Operational guidance.* Coventry: College of Policing. Retrieved from http://www.report-it.org.uk/files/hate_crime_operational_guidance.pdf. Accessed 2.2.20.

Copsey, N. (2010). *The English Defence League: Challenging our country and our values of social inclusion, fairness and equality.* London: Faith Matters. Retrieved form http://faith-matters.org/images/stories/fm-reports/english-defense-league-report.pdf.

Grieve, J. D., & French, J. (2002). Does institutional racism exist in the metropolitan police service? In D. G. Green (Ed.), *Institutional racism and the police: Fact or fiction?* London: Institute for the Study of Civil Society (Civitas).

Guardian. (2015, September 27). *Shoreditch cereal killer cafe targeted in anti-gentrification protests.* Retrieved from https://www.theguardian.com/uk-news/2015/sep/27/shoreditch-cereal-cafe-targeted-by-anti-gentrification-protesters.

Hall, N. (2005). *Hate crime*. Cullompton: Willan Publishing.

Hall, N. (2014). *Foreword*: *College of policing hate crime*: *Operational guidance.* Coventry: College of Policing. Retrieved from http://www.report-it.org.uk/files/hate_crime_operational_guidance.pdf.

Lambert, R. (2011). *Countering Al-Qaeda in London: Police and Muslims in partnership*. London: Hurst.

Lambert, R., & Parsons, T. (2017). Community-based counter-terrorism policing: Seven recommendations for practitioners. *Studies in Conflict & Terrorism, 40*(12), 1054–1071.

Macpherson, L. (1999). *The Stephen Lawrence inquiry: Report*, Cm. 4262–1. Retrieved from https://assets.publishing.service.gov.uk/government/uploads/system/uploads/attachment_data/file/277111/4262.pdf.

Mawby, R. C. (2002). *Policing images: Policing, communication and legitimacy*. Abingdon: Routledge.

Perry, B. (2001). *In the name of hate: Understanding hate crimes*. London: Routledge.

Police Federation. (2018). *The office of constable*. Retrieved from https://www.polfed.org/documents/The%20Office%20of%20Constable%20with%20links.pdf.

Reiner, R. (1985). *The politics of the police*. Brighton: Wheatsheaf.

Rowe, M., & Garland, J. (2007). Police diversity training: A silver bullet tarnished? In M. Rowe (Ed.), *Policing beyond Macpherson: Issues in policing, race and society* (pp. 43–65). Cullompton, Devon: Willan.

Souhami, A. (2007). Understanding institutional racism: The Stephen Lawrence inquiry and the police service reaction. In M. Rowe (Ed.), *Policing beyond Macpherson: Issues in policing, race and society* (pp. 66–87). Cullompton, Devon: Willan.

7

Police Responses to Islamist Radicalisation and Violent Extremism

Timothy Parsons

The study of Islamist radicalisation and violent extremism is both topical in terms of the threat posed by this phenomenon across Europe, the Middle East and many other parts of the world, and as a highly contested area of academic debate and policy development. Accepting that this is a controversial area of debate in academic circles means acknowledging that there are alternative critiques and different interpretations. Due to some of the controversies and confusion that can arise when conducting a detailed study of Islamism and violent extremism, scholars can find themselves trapped between two extreme positions, the adoption of which is deliberately intended to stifle debate and obscure learning. The first of those extreme positions is that any criticism of fundamentalist interpretations of Islam or the violent extremism that they might inspire is, of and in itself, Islamophobic. Such claims are both unfair and unhelpful to researchers with a genuine interest in analysing

T. Parsons (✉)
School of Justice Studies, Liverpool John Moores University, Liverpool, UK
e-mail: t.f.parsons@ljmu.ac.uk

J. J. Nolan et al. (eds.), *Policing in an Age of Reform*,
Palgrave's Critical Policing Studies,
https://doi.org/10.1007/978-3-030-56765-1_7

and comprehending the various complex and intertwined issues at play. Those that adopt this position are more interested in closing down debate and discouraging scrutiny and understanding than they are in offering education and enlightenment.

The other extreme position is similar in nature but opposite in form. The exponents of this position choose to envisage the entire faith of Islam and those who adhere to it as in some way sinister, threatening and malign. Just as with the position outlined above those who adopt this stance are too, against the promulgation of insight and understanding and supportive of an absolutist, hostile and intolerant stance towards one of the world's great religions. The conscientious scholar has to negotiate their way between these two extreme critiques and seek out the facts, the evidence and something that approaches the objective truth. In this more than in any field of study it is perhaps appropriate to accept that there are limitations to human knowledge and understanding.

Across the national and international policymaking landscape there are a number of competing discourses on violent extremism, its nature, definition, causes and contributory factors. This matters for without some clarity of thought and consensus view the development of effective policy responses by governments, security agencies and other arms of the state, becomes impossible. It is a regrettable, but perhaps inevitable, fact that policy, strategy and tactical approaches to the threat posed by violent extremism becomes mired in narrow and partisan political doctrines that all too often obscure the real issues and ignore inconvenient evidence. This lack of clarity at policy level affects the operational focus of the police and influences where finite resources are deployed. During the thirty-year terror campaign waged by republican paramilitaries in Northern Ireland, many young men and women were recruited to the cause and encouraged to engage in terrorist activity. At no point was this phenomenon described as "radicalisation", neither were resources allocated to de-radicalisation programmes. It was simply and accurately described as terrorist recruitment, which is what it was. The quasi-religious language of radicalisation is a recent innovation that has only emerged as the threat from Islamist terror groups has come to prominence.

Following the carefully planned and executed Al Qaeda terror attacks in the USA in 2001, the United Kingdom developed a new Counter-Terrorism Strategy, widely referred to as CONTEST. The initial version was published in 2003. It was then revised in 2006 and subsequently went through several revisions under the last Labour government (1997–2010) and here being updated again by the new coalition government in 2011, it has now re-emerged in yet another revised version, June 2018. This new strategy refers to the threat posed by Islamist terror groups identified as Daesh (Islamic State or ISIL) and Al Qaeda. Much is also made of an equivalent threat posed by far-right terror groups although the evidence to support this claim is decidedly sparse (HM Government, 2018, p. 13). The fact that the British government has harnessed an Arabic word "Daesh", which is meaningless to English speakers, to describe a group with a clear and identifiable English title "Islamic State" is revealing in itself. The Government has attempted to tread a narrow path between trying to avoid implying any link between violent extremism and the Islamic faith and confronting the reality of the threat posed by groups that identify very strongly with Islam as their motivation and inspiration. The strategy develops an apparently deliberate ambiguity about the nature of these groups and where the Government believes their motivation comes from. The UK Government strategy reads as follows: "*The existence of a broadly consistent set of ideas and narratives is an important factor in motivating terrorist groups of all kinds, including Daesh, Al Qaeda and extreme right-wing organisations*" (HM Government, 2018, p. 16). Conflating Islamist ideology with Fascist or far-right ideology seems a stretch and does not assist in the formulation of clear policy responses. The defining ideological characteristics of Daesh and Al Qaeda are described thus—"*Their shared ideological anchor is Salafi-Jihadism, a violent hybrid ideology*" (HM Government, 2018, p. 16). This description appears not only to be lazy and inaccurate, but also illustrative of a lack of any attempt by policymakers to understand and objectively define the nature of the threat. From this must flow flawed policy and misdirected interventions.

As to efforts to combat underlying factors that may lead to violent extremism or terrorism the strategy states—"*This includes tackling the promotion of hatred, the erosion of women's rights, the spread of intolerance, and the isolation of communities. We judge that communities which do not or cannot participate in civic society are more likely to be vulnerable to radicalisation*" (HM Government, 2018, p. 23).

What is not clear from this, and it appears to have been left deliberately vague perhaps to avoid attributing blame, is who these communities are and whether they are really incubators for violent extremism. In a detailed piece of research conducted by Frampton, Goodhart, and Mahmood (2016, p. 70), British Muslims were surveyed about a wide range of topics including integration, exclusion and violent extremism. The survey showed that "From the dataset assembled as a result of our survey, it is possible to state that those inclined to sympathise with the use of either violence or terrorism are more likely to be:

- Male
- In full-time work (or to be students)
- Owners of their own house, or have a mortgage
- In possession of educational qualifications – at least to a secondary level".

This is remarkable, as it directly contradicts the picture painted in the UK Government' strategy of "vulnerable" people from socially isolated communities. Indeed, the Government's fixation with the term vulnerable not only removes any sense of personal agency or individual responsibility but conjures up an image of listless individuals wandering aimlessly about our streets waiting to be targeted by ruthless terrorist recruiters. Such a glaring misalignment between political perception and evidenced reality might be comical, if the subject were not so serious. But the Government's strategy is also illuminating for what it does not say, as much as for what it does. In the 2011 UK Government prevent strategy, much is made of the importance of promoting British values, variously described as "values of democracy", "core values", "mainstream British values" (HM Government, 2011, pp. 39, 48, 57, 61). This contrasts with the approach taken in the 2018 version, where mention of "our values" has been deliberately downplayed and features very little in the 98-page document. This is a revealing omission and perhaps a belated acknowledgement that "our values" or rather the values subscribed to by a global liberal elite are not necessarily the values that are dear to the hearts of all British citizens, a point made succinctly here:

> Liberal evasions have been perpetuated by many people who should know better. But for many people of goodwill it may be the only way to avoid confronting an inconvenient truth: that some minority groups hold very different values and ambitions than those commonly held amongst the dominant majority. (Phillips, Goodhart, & Davies, 2016, p. 15)

This seems to accurately sum up the dilemma at the heart of the UK's preventing violent extremism strategy. What Phillips, Goodhart and Davies make explicit is merely implicit in the strategy document. The liberal world view and dominant political narrative is hinted at rather than overtly articulated. The pious Salafi or the Brotherhood activist is painted as extreme, foreign, backward, third world. This neo-colonial vision of the world denies the reality of demographic change, of a large and growing indigenous Muslim population, that simply does not subscribe to the liberal values of polite society.

And there is another notable omission in the new 2018 strategy. It talks about mental health. "*While no links have been established between mental disorder and group-based terrorism, terrorists who act alone may be more likely to have a background that includes mental ill-health*" (HM Government, 2018, p. 36) A reasonable enough observation as far as it goes, but from that position must surely come a further analysis of the impact of drugs and specifically cannabis. There is ample evidence of a link between terrorism/violent extremism and cannabis use, and yet no mention is made of this as a possible causal factor or enabling activity. This is despite the fact that the link between so-called Islamist terrorists, violent extremists and drug-taking and dealing is long-established and a constantly recurring characteristic in those who have engaged in such violence. See for instance Richard Reid "shoe bomber" 2001, killers of Fusilier Lee Rigby 2013, Boston bombers 2013, Killers of staff at Charlie Hebdo 2015, all widely reported as cannabis users, most as heavy users.

In a UK context it is worthwhile considering the role played by masjids (mosques) in either fuelling Islamist violent extremism or in militating against it. The situation in other European countries will be quite different, although some of the underlying issues and challenges are likely to be the same. There is a considerable amount of misunderstanding about the organisation and distribution of UK masjids and the influence that they exert upon Muslim life. One of the most up-to-date and carefully researched databases on British masjids can be found at www.MuslimsinBritain.org, a privately supported and administered website whose author Mehmood Naqshbandi is a British convert to Islam who has made it his mission to compile and update an accurate directory of UK masjids. This service is principally provided for worshippers who may be seeking a masjid in their local area but the data is open source and therefore available to scholars, researchers and policymakers alike. First Naqshbandi notes that the vast majority of UK masjids are established and sustained through small private donations and not, as some may suppose, through large donations from Arab gulf countries or other overseas sources. He comments too on the size and significance of the South Asian demographic among British masjids. This of course will surprise no one and is as a direct consequence of British imperial conquest, colonisation of the Indian sub-continent and subsequent de-colonisation after the Second World War. Naqshbandi (2017, p. 11) describes the "*Overwhelming domination of South Asian influence in UK masjids' management, 86%*". And goes on to say:

> Adding to that, the fact that most masjid managements are age-biased towards the elder generation, and that many masjids were founded as much to preserve mother-country culture as to provide a religious service, and the ethnic make-up takes on a much more challenging significance. Along with factionalism, one of the biggest alienating factors for Muslim youth and converts in the UK is the way in which masjids fail to meet their needs or interests, and through ethnic parochialism, how their adherents fail to be able to tackle the influence of extremism. (Naqshbandi, 2017, p. 11)

The lack of suitable pastoral and spiritual provision for young British Muslims in UK masjids was a theme that was unpacked in some detail in a publication by the Quilliam Foundation: Hart Dyke (2009, p. 15). (Quilliam presents itself as a counter-extremist think tank and has in the past received considerable financial support from the UK government. It is staffed by a mixture of reformed extremists, scholars and UK Orientalists.) The Quilliam report drew heavily upon work published by Naqshbandi and drew some similar conclusions. For instance, it identified the lack of imams that were British-born and competent in the English language. It also highlighted another pressing concern, that it "*... is simply not enough for imams to merely 'understand' Britain; where are the mechanisms for ensuring that they believe in and seek to uphold Britain's liberal democratic principles?*" Of course, this quote is telling, as it reveals a form of post-colonial paternalism where the un-integrated "other" has to be managed and tutored in what is expected of them. What other community is held to the same standard? The truth is that Muslim communities, masjids and imams are under no obligation to promote liberal values (that many secular British citizens don't in any case subscribe to), or to uphold Britain's democracy.

There is and continues to be a so-far intractable problem of the disconnect between UK masjids and the committees of mainly elderly males who manage them and young British Muslims who are looking for answers to some very modern problems. This issue was explored in some detail more than a decade ago by Policy Exchange researchers, Mirza, Senthilkumaran, and Jafar (2007, p. 40) They included a quote from the late Dr. Ghayasuddin Siddiqui speaking at a Birmingham conference in 2005, who opined that "Most mosques are not equipped to deal with young people...Our mosques are largely tribal and controlled by old men on the dole with no understanding of the changing world around them". The report authors developed the point further—"Some of the respondents we spoke to complained that Islam had become 'Pakistanised' and that they wanted to identify with something unadulterated, and not tied to the received ideas of their parents" (ibid., p. 40).

And it is not just young British Muslims who feel that UK masjids do not meet their needs. There is also evidence that for British converts to Islam many masjids are neither particularly welcoming or in a position to assist and support them as fellow Muslims. Once again, it is the thorny problems of culture, nationality and ethnic difference that stand in the way of integration and acceptance. Researching the lived experience of British converts to Islam, Suleiman (2016) highlighted some of these issues. The experiences of those interviewed are worth recounting in some detail here. One interviewee observed that "upon his return to Britain as a Muslim and his visit to a London mosque (masjid), he encountered 'the tribal mentality' that other participants had complained of and that he felt Islam was supposed to abolish. Explaining that he had converted in Turkey, he had been told that there were "no Muslims in Turkey, only Sufis" (p. 43). Another British convert to Islam who had converted in Indonesia and had married an Indonesian Muslim woman, also found the attitude he encountered at British mosques unnerving. His experience upon returning to the UK was one of sharp and uncomfortable contrast. While he had come back once before and studied in a mosque, it had been a "very definite Arab mosque", and he was eventually to learn that the ethnic composition of British mosques could matter a great deal. His permanent move back led him and his wife to encounter South Asian Islam for the first time. Not only was he—a white convert–seen as an outsider, so was his wife, despite the fact that she was a born Muslim who could speak Arabic and held a degree from an Islamic university (Suleiman, 2016, p. 67).

As outlined above, the issue of culture, nationality and ethnicity are so closely interwoven with religious identity in many British Muslim communities and, therefore, reflected in the make-up of UK masjids or mosques that the environment can appear daunting for the English-speaking, white British convert trying to navigate their way around an, as yet, unfamiliar and theologically complex faith. These experiences take on an added significance when juxtaposed with the large number of terrorist plots that have included one or more converts. The fact that UK masjids clearly do not, on the evidence available, cater for the religious and cultural needs of an increasing community of British converts, should be a topic of concern to policymakers. The activities of UK masjids are tightly controlled by their respective management committees (not the imams who are simply regarded as employees and not particularly well paid ones at that) and therefore not open to wide-ranging theological discussion or political debate is clearly apparent from testimony of those familiar with these institutions. This has the effect of denying to both young British Muslims and British converts to Islam, any obvious avenue to spiritual enlightenment or resolution to powerful feelings of cultural and religious dissonance. Conversations around difficult and complex issues confronting conscientious Muslims are discouraged or actively closed-down in the masjid environment, partly due to the lack of linguistic skills and the intellectual depth available to many imams and spiritual leaders. Added to this may be concerns about attracting the unwanted attention of police and security services if topics such as jihad, violent extremism and the restoration of a caliphate are openly discussed within the environs of a masjid.

The strange and convoluted relationship between Western policy-makers and the Muslim populations of Middle Eastern countries can be traced back to an earlier period in which Britain, France and later the USA occupied the role of colonial powers and imperial oppressors (albeit that America chose to perform this function largely at arms-length). This relationship was examined exhaustively by the great Palestinian-American scholar Edward Said in his seminal work Orientalism (Said, 1978, p. 347). Said described Orientalism as a discourse of power originating in an era of colonialism. One of the earliest phases in the development of Orientalism that Said describes, is a process of classification, description and translation, through which process could occur a "cultural decoding – restored, fleshed out" (ibid., p. 121). Said explains that this process "had the effect of releasing the Orient generally, and Islam in particular, from the narrowly religious scrutiny by which it had hitherto been examined (and judged) by the Christian West" (ibid., p. 120). It is increasingly apparent that a strong vein of continuity runs from these early Orientalist methods and approaches through documents being produced by and on behalf of Western governments today. The key difference between now in the early twenty-first century and the situation in the nineteenth and early twentieth centuries, is that today not only does the West have to define and articulate the nature of its relationship with the Muslim East, but also Western politicians and policymakers have to define and articulate the nature of our relationship with, and attitude towards, the substantial and growing Muslim communities at home: the legacy of that earlier colonial expansion.

Current government thinking in Britain highlights a threat posed by *Salafi-jihadism.* What is it and why is it a threat? There are in the UK and across Europe an increasing number of Salafi-themed masjids. The politically active Salafi or Salafi-inspired activist is clearly the focus of Government attention and disapproval, i.e. specifically, organisations such as the Muslim Brotherhood and the Jamaat Islami. These organisations established in the early part of the twentieth century when both pre-partition India and Egypt were under colonial rule have continued to evolve and flourish in a number of different countries. Both organisations have members and networks in the UK. In April 2014 Prime Minister, David Cameron, commissioned an internal review of the Muslim Brotherhood including its origins, ideology and activities in the UK. The review was conducted by Sir John Jenkins, a senior British diplomat and Charles Farr the Director General of the Office for Security and Counter Terrorism at the Home Office. Although the full text of the report has not been published a summary of the key findings was submitted to Parliament in December 2015. The paper stated that the "Muslim Brotherhood dominated the Muslim Association of Britain (MAB) and that the MAB has links to the Cordoba Foundation, a think tank which is associated with the Brotherhood". The paper also acknowledged that the MAB were "active partners in a security dialogue with the police". The paper concluded that the "Muslim Brotherhood has not been linked to terrorist related activity in and against the UK". Despite this confident assertion it is clear that organisations such as the MAB remain objects of suspicion within government. In October 2019 the UK's Commission for Countering Extremism published a report into what is described as "Hateful Extremism". The report is the culmination of many focus-groups, community consultations and commissioned pieces of academic research. The report authors acknowledge that there is "no legal definition of extremism" (p. 26) and that "The Government's Muslim Brotherhood Review found that some UK-based groups with links to the Muslim Brotherhood Jamaat-e-Islami network praised or equivocated on the use of violence by organisations such as Hamas" (p. 45). It is observations such as this that lead Government ministers and appointed civil servants down a political and ethical rabbit hole from which they may struggle to emerge. If the UK Government is to make the protection of human rights a central theme in its effort to combat violent (and "hateful") extremism, which it does explicitly in the forward to the above report, then there must be a consistent and unwavering commitment to human rights which cannot be, when convenient, brushed aside or subordinated to other economic or political imperatives.

The UK Government classifies Hamas and Hezbollah as terrorist organisations; this regardless of the fact that both administer territories as the democratically elected representatives of their people. In the above report into hateful extremism it is observed that "the beliefs that drive terrorism and violence can be varied, but all draw on an ideological or supremacist view of the world or society" (p. 34). This is quite wrong and leads to further confusion and muddle in the government approach to combating terrorism and violent extremism. The central goal and political objective of groups such as Hamas and Hezbollah is to protect their territory from foreign invasion and to liberate land already occupied from foreign occupation. If the defence of human rights is central to our policy approach, then we may well condemn the actions of groups like Hamas and Hezbollah regardless of their democratic legitimacy. And at the same time we would condemn and place under sanction the Chinese communist party and the House of Saud who are also guilty of widespread and grotesque human rights abuses and who have no democratic legitimacy—but of course, we do not. As a consequence, we undermine all our other efforts to combat the spread of extremist ideologies and the threat of terrorism. Despite the suspicions of government as to the activities and intentions of Salafi groups operating in the UK, the fact is that as has been acknowledged in the Government's own report, representatives from Salafi groups have been actively involved in a dialogue with and support for, police forces in London. Following the Al Qaeda organised attacks in the USA in 2001, the Metropolitan Police Service established the Muslim Contact Unit (MCU), a unit intended to counter terrorism and violent extremism through active and constructive engagement with diverse Muslim communities in London. Staffed in the main with Muslim police officers (including some with Salafi leanings), the MCU enjoyed considerable success, including working with local communities and the MAB to drive an extremist preacher and his followers out of the Finsbury Park Mosque (Lambert, 2008). In addition to this the City of London Police and British Transport Police commissioned a series of public information leaflets on Islam from Salafi Publications in Birmingham. The leaflets were intended to educate the wider public about Muslim communities and to combat Islamophobia. Widely distributed they attracted no comment or criticism from the public, the media or the government. Officers from the City of London Police had regular meetings with officials from the MAB in their London offices and were present when MAB members were speaking by mobile phone to Hamas fighters in Gaza resisting the assault by Israeli forces in 2006.[1] The MAB were also instrumental at the time in providing advice and support to the City Police when the Force was carrying out a community impact assessment of their prevent implementation strategy. For law enforcement officers and frontline practitioners the more esoteric debates about doctrinal differences in Europe's Muslim communities or political tensions between the United Kingdom and various governments in the Middle East are not matters that impact upon day-to-day service delivery in community safety activities, or counter-terrorism operations. Experience has shown that community police officers and trained counter-terrorism liaison officers can build trusting, enduring and mutually beneficial relationships with Salafi and Islamist political groups. Adopting an aggressive and confrontational stance towards these groups and organisations is likely to be damaging to good police-community relations and efforts to maintain public safety in the long term.

It has often been the case that imams in UK masjids, anxious not to incur the displeasure of their employers have tended to steer clear of discussing problematic doctrinal topics, which might include how a young British Muslim should respond to the dramatic and shocking events unfolding in Iraq, Syria, Libya, Yemen and Somalia. Such foreign-born imams then find themselves unable to answer even

[1]This is the author's personal recollection of meetings he attended.

the most basic questions of doctrine, due to their own lack of knowledge, lack of education and lack of fluency in the English language. As a consequence, dissent is driven out of the confines of the mosque and underground. Time and again this failure to respond to the needs of often young dissenters and most particularly young dissenting converts has led to vulnerable individuals being drawn into the welcoming embrace of violent extremists and terrorists. Whether it is 7/7 bomber Germaine Lindsay and his young wife Samantha Lewthwaite, or al-Shabab commander Tom Evans from High Wycombe who was killed in combat by the Kenyan Army, the number of British converts to Islam who have become involved in terrorist plots, is highly significant and indicative of the inability of most UK mosques to satisfy their spiritual and pastoral needs.

Into such a complex and challenging environment ventures the community police officer. The complexity of the task of attempting to successfully negotiate inter-factional and inter-ethnic tensions in UK masjids cannot be over-emphasised. The very real danger of one faction playing naïve and uninformed police officers, against another faction is all too real. And this turgid inter-religious and inter-ethnic landscape can quickly become yet more perilous for law enforcement officers as a consequence of inappropriate staffing and deployment decisions made by local police leaders. All too often police commanders with naïve but benign intent, assign police officers drawn from the local Muslim community to conduct sensitive and delicate engagement activity. The rationale behind such decisions is clear: a police officer with a shared cultural, ethnic and religious background will be able to interact seamlessly with individuals and groups in the local community. Except that it is not quite as straightforward as this. For example, a Sufi-oriented police officer may not necessarily empathise with the management of a mosque run by Salafi inclined Muslim converts. Equally, British-Pakistani, or British-Bangladeshi police officers may sometimes find themselves in highly conflicted positions. Both loyal and committed to the police service of which they are members, while at the same time feeling the pervasive influence of *biraderi* and caste (Metcalf & Rolfe 2010) that permeates many South Asian communities in Britain. It is still unfortunately the case that senior politicians and policymakers appear ignorant of the presence of these deep and complex dynamics within British Muslim communities. The police, on the other hand, encounter them on a daily basis and have the means and opportunity to understand them, accept them as they are and to engage and activate a willingness on the part of these fractured communities to collaborate constructively in the shared endeavour of maintaining public security and personal safety.

Conclusion

In a democratic society it is perfectly legal and legitimate to want to change the system, including changing it so that a country becomes an Islamic republic governed by Quranic injunctions and sharia law. So long as such ambitions for change are not driven by crime or terrorism they are frankly of no business to law enforcement or other security structures of the state. What clearly *is* possible is that police officers can develop a meaningful dialogue with Salafi groups and further to that evolve constructive working relationships. Allied to that is the duty of those same police officers to negotiate the complexity of inter-doctrinal and factional difference within Muslim communities and to accept those communities as they are, rather than attempting to coerce them into being something more socially and politically palatable to central government. Ultimately the most effective way to resist the infiltration of our Muslim communities by either foreign governments or terrorist organisations is to build solid and enduring relationships between law enforcement and local populations constructed around mutual trust, respect and acceptance of diversity and difference.

References

Commission for Countering Extremism. (2019). *Challenging Hateful Extremism*. Retrieved from https://www.gov.uk/government/publications/challenging-hateful-extremism.

Frampton, M., Goodhart, D., & Mahmood, K. (2016). *Unsettled belonging: A survey of Britain's Muslim communities*. London: Policy Exchange.

Hart Dyke, A. (2009). *Mosques made in Britain*. London: Quilliam Foundation.

HM Government. (2009). Pursue prevent protect prepare: The United Kingdom's strategy for countering international terrorism. *Cm 7547*. Retrieved from https://assets.publishing.service.gov.uk/government/uploads/system/uploads/attachment_data/file/228644/7547.pdf.

HM Government. (2011). CONTEST: The United Kingdom's strategy for countering terrorism. *Cm 8123*. Retrieved from https://assets.publishing.service.gov.uk/government/uploads/system/uploads/attachment_data/file/97995/strategy-contest.pdf.

HM Government. (2018). CONTEST: The United Kingdom's strategy for countering terrorism. *Cm 9608*. Retrieved from https://assets.publishing.service.gov.uk/government/uploads/system/uploads/attachment_data/file/716907/140618_CCS207_CCS0218929798-1_CONTEST_3.0_WEB.pdf.

HM Government, Countering International Terrorism: The United Kingdom's Strategy, *Cm 6888* (July 2006). Retrieved from https://assets.publishing.service.gov.uk/government/uploads/system/uploads/attachment_data/file/272320/6888.pdf.

House of Commons. (2015). *Muslim Brotherhood review: Main findings* (House of Commons Paper HC679 (17/12/15)). Retrieved from https://assets.publishing.service.gov.uk/government/uploads/system/uploads/attachment_data/file/486932/Muslim_Brotherhood_Review_Main_Findings.pdf.

Lambert, R. (2008). Empowering Salafis and Islamists against al-Qaeda: A London counterterrorism case study. *PS: Political Science and Politics, 41*(1), 31–35.

Metcalf, H., & Rolfe, H. (2010). *Caste discrimination & harassment in Great Britain*. London: National Institute of Economic & Social Research.

Mirza, M., Senthilkumaran, A., & Jafar, Z. (2007). *Living apart together: British Muslims and the paradox of multiculturalism*. London: Policy Exchange.

Naqshbandi, M. (2017). *UK Mosque statistics/masjid statistics*, 1–15. Retrieved from http://www.muslimsinbritain.org/index.php.

Phillips, T., Goodhart, D., & Davies, J. G. (2016). *Race and faith: The deafening silence*. London: CIVITAS.

Said, E. (1978). *Orientalism*. London: Routledge & Kegan Paul.

Suleiman, Y. (2016). *Narratives of conversion to Islam in Britain: Male perspectives*. UK: University of Cambridge.

8

Forensic Science Understanding by Police Managers: New Opportunities to Re-think Its Involvement in Policing

Frank Crispino, Vincent Mousseau, Simon Baechler, Olivier Delémont, Claude Roux, and Olivier Ribaux

Police Management and Policing

Police management is defined as a set of individual, collective and organisational practices with the aim of producing useful knowledge to ensure the satisfaction of staff members and the performance of the organisation

F. Crispino (✉)
Université du Québec à Trois-Rivières (UQTR), Trois-Rivières, QC, Canada
e-mail: frank.crispino@uqtr.ca

V. Mousseau
School of Criminology, University of Montreal, Montréal, QC, Canada
e-mail: Vincent.mousseau.1@umontreal.ca

S. Baechler
School of Criminal Justice, University of Lausanne, Lausanne, Switzerland
e-mail: simon.baechler@unil.ch

O. Delémont
School of Criminal Justice, University of Lausanne, Lausanne, Switzerland
e-mail: Olivier.delemont@unil.ch

J. J. Nolan et al. (eds.), *Policing in an Age of Reform*,
Palgrave's Critical Policing Studies,
https://doi.org/10.1007/978-3-030-56765-1_8

in terms of cohesion and policing (Roberg, Kuykendall, & Novak, 2002). To attain those goals, modern law enforcement agencies are increasingly moving towards a more proactive approach to address offending, disorder and crime. Consequently, it seems that community policing, problem-oriented policing and intelligence-led policing are gradually becoming standard ways of administering the police—at least in its organisational rhetoric (National Academies of Sciences, Engineering and Medicine, 2017). As "[a] number of writers have drawn attention to the increased reliance on science and technology for the successful performance of contemporary policing" (Ludwig, Fraser, & Williams, 2012, p. 53) we postulate that forensic science has a role to play in these modern forms of policing. Therefore, the understanding of forensic science contributions among police senior managers ought to be questioned.

In charge of policy, they act as strategic planners who define short-, medium- and long-term goals and objectives in order to meet expectations and needs of their stakeholders (state, counties, cities) and other partners such as community groups. They are also in charge of the financial, material and human resources allocation within the organisation they lead (Aepli, Ribaux, & Summerfield, 2011; Lynch & Lynch, 2005). Police managers therefore certainly have powers and responsibilities that influence the quality and use of forensic science (Guéniat, 2017). Indeed, they assign tasks and objectives to crime scene units and crime labs and define the conditions that guide their involvement and standards. A recent publication revealed the underestimation by police managers of the scope and possibilities of forensic science, hence limiting its exploitation and potential involvement in law enforcement and policing

C. Roux
Centre for Forensic Science, University of Technology Sydney, Ultimo, NSW, Australia
e-mail: Claude.roux@uts.edu.au

O. Ribaux
School of Criminal Justice, University of Lausanne, Lausanne, Switzerland
e-mail: Olivier.ribaux@unil.ch

(Mousseau, Baechler, & Crispino, 2019). Although limited to the Canadian Province of Quebec, this study does not "identify specific reasons why such a perception from police leaders would be exclusive to Quebec" (p. 530).

Indeed, those results are in line with the findings of previous studies over the last decades in the United Kingdom, which indicated that crime scene examiners were essentially considered (including by themselves) as "technical assistants" in charge of collecting evidence (Ludwig et al., 2012; Williams, 2004). For Quebec police senior managers, crime scene units are viewed essentially as support units for criminal investigations. They therefore tend to associate forensic science to a reactive (i.e. on request) and somewhat auxiliary process initiated by the commission of crimes and other types of incidents requiring investigation (e.g. car accidents). Many police managers admitted having neither tight relationships with forensic laboratories or research institutions, nor dedicated protocols or standards to assess the performance of their crime scene units (Mousseau, 2019).

In the eyes of police managers, forensic science appears to be a complementary and powerful resource to the work of investigators, but mainly dedicated to Court, focused on the exclusion of bystanders and the identification of suspects, who could not be identified by other so-called conventional investigation methods. However, according to a body of research, only a small ratio of criminal cases is solved with the help of forensic science, which plays a minimal role in resolving homicide and even burglary cases in the United States, England, Australia, France and Quebec. Rather, human sources (witnesses, informants) and police activities (patrol intervention, surveillance) seem to be the factors contributing to the elucidation of homicide cases (Baskin & Sommers, 2010; Brodeur, 2010; McEwen & Regoeczi, 2015).

In the police managers view, forensic science is strongly associated with supporting the Court decision-making process. In this context, they seem to ignore governmental and academic controversies about the implementation and practices of forensic science (Margot, 2011; NAS, 2009; PCAST, 2016; Roux, Crispino, & Ribaux, 2012). The contribution of forensic science in the investigative process is found limited over the past decades, despite abilities to answer and raise questions about a perpetrated crime (Bitzer et al., 2017; Jackson, Jones, Booth, Champod, & Evett, 2006; Kruse, 2015), and the potential to link cases through traces, the best example being burglary series (Bond, 2007; Coupe & Griffiths, 1996). To process traces is not a guarantee of investigative and judicial success per se. Beside that, the efficiency of forensic science can also be challenged since few traces are collected from crime scenes (e.g. physical evidence is collected in less than a third of the assault and burglary cases reported to the police), and only a tinier fraction ends up into Court. Obviously, many traces remain unexploited and sleep in investigative files or databases, whereas these traces hold relevant information on prolific offenders, criminal activity and new threats (Laurin, 2012; Robertson, 2012; Strom & Hickman, 2010).

Traces, as weak signals, constitute many missed opportunities to elicit forensic intelligence useful to support policing (Raymond & Julian, 2015), as will be discussed below. In this regard, managerial (e.g. quality management) and academic efforts (cognitive science, analytics, forensic interpretation) miss out more often than not the potential contribution of forensic science to policing since their main focus is on a better support of justice decisions. Although traces are available to be used in a greater scheme of inferences than systems are able to figure out (Ribaux, Roux, & Crispino, 2017), operational practitioners are able to deploy abundant and imaginative schemes that may take them into account, but they are not necessarily solicited and remain under the radar of academic studies.

It must be acknowledged that this problem is not limited to forensic science. It is systemic inside the complex policing system, difficult to frame itself coherently through various and different organisations that compose the security and justice apparatus (Brodeur & Shearing, 2005). For instance, databases expansion, including their interconnection upgrade, cannot alone provide a more efficient impact on security, if the efficiency criterion is strictly limited to the jurisdictional answer in Court (Jeuniaux et al., 2015; Ribaux & Hicks, 2013).

Forensic Science as a Provider of Policing Intelligence: Some Examples

Forensic intelligence is "the accurate, timely and useful product of logically processing forensic case data" (Ribaux et al., 2003, p. 49). This concept relies on the analogy that similar criminal activities will leave traces that are likely to be—at least partly—similar, while distinct activities will mostly produce distinct traces. This systematic comparison of traces can contribute to the study of crime patterns and serial crimes (Ribaux, Baylon, Lock, et al., 2010; Ribaux, Baylon, Roux, et al., 2010; Ribaux, Walsh, & Margot, 2006).

Using forensic science in an intelligence perspective is beneficial for supporting decision-making at strategic, operational and tactical levels for law enforcement agencies (Bell, 2006; Ribaux, 2014; Ribaux et al., 2017). It even becomes useful at a macroscopic level as a tool for managers and researchers through the development of scientific knowledge. Since traces are, by definition, dependent on the criminal activities at their origin, using them in a criminological perspective creates knowledge on "forms of crime, modus operandi, typologies of crime situations and problems" (Free translation) (Baechler, 2018, p. 143). Forensic science can contribute to the understanding of particular crime systems, criminal trajectories and the evolution of certain offending behaviours, including new criminal trend detection (crime epidemiology), thus becoming an interesting tool for the detection of innovations used by offenders and for resource allocation (Rossy, Décary-Hétu, Delémont, & Mulone, 2017).

Roux, Talbot-Wright, Robertson, Crispino, and Ribaux (2015) pointed out that forensic science should focus on the trace and its potential contribution to security and policing rather than on the specialisation of laboratory techniques and the mere presentation of evidence to the Court. In order to remedy the widespread underutilisation of traces, forensic science should be extended to a proactive role of detection and resolution of problems faced by law enforcement agencies and other actors in the field of security. These problems here refer to disrupting criminal activities which, by their frequency or their gravity, threaten social order and the security of the community (Goldstein, 1990).

The scientific literature is also increasingly recognising that traces can be exploited in a proactive perspective of operational and strategic intelligence, by participating in the definition of problems and objectives, in the resource prioritisation and allocation, as well as in the development of standards and strategies regarding crime prevention (Bruenisholz et al., 2016; Ribaux et al., 2017).

For example, Fortin (2014) was interested in digital traces not to identify offenders, but to better understand child pornography cyber behaviours as a whole in order to propose an optimisation of tools to fight against predators. He developed a method based on digital traces to decipher the interactions of criminals on the Web. It is interesting to note that this approach is fundamentally similar to the one already implemented by using physical, biological and image traces to assess the social and economic structure of crime, the mobility and interaction of criminal groups and the emergence of new trends (Rossy, Ioset, Dessimoz, & Ribaux, 2013).

This approach relying on the use of traces to gain knowledge about a "criminal ecology" is indeed experiencing some success in:

- understanding the structure and extent of criminal networks as well as distribution routes through the analysis of seized illicit drugs specimens (Esseiva et al., 2007; Morelato et al., 2013; Ouellet & Morselli, 2013);
- identifying prolific authors through the comparison of shoemarks helping to decide where and when to allocate investigative resources (Ribaux et al., 2003; Rossy et al., 2013);
- detecting links between forged and counterfeit documents revealing the activity of criminal networks, such as human trafficking rings, and inviting to focus on the traffickers instead of the victims (Baechler & Margot, 2016; Baechler, Ribaux, & Margot, 2012);
- refuting criminological and police hypothesis of watertight separations between street gangs, when firearms traces support the sharing of weapons between gangs (Braga & Pierce, 2004; Hannam, 2010);
- mitigating methodological biases in the evaluation of spatial patterns of serial offenders' criminal activity through the use of DNA evidence

for intelligence purpose (Lammers, 2013; Lammers, Bernasco, & Elffers, 2012; Palmbach, Blom, Hoynes, Primorac, & Gaboury, 2014).

This perception of social reality by traces does not interest only investigators or social researchers (through the emerging interdisciplinary concept of traceology [Rossy et al., 2017]), but also authorities in charge of policing, including economy, public health and prevention, as illustrated by four last examples:

- The assessment of the legal response to public health and economic harm caused by counterfeit medicines concluded that the legal measures were not applicable. The establishment of forensic monitoring was proposed, which initiated the mobilisation of the Swiss agencies and relevant international agencies (Dégardin, Roggo, & Margot, 2014).
- The estimation of drug addiction habits and the identification of new substances using wastewater analysis provided also an assessment of the effectiveness of police operations, all aimed at optimising the resources of prevention and control available (Been, Esseiva, & Delémont, 2016).
- The assessment of the doping trade magnitude through the study of online doping market on biological markers and digital traces highlighted the problem being more significant than what was perceived by the laboratories in charge of security and health problems (Marclay, Mangin, Margot, & Saugy, 2013; Pineau et al., 2016).
- The call for awareness-raising among European web hosts about their responsibility in the area of counterfeits through the combined analysis of physical and chemical traces arising from the production of watches (on the watches themselves) as well as digital traces linked to distribution websites, which led to favourable developments to protect this art craft (Hochholdinger, Marvin, Arnoux, Esseiva, & Delémont, 2019).

The common key to these strategies lies naturally in the identification of patterns. However, the detection and recognition of these patterns can hardly occur without the transformation of a reactive criminal justice strategy into a proactive security approach. This transformation, in turn, makes it possible to anticipate the means to be implemented in face of criminal innovations. Such a paradigm shift has certainly some consequences on traditional policing, addressing also communities, public health, industry or commerce.

The adoption of such a proactive forensic pathway on serial crime and prolific offenders could look locked by operational or even "pathological" obstacles in law enforcement agencies (Sheptycki, 2004), but forensic data beholds interesting qualities for democratic rights (Grossrieder & Ribaux, 2017). For instance, there is no need of coercive measures (house search, arrest, etc.) to collect traces available in public area or at victims' homes at their request. The use of forensic data for crime understanding and policing has an undeniable potential. But this use must be well regulated and ethically justified to avoid being perceived—rightly or wrongly—as an expansion of governmental intervention and surveillance (Dahl & Sætnan, 2009).

Back to Quebec Practice with Some Positive Forecast

The tendency to focus on a low diversity of traces, typically DNA and fingerprints, which emerges from the police senior managers' interviews conducted by Mousseau et al. (2019), is consistent with the more general lack of knowledge of the concept of forensic intelligence (Crispino, Rossy, Ribaux, & Roux, 2015).

However, three interviewees (over 18) attributed to forensic science a proactive role similar to the concepts on which forensic intelligence is based. They suggested that forensic science might be useful in identifying a particular modus operandi, in detecting a crime series, in discovering new techniques used by offenders and in acquiring knowledge on offenders' habits. Practically, these police managers would ask their crime scene officers to intervene more frequently and systematically on different cases where links are anticipated, i.e. when those cases could be connected to the activity of a serial offender. Still, their primary rationale for such strategies remains first and foremost built on other types of information and intelligence than forensic science, based for instance on the analysis of spatiotemporal and digital data. It should thus be noted that these three interviewees only very briefly mentioned this extension of the role of forensic science, appearing rather as the result of a thought emerging from the ongoing interview than an entrenched perception (Mousseau et al., 2019).

Nevertheless, such an opening suggests that basic and/or continuing training dedicated to the various roles of forensic science and to the possibilities offered by the discipline should be developed to supplement the knowledge of police decision-makers. To maximise the scope of their reflections on this subject, success story examples showcasing the usefulness to policing might be privileged, including ones in the proactive fight against volume crimes, as such as burglaries, car thefts, etc. only potentially serial.

With proper forensic science training and, why not, a forensic scientist attached at the right level of command, police senior managers could have a leading role in supporting and extending the use of forensic science for criminal intelligence and more generally policing.

Conclusion

The present analysis, corroborated by a survey of Quebec police managers, supports that police managers as well as some other practitioners and researchers do not perceive the full potential of traces in a holistic approach. Indeed, by concentrating their attention mainly, if not exclusively, on the ability of forensic science to serve justice, they tend to restrict forensic science to a set of scientific disciplines used in a laboratory context, without a clear understanding and a real reflection of its potential within a broader security challenge (Crispino, Ribaux, Houck, & Margot, 2011; Kelty, Julian, & Ross, 2013; Pietro, Kammrath, & De Forest, 2018). They thus seem little informed about the demonstrated usefulness of traces in a proactive perspective that goes beyond the investigation of singular cases, and in the knowledge acquisition on volume crimes. Further, most police forces have been struggling with the challenges caused by the digital transformation of society. In this context, forensic intelligence provides an additional avenue to exploit the large variety of commonly encountered digital traces. As a result, forensic intelligence may provide a framework to police organisations to design and integrate policing strategies, methods and tools that are adapted to an increasingly digitalised society (see Ribaux et al., Chapter 11).

Reducing forensic science to an ancillary service to the justice system deprives police managers of an effective perception tool complementary to their traditional methods of policing, to unveil actual or emergent threats on their fellow citizens, and rationalise the allocation of resources to remedy them.

References

Aepli, P., Ribaux, O., & Summerfield, E. (2011). Decision making in policing: Operations and management (1st ed.). Lausanne: EPFL Press.

Baechler, S. (2018). Science forensique et innovations criminelles: Opportunité méthodologique ou jeu du chat et de la souris? In D. Décary-Hétu & M. Bérubé (Éds.), *Délinquance et Innovation* (pp. 139–158). Montreal: Les Presses de l'Université de Montréal.

Baechler, S., & Margot, P. (2016). Understanding crime and fostering security using forensic science: The example of turning false identity documents into forensic intelligence. *Security Journal, 29*(4), 618–639. https://doi.org/10.1057/sj.2015.26.

Baechler, S., Ribaux, O., & Margot, P. (2012). Toward a novel forensic intelligence model: Systematic profiling of false identity documents. *Forensic Science Policy & Management: An International Journal, 3*(2), 70–84. https://doi.org/10.1080/19409044.2012.744120.

Baskin, D., & Sommers, I. (2010). The influence of forensic evidence on the case outcomes of homicide incidents. *Journal of Criminal Justice, 38*(6), 1141–1149. https://doi.org/10.1016/j.jcrimjus.2010.09.002.

Been, F., Esseiva, P., & Delémont, O. (2016). Analysis of illicit drugs in wastewater—Is there an added value for law enforcement? *Forensic Science International, 266,* 215–221. https://doi.org/10.1016/j.forsciint.2016.05.032.

Bell, C. (2006). Concepts and possibilities in forensic intelligence. *Forensic Science International, 162*(1–3), 38–43. https://doi.org/10.1016/j.forsciint.2006.06.030.

Bitzer, S., Heudt, L., Barret, A., George, L., Van Dijk, K., Gason, F., & Renard, B. (2017). The introduction of forensic advisors in Belgium and their role in the criminal justice system. *Science & Justice*. https://doi.org/10.1016/j.scijus.2017.11.002.

Bond, J. W. (2007). Value of DNA evidence in detecting crime. *Journal of Forensic Sciences, 52*(1), 128–136. https://doi.org/10.1111/j.1556-4029.2006.00323.x.

Braga, A. A., & Pierce, G. L. (2004). Linking crime guns: The impact of ballistics imaging technology on the productivity of the Boston Police Department's Ballistics Unit. *Journal of Forensic Sciences, 49*(4), 1–6. https://doi.org/10.1520/JFS2003205.

Brodeur, J.-P. (2010). *The policing web*. New York: Oxford University Press.

Brodeur, J.-P., & Shearing, C. (2005). Configuring security and justice. *European Journal of Criminology, 2*(4), 379–406. https://doi.org/10.1177/1477370805056055.

Bruenisholz, E., Prakash, S., Ross, A., Morelato, M., O'Malley, T., Raymond, M. A., ... Walsh, S. (2016). The intelligent use of forensic data: An introduction to the principles. *Forensic Science Policy & Management: An International Journal, 7*(1–2), 21–29. https://doi.org/10.1080/19409044.2015.1084405.

Coupe, T., & Griffiths, M. (1996). *Solving residential Burglary*. London: Home Office, Police Research Group.

Crispino, F., Ribaux, O., Houck, M., & Margot, P. (2011). Forensic science—A true science? *Australian Journal of Forensic Sciences, 43*(2–3), 157–176. https://doi.org/10.1080/00450618.2011.555416.

Crispino, F., Rossy, Q., Ribaux, O., & Roux, C. (2015). Education and training in forensic intelligence: A new challenge. *Australian Journal of Forensic Sciences, 47*(1), 49–60.

Dahl, J. Y., & Sætnan, A. R. (2009). "It all happened so slowly"—On controlling function creep in forensic DNA databases. *International Journal of Law, Crime and Justice, 37*(3), 83–103. https://doi.org/10.1016/j.ijlcj.2009.04.002.

Dégardin, K., Roggo, Y., & Margot, P. (2014). Understanding and fighting the medicine counterfeit market. *Journal of Pharmaceutical and Biomedical Analysis, 87*, 167–175. https://doi.org/10.1016/j.jpba.2013.01.009.

Esseiva, P., Ioset, S., Anglada, F., Gasté, L., Ribaux, O., Margot, P., ... Ottinger, E. (2007). Forensic drug Intelligence: An important tool in law enforcement. *Forensic Science International, 167*(2), 247–254. https://doi.org/10.1016/j.forsciint.2006.06.032.

Fortin, F. (2014). *C'est ma collection mais c'est bien plus que ça: Analyse des processus de collecte et de l'évolution des images dans les collections de pornographie juvénile*. Thèse de doctorat. Université de Montréal.
Goldstein, H. (1990). *Problem-oriented policing*. New York: McGraw-Hill.
Grossrieder, L., & Ribaux, O. (2017). Towards forensic whistleblowing? From traces to intelligence. *Policing: A Journal of Policy and Practice, 13*(2), 80–93. https://doi.org/10.1093/police/pax039.
Guéniat, O. (2017). In vestige @ and police management? *Policing: A Journal of Policy and Practice, 13*(1), 35–46. https://doi.org/10.1093/police/pax044.
Hannam, A. G. (2010). Trends in converted firearms in England & Wales as identified by the National Firearms Forensic Intelligence Database (NFFID) between September 2003 and September 2008. *Journal of Forensic Sciences, 55*(3), 757–766. https://doi.org/10.1111/j.1556-4029.2009.01293.x.
Hochholdinger, S., Marvin, L., Arnoux, M., Esseiva, P., & Delémont, O. (2019). Elemental analysis for profiling counterfeit watches. *Forensic Science International, 298,* 177–185. https://doi.org/10.1016/j.forsciint.2019.03.006.
Jackson, G., Jones, S., Booth, G., Champod, C., & Evett, I. W. (2006). The nature of forensic science opinion—A possible framework to guide thinking and practice in investigation and in court proceedings. *Science & Justice, 46*(1), 33–44.
Jeuniaux, P., Renard, B., Duboccage, L., Steuve, S., Stappers, C., Gallala, I., … Vanvooren, V. (2015). Managing forensic DNA records in a divided world: The Belgian case. *Records Management Journal, 25*(3), 269–287. https://doi.org/10.1108/RMJ-05-2015-0018.
Kelty, S. F., Julian, R., & Ross, A. (2013). Dismantling the justice silos: Avoiding the pitfalls and reaping the benefits of information-sharing between forensic science, medicine and law. *Forensic Science International, 230*(1–3), 8–15. https://doi.org/10.1016/j.forsciint.2012.10.032.
Kruse, C. (2015). *The social life of forensic evidence*. Oakland: University of California Press. https://www.ucpress.edu/book/9780520288393/the-social-life-of-forensic-evidence.
Lammers, M. (2013). Are arrested and non-arrested serial offenders different? A test of spatial offending patterns using DNA found at crime scenes. *Journal of Research in Crime and Delinquency, 51*(2), 143–167. https://doi.org/10.1177/0022427813504097.
Lammers, M., Bernasco, W., & Elffers, H. (2012). How long do offenders escape arrest? Using DNA traces to analyse when serial offenders are caught:

How long do offenders escape arrest? *Journal of Investigative Psychology and Offender Profiling, 9*(1), 13–29. https://doi.org/10.1002/jip.1353.
Laurin, J. E. (2012). Remapping the path forward: Toward a systemic view of forensic science reform and oversight. *Texas Law Review, 91,* 1051–1118.
Ludwig, A., Fraser, J., & Williams, R. (2012). Crime scene examiners and volume crime investigations: An empirical study of perception and practice. *Forensic Science Policy & Management: An International Journal, 3*(2), 53–61. https://doi.org/10.1080/19409044.2012.728680.
Lynch, R. G., & Lynch, S. R. (2005). *The police manager* (6th ed.). Philadelphia, PA: Matthew Bender & Company.
Marclay, F., Mangin, P., Margot, P., & Saugy, M. (2013). Perspectives for forensic intelligence in anti-doping: Thinking outside of the box. *Forensic Science International, 229*(1), 133–144. https://doi.org/10.1016/j.forsciint.2013.04.009.
Margot, P. (2011). Forensic science on trial—What is the law of the land? *Australian Journal of Forensic Sciences, 43*(2–3), 89–103. https://doi.org/10.1080/00450618.2011.555418.
McEwen, T., & Regoeczi, W. (2015). Forensic evidence in homicide investigations and prosecutions. *Journal of Forensic Sciences, 60*(5), 1188–1198. https://doi.org/10.1111/1556-4029.12787.
Morelato, M., Beavis, A., Tahtouh, M., Ribaux, O., Kirkbride, P., & Roux, C. (2013). The use of forensic case data in intelligence-led policing: The example of drug profiling. *Forensic Science International, 226*(1–3), 1–9. https://doi.org/10.1016/j.forsciint.2013.01.003.
Mousseau, V. (2019). La sélection et l'évaluation des techniciens en scène de crime: Compétences attendues des techniciens en identité judiciaire par les dirigeants policiers du Québec. *Criminologie, 52*(2), 193–217. https://doi.org/10.7202/1065861ar.
Mousseau, V., Baechler, S., & Crispino, F. (2019). Management of crime scene units by Quebec police senior managers: Insight on forensic knowledge and understanding of key stakeholders. *Science & Justice, 59*(5), 524–532. https://doi.org/10.1016/j.scijus.2019.04.004.
NAS. (2009). *Strengthening forensic science in the United States: A path forward.* Washington, DC: National Research Council of the National Academies, National Academies Press.
National Academies of Sciences, Engineering, and Medicine. (2017). *Proactive policing: Effects on crime and communities.* Washington, DC: The National Academies Press. https://doi.org/10.17226/24928.

Ouellet, M., & Morselli, C. (2013). Precursors and prices: Structuring the Quebec synthetic drug market. *Journal of Drug Issues, 44*(1), 37–55. https://doi.org/10.1177/0022042613491104.

Palmbach, T., Blom, J., Hoynes, E., Primorac, D., & Gaboury, M. (2014). Utilizing DNA analysis to combat the world wide plague of present day slavery—Trafficking in persons. *Croatian Medical Journal, 55*(1), 3–8. https://doi.org/10.3325/cmj.2014.55.3.

Pietro, D. S., Kammrath, B. W., & De Forest, P. R. (2018). Is forensic science in danger of extinction? *Science & Justice, 59*(2), 199–202. https://doi.org/10.1016/j.scijus.2018.11.003.

Pineau, T., Schopfer, A., Grossrieder, L., Broséus, J., Esseiva, P., & Rossy, Q. (2016). The study of doping market: How to produce intelligence from Internet forums. *Forensic Science International, 268,* 103–115. https://doi.org/10.1016/j.forsciint.2016.09.017.

President's Council of Advisors on, & Science and Technology. (2016). *Forensic science in criminal courts: Ensuring scientific validity of feature-comparison methods* (p. 174). Executive Office of the President.

Raymond, T., & Julian, R. (2015). Forensic intelligence in policing: Organisational and cultural change. *Australian Journal of Forensic Sciences, 47*(4), 371–385. https://doi.org/10.1080/00450618.2015.1052759.

Ribaux, O. (2014). *Police scientifique: Le renseignement par la trace*. Lausanne: Presses Polytechniques Universitaires Romandes (PPUR).

Ribaux, O., Baylon, A., Lock, E., Delémont, O., Roux, C., Zingg, C., & Margot, P. (2010). Intelligence-led crime scene processing. Part II: Intelligence and crime scene examination. *Forensic Science International, 199*(1–3), 63–71. https://doi.org/10.1016/j.forsciint.2010.03.011.

Ribaux, O., Baylon, A., Roux, C., Delémont, O., Lock, E., Zingg, C., & Margot, P. (2010). Intelligence-led crime scene processing. Part I: Forensic intelligence. *Forensic Science International, 195*(1–3), 10–16. https://doi.org/10.1016/j.forsciint.2009.10.027.

Ribaux, O., Girod, A., Walsh, S. J., Margot, P., Mizrahi, S., & Clivaz, V. (2003). Forensic intelligence and crime analysis. *Law, Probability and Risk, 2*(1), 47–60. https://doi.org/10.1093/lpr/2.1.47.

Ribaux, O., & Hicks, T. (2013). Technology and database expansion: What impact on policing? In S. Leman-Langlois (Ed.), *Technocrime, policing and surveillance* (pp. 91–108). London and New York: Routledge.

Ribaux, O., Roux, C., & Crispino, F. (2017). Expressing the value of forensic science in policing. *Australian Journal of Forensic Sciences, 49*(5), 489–501. https://doi.org/10.1080/00450618.2016.1229816.

Ribaux, O., Walsh, S. J., & Margot, P. (2006). The contribution of forensic science to crime analysis and investigation: Forensic intelligence. *Forensic Science International, 156*(2–3), 171–181. https://doi.org/10.1016/j.forsciint.2004.12.028.

Roberg, R. R., Kuykendall, J. L., & Novak, K. (2002). *Police management* (3rd ed.). Los Angeles, CA: Roxbury Publishing.

Robertson, J. (2012). Forensic science, an enabler or dis-enabler for criminal investigation? *Australian Journal of Forensic Sciences, 44*(1), 83–91. https://doi.org/10.1080/00450618.2011.595736.

Rossy, Q., Décary-Hétu, D., Delémont, O., & Mulone, M. E. (2017). *The Routledge international handbook of forensic intelligence and criminology.* Abingdon, Oxon, UK: Routledge.

Rossy, Q., Ioset, S., Dessimoz, D., & Ribaux, O. (2013). Integrating forensic information in a crime intelligence database. *Forensic Science International, 230*(1–3), 137–146. https://doi.org/10.1016/j.forsciint.2012.10.010.

Roux, C., Crispino, F., & Ribaux, O. (2012). From forensics to forensic science. *Current Issues in Criminal Justice, 24*(1), 7–24.

Roux, C., Talbot-Wright, B., Robertson, J., Crispino, F., & Ribaux, O. (2015). The end of the (forensic science) world as we know it? The example of trace evidence. *Philosophical Transactions of the Royal Society B: Biological Sciences, 370*(1674), 20140260. https://doi.org/10.1098/rstb.2014.0260.

Sheptycki, J. (2004). Organizational pathologies in police intelligence systems: Some contributions to the lexicon of intelligence-led policing. *European Journal of Criminology, 1*(3), 307–332. https://doi.org/10.1177/1477370804044005.

Strom, K., & Hickman, M. J. (2010). Unanalyzed evidence in law-enforcement agencies: A national examination of forensic processing in police departments. *Criminology & Public Policy, 9*(2), 381–404.

Williams, R. (2004). *The management of crime scene examination in relation to the investigation of burglary and vehicle crime.* Home Office.

9

"So, How Are We Doing…?" Issues and Considerations in the Design of Police Performance Measurements

James Brown

Background

While much has been written on police performance measurements and performance evaluation, each department provides a different focus based upon the needs of their respective communities. In an age of reform, where the functions of the police are being questioned anew, it is essential that officers and police leaders understand what they are expected to do, how to successfully measure it, and how to adapt it to new methods or mandates. For example, harnessing the power of big data and using it pro-actively to inform and implement police reform will require a new cohort of highly skilled police specialists. Efforts to identify, recruit, and evaluate the work of these data experts needs to begin right away. New skills in policing may also be required to strengthen

J. Brown (✉)
University of Ontario Institute of Technology, Oshawa, ON, Canada
e-mail: james.brown@UOIT.ca

J. J. Nolan et al. (eds.), *Policing in an Age of Reform*,
Palgrave's Critical Policing Studies,
https://doi.org/10.1007/978-3-030-56765-1_9

community ties and solve local problems in new ways. Again, these new approaches will have to be evaluated.

However, many challenges lie ahead as police services and performance appraisal systems in North America are decentralised and fragmented. This is not the case in Great Britain which has a nationally mandated performance measurement system. In Canada, a national report identified performance measurement as organisation-specific initiatives with little coordination and metrics which is incomparable (Expert Panel on the Future of Canadian Policing Models, 2014). While the 2013 report of *Canadian Police Board Views on the Use of Police Performance Metric* (Kiedrowski, Petrunik, Macdonald, & Melchers, 2013) revealed that the majority of police services across the country had rudimentary performance evaluation models, it was perhaps more poignant to note that over 50% of the police services in Canada had no model by which to measure performance. Conversely, a recent European study of police performance measures noted that performance measures are also political issues and subject to continuous improvement for the long-term good of police organisations (Rautiainen, Urquía-Grande, & Muñoz-Colomina, 2017).

There are currently significant variances in performance measures within jurisdictions, illuminating the expectations of police executives as well as the community. Some countries focus their efforts (and measures) around containing or constraining police actions and intrusions (such as the United States). Others tend to focus their measures around meeting community expectations (such as in the U.K.), while others are principally focused on cost control (such as Canada). While these are generalisations of current police performance measurements, we will explore the consequences of performance measures on service delivery and organisational performance. Hence, this chapter will describe the importance of police performance assessment in the evolution of policing especially in times of change.

The Value of Performance Measures

With seemingly inconsistent performance measures across police agencies, why should police leaders and police governance bodies even consider them? Robert Behn (2003) suggests eight purposes for performance measures which included: (1) Evaluating organisational performance; (2) Controlling organisational activities; (3) Budgeting for people. Programmes and projects; (4) Motivating all staff members in their work; (5) Promoting the work of the organisation to the public and politicians; (6) To celebrate personal and organisational achievements and promote success; (7) To help the organisation learn about its successes and challenges; and (8) To determine how to improve the organisation and its service delivery. Within these areas are specific grouping that are of interest to police leaders.

Evaluate Organisational Performance Against Set Goals

Police leaders and their governance bodies frequently commit significant time and effort to the development of organisational goals and objectives, both of which have a strong desire to determine if those goals and objectives are achieved, and with how much success, and at what cost. Hence, "Performance measures need to be linked directly with the strategies and plans of the organisation which, in turn derive from the overall vision and direction that has been established" (Wisniewski & Dickson, 2001), and are clearly critical if the leadership team is to evaluate the organisations' performance towards achieving those goals.

Accountability (Fiscal and Operational)

"The public cannot judge the police, as democracy requires, in their performance is invisible" (Bayley, 1996). Publicly funded agencies are accountable to elected officials, and ultimately the public, for both the allocation of the tax dollars that are spent for their operations, as well as to the publicly funded services that they provide. "Accountability also contributes to police legitimacy, which underpins public support for the police and the public's willingness to cooperate with police" (Expert Panel on the Future of Canadian Policing Models, 2014). Performance measures allow police leaders to inform those constituents about how funds were allocated and what results they produced.

Organisational Focus

Drawing upon the premises "that which gets measured, gets done", those actions, services, behaviours, and efforts that are captured as part of the organisations performance measurement process, tend to be areas in which members of the organisation give focus, especially when performance that is measured is linked to discipline and reward outcomes.

Resource Allocation

While resource allocation (fiscal and human) across the organisation may be based solely on anecdotal evidence, geography, hierarchical and/or power positions, or even relationships, each of these models has significant failings, not the least of which is the lack of evidence from performance measures to assist the organisational leaders in their decision to allocate resources.

Benefits from Performance Measures

While establishing performance measures clearly has an impact on many of the strategic areas of the police organisation, police leaders and governance bodies need to determine what it is that they hope to gain from gathering performance measurements. Simply asking for data on performance without having a clear goal in mind is both wasteful and potentially harmful to the organisation. If the organisation is counting the number of speeding tickets that are generated, what is the purpose?

How is the information going to be used? What is the cost of data collection? What are the organisational as well as performance (behaviour) impacts that result?

The question of whether the organisation is doing "a good job" is completely dependent upon the lens through which the evaluation is undertaken, and that lens is "owned" by the viewer. Hence, those responsible for finance will look at fiscal accountability, those responsible for governance will look at compliance, and those responsible for service delivery will look at success. Therefore, when building performance measurements systems, designers and leaders need to understand the needs of each of the respective constituencies and equally importantly, how the needs of each constituency interact, overlap, and sometimes conflict with.

Some organisational leaders would prefer to be judged on the qualitative aspects of their leadership capacity, and may ask the question, if I create a performance measurement system, will it be used against me? The answer is "yes you should" and "yes it can". However, a performance measurement system is also a shield by which it protects police leaders against political interference or personality clashes with their governance boards. Without this, the evaluation of police leaders can be superficial (personality based instead of performance based), politically motivated or personality based. However, a performance measurement system provides an established and politically unbiased method by which to measure the organisations performance as well as the leadership. While poor organisational performance may reflect poorly on the police leadership, positive performance will reflect positively. Thus, a police leader who is successfully leading a successful organisation is in a much stronger position in dealings with their governance boards or politicians than one that lacks that kind of information.

Common Principles Emerging in the Design of Performance Measurement Systems

There are some underlying principles that should be considered when developing organisational performance measurements.

- Accessibility of performance measurements to those being measured.
- Consistency of performance measurements across the spectrum of those being measured.
- Transparency and clarity for the rationale of those things being measured.

Further, these are principles against which such systems should be tested once they have been developed. They include: accessibility, consistency, transparency and clarity of purpose, what gets measured, and outcomes vs. outputs.

Accessibility

Those being measured should have access to the measurement system and its data. Police leaders who keep their measurement data behind a "wall", and then pull it out in order to "hit people over the head with it" fail themselves and their staff. The New South Wales Police Commissioners introduction of Operational Performance Reports in 1998 "adopted a confrontational approach. This was bitterly resented by senior police who were given no access to the Commissioner's local statistics until they arrived at the meeting. Tales of bullying and confrontation obscured any positive aspects of the system and the OPR quickly became enmeshed in organisational politics" (Fleming & Scott, 2008). Staff members that are being measured should have access to the data, and their measurement results, and they should be encouraged to review that data as frequently as their supervisers and managers do.

Consistency

Performance measure processes (and the data that they use) should be consistent across all the groups and individuals being measured. Creating systems that are inconsistent at the design phase results in loss of credibility for both the systems, the designers, and the organisational leadership. However, consistency results in greater usability of the measurement system and greater confidence by the organisational membership. Consistency does not mean that every member of the organisation is measured on the same criteria (the Chief and front-line officers have much different measurement criteria). However, it does mean that members doing similar work would have similar measurement criteria.

Transparency and Clarity of Purpose

Performance measurement systems should have transparency on data collection (organisational members should know what data is getting collected on their performance) as well as transparency of purpose, so that it should be clear why data is being collected.

What Gets Measured?

This is the question for which there is no single answer, but rather draws upon the "socially constructed and locally developed institutional logic" (Rautiainen et al., 2017) to determine the organisations performance measurement needs, which also needs to address the legislative environment, the governance and control environment, the organisations policies and procedures as well as the community's expectations. Behn's (2003) comments about what public sector managers should measure does help inform the discussion on police performance measures. Herman Goldstein's discussion on the scope of the policing mission from his 1977 book "Policing a Free Society" (Goldstein, 1977) summarised the core functions of a police service, and included:

1. To prevent and control conduct widely recognised as threatening to life and property (serious crime).
2. To aid individuals who are in danger of physical harm, such as the victim' of a criminal attack.
3. To protect constitutional guarantees, such as the right of free speech and assembly.
4. To facilitate the movement of people and vehicles.

5. To assist those who cannot care for themselves: the intoxicated, the addicted, the mentally ill, the physically disabled, the old, and the young.
6. To resolve conflict, whether it be between individuals, groups of individuals, or individuals and their government.
7. To identify problems that have the potential for becoming more serious problems for the individual citizen, for the police, or for government.
8. To create and maintain a feeling of security in the community.

While these macro level elements can help guide police executives into relevant directions for performance measurement, they do not provide specific details on what should be examined.

This begs the questions of "What specifically as a police leader should I be looking at?" Does the police leader focus on the number of arrests, the number of occurrences, or is it the clearance or solve rates from crime? Do these numbers tell them how successful the organisation is in achieving its mission or are they an indicator of how efficient the organisation is at gathering information or preparing criminal cases or how effective prosecution efforts are? Police executives and governing authorities also need to be mindful that "key performance indicator use is often adjusted for political reasons…to measure only some suitable aspects of performance" (Rautiainen et al., 2017). However, the larger question is whether the organisation is measuring its outputs, or are they measuring societal outcomes?

Outcomes vs Outputs

For years, many police agencies have used output measures to evaluate officer and organisational performance, these range from speeding tickets, to field interview reports, numbers of arrests, accidents, occurrence reports, vehicles stops, bank checks, parking tags, and school visits. Within Pierre Bourdieu's framework (Littleton, 1979) this system of measurement forms the "field", on which officer performance is measured and which largely forms the motivation for officers' actions.

Financial compensation and organisational prestige (capital) both stem from these measures as well, which are designed as significant motivators for officer actions. There is obviously a never-ending list of "things" that can be measured, and many of these are in response to politically motivated inquiries, comments from the media or demands from the community, all of which reinforce the existing environment (field). While this type of data is usually easy to acquire, and states our natural desire for tangible (and numeric) information, it unfortunately seldom answers the key question that needs to be asked; "are the actions of the police achieving the desired goals?"

Example: *Our community has been impacted by knife violence in our schools. The immediate questions that arises are:*

"How many times have the police visited our schools";
"How many interactions have police officers had with students"
"How many arrests involving knife violence involving school aged children have the police made in the community?"
"How many incidents involving knife violence have there been at our schools?"

These are all valid questions, but the desire of the community is to reduce the number of incidents of knife violence in schools, and yet none of the typical questions relates to changes to behaviour or desired outcomes.

While outputs are under the direct control of the police, outcomes are the impact of police action (Bayley, 1996; Davis, 2012). The challenge of measuring outcomes is that they seldom have readily available numeric values, and frequently are subjective and require interpretation (Nolan & Hinkle, n.d.). The example of outcome measurements in Chapter 5 provides some insight about the type of things that might be measured as a community or neighbourhood outcome of policing outputs (Chapter 5).

In the above example, the outcome that the community wants to know is whether the number of incidents of knife violence has decreased in their schools. This however has a direct correlation to the level of hostility and anger among students, their sense of justice, their perception of power, being held to account, the alternatives to violence, as well as their understanding and perception of control, the ease and availability of edged weapons, their sense of retribution, security for themselves and their family and/or their perception of future consequences. Simply counting the number of times that a police officer visits a school has little impact on any of these factors, but it is easy to count.

To achieve the desired outcome (lower levels of violence) requires the police (and many other stakeholders) to engage in a strategy that impacts on most of the above identified issues. This would require broader engagement with other stakeholders in data collection (as well as coordinated strategy and response). The outcome measures will likely reflect the qualitative nature of the issue, examining how staff and students feel, their perceptions of safety and security, whether they perceive (and understand) that there are alternative dispute resolution strategies (including what they are and how they would be accessed).

Simon Guilfoyle undertook research in this area to conclude that not only did output data fail to assist with outcome evaluation, but that output data was frequently misinterpreted. His comments pertain to the use of numeric comparisons over time (year to date arrest numbers, as an example). He found that a "common method of presenting data in the police performance environment is the use of binary comparisons. This involves comparing two isolated numeric values, then interpreting the difference between them as a trajectory, or assuming it is significant. The practice is commonplace within UK police forces, appearing at face value to be a simple method for interpreting data. However, concerns exist about the efficacy of the approach; furthermore, experience suggests the practice leads to unwarranted assumptions, which impair decision-making and encourage inappropriate behavioural responses" (Guilfoyle, 2015).

Broader community outcomes frequently require the police to understand how the community "feels" and how they behave. The impact of crime on a community is a measure of the community's perception of safety as well as the change in their behaviour as a result of crime. Neither of these factors is either within the control of the police, nor are they elements that have quantitative values. Other researchers such as Bayley suggests that the outcome (direct measures) and outputs (indirect measures) are further broken down into hard (quantifiable) and soft (subjective) elements (Bayley, 1996), and Bayley identifies elements such as real estate value as a hard direct indicator, while officer morale would be a soft indirect indicator. Hence, while police agencies have internal measures in place to provide quantitative performance measures, a small percentage of police agencies have structured processes in place to provide regular qualitative data from the community, which is normally undertaken through public surveys and examination external data.

Police Reform as Welcome Outliers?

Managing Unintended Consequences

Unintended consequences are outcomes that were not envisioned during the design of the measurement system. They typically can appear during times of changes within the population and the police. These consequences can be positive, neutral, or negative, and need to be evaluated by the organisation to determine if they have a positive impact, can they operate having absorbed the unintended consequences or will the organisation need to change or even abandon the measurement systems because the unintended consequences are so impactful.

A common consequence of this in policing has been monitoring the productivity of officers by counting the number of violation notices they issue. These have historically been in relation to vehicle moving violations, such as travelling over a posted speed limit on a highway (speeding tickets). This originated when police officers had a significant amount of unstructured time (such as when undertaking random patrols), and this was an easy way for supervisers to determine if police officers were watching citizen behaviour and taking appropriate action.

However, this practice quickly got distilled done to an output measurement practice for supervisers, who would set a numeric value for satisfactory performance (1 ticket per day). Officers could then determine that in their week of work (5 days), they would been to issue 5 tickets. As a consequence, officers may take up traffic observation in an area in which drivers frequently committed traffic violations (such as changes in speed limit on a highway). Officers could then quickly get the number of moving violations required to maintain an acceptable performance level by their supervisers (5 tickets for the week), and then continue their regular duties throughout the week. The consequence of setting this practice as a performance measure is that it is not reflective of the officers ongoing efforts to ensure a safe community and may in fact bring about negative consequences in relation to the community. Such performance measures can also quickly morph from an "Community engagement performance measure" to be perceived as a quota, and can have a negative impact on officer performance, and a negative impact on the police relations with the community.

Unintended consequences may include undesired outcomes that police services simply choose to accept. For many police agencies, they provide financial compensation for their officers when they attend court during their off-duty hours. As a result, there is a direct financial incentive to arrest a person and bring them before the courts, so while there may be other alternatives, those other alternatives may not be financially incentivised. Police agencies may accept this unintended consequence (and its associated optics) as it drives organisational action (and the optics of organisational impact), but it may not drive officers to work towards outcomes that necessarily achieve the greatest community good or that are focused on harm reduction.

While "indiscriminate use (of quantitative measures) may result in side effects and reactions outweighing the benefits" (Ridgeway, 1956), recent research in this field has suggested that differing data presentation methods (such as statistical process control) have value, as "It found that respondents were significantly likely to draw un- warranted conclusions and engage in disproportionate or unwarranted behavioural responses (DUBR) when performance information was presented in binary comparison format" (Guilfoyle, 2016).

Unintended consequences are inevitable in performance measurement systems not only because it is virtually impossible to see all the consequences of a system prior to implementation, but even more far reaching is that the impact on behaviours, the breadth of perceptions and the practical elements stemming from the introduction of a performance management system are simply too diverse and extensive to be envisioned during system design. Therefore, while broad-based consultation is a critical element during system design, it is always advisable to undertake pilot testing with such systems prior to implementation.

Countering Unintended Consequences

There are some principals that can be taken into consideration during the design phase of performance measurement methodologies and practices that may reduce the incidents of unintended consequences or at least mitigate their impact and provide a path to remediation.

1. The performance measures should be transparent to those being measured, as well as impacted stakeholders, and the validity and the expected benefits of improving performance should be clearly articulated.
2. When determining a performance measurement practice, the benefits of the measurement practice should be measured against associated risks, which should include the anticipated reaction of those being measured.
3. All measurements should routinely allow for those being measured (and supervisers) to report exceptions.
4. Finally, to reduce any risk that may be associated with the capture of the performance measure, alternative pathways to information capture should be considered.

Pilot Testing

Performance measurement systems should be tested in a confined field environment, not just in a theoretical application or a "sandbox", but with personnel in the field who can provide detailed feedback and input into system design and modification.

Pilot testing should reveal challenges or hurdles associated with data collection, with data analysis, with data reporting, and with impacts on behaviours. System shortfalls, work arounds, shortcuts, and unintended consequences should become visible to the assessment team through those being measures, their supervisers, and managers. System design teams need to be sensitive to all these elements and be prepared to accept feedback and make system or process changes are required.

Measuring What Matters

Mike Moore and Anthony Braga's work in the field of police performance measures (Moore & Braga, 2003) was based upon extensive discussions with police leaders from across the United States. Their work has been extensively referenced in Canada and the United Kingdom and has been recommended to Police Service Boards (in Canada) and Police and Crime Commissioners (PCC's) in the United Kingdom. However, measuring police performance is not a stagnant process, nor one is which there is a single end goal that can be achieved, but rather it is an evolutionary process that requires ongoing evaluation and maintenance. Therefore, while Moore and Braga provide a macro level framework that is still valid today, police leaders and governance boards need to continually evaluate this framework to ensure it is still valid and meets their needs.

Although the Moore/Braga framework provides large "buckets" into which to place data elements to evaluate performance, they do not provide the micro level structure to assist police managers in designing performance measures for specific areas. The seven dimensions of police performance metrics identified by Moore and Braga in their work for the Police Executive Research Forum in the United States (PERF) are provided here along with the recommended statistical indicators. These metrics are reflected in the recommendations from the 2013 report on Canadian Police Board views on the use of police performance metrics prepared for Public Safety Canada (Kiedrowski et al., 2013), and "Measuring the Performance of the Police: The Perspective of the Public" 2015 Research report for Public Safety Canada (Maslov, 2016). While the dimensions of police performance metrics that are detailed in Moore's work are certainly applicable in the U.S. environment, there are additional areas of focus that would be applicable in most other communities.

Some Specific Areas of Focus

A measure of efficiency for any police service includes problem resolution at the first available opportunity. The transfer of problems to other areas within the organisation, or multiple visits to the same problem without resolving it suggests an inefficient process, which by its very nature is also ineffective and uneconomical. Therefore, consideration should be given to measuring problem resolution at the first point of contact.

Problem resolution can take many forms, including securing agreement on the resolution of the problem by the involved parties. Therefore, a resolution to an ongoing noise complaint may be secured through discussions with the involved parties to determine the underlying problem, while in the case of a domestic dispute, problem resolution may take the form of community service engagement and ongoing monitoring.

While resolution to problems may therefore take many forms, the monitoring and evaluation of effective police performance therefore needs to examine a broad spectrum of metrics to determine if police actions and activity are being effective in problem solving and issue resolution.

Conclusions

Measuring police performance not only provides an opportunity to accurately assess the impact that resources have had on an issue, or the degree of success that a specific strategy has brought to bear on a problem, but it also helps to place into context for the organisation and its membership, those priorities that are of concern to the organisation's leadership and governance team. By harnessing the power of performance measures police leaders can justify current expenditure and evidence the need for any budgetary increase. Data can be provided to illustrate where police resources are being deployed effectively as well as highlighting waste and inefficiency. Police reforms invariably require a reallocation of personnel, equipment, and money. The deployment of accurate and detailed performance measures will assist policymakers and police leaders to justify and explain the reform process. It may also provide the opportunity to shift the objective structures of the "field" in the practice of policing by shifting reward and recognition activities (capital).

References

Bayley, D. H. (1996). *Police for the future*. New York, USA: Oxford University Press.

Behn, R. D. (2003). Why measure performance? Different purposes require different measures. *Public Administration Review, 63*(5), 586–606. https://doi.org/10.1111/1540-6210.00322.

Davis, R. C. (2012). *Selected international best practices in police performance measurement: Rand corporation*. Santa Monica, CA. Retrieved from https://www.rand.org/pubs/technical_reports/TR1153.html.

Expert Panel on the Future of Canadian Policing Models. (2014). *Policing Canada in the 21st century: New policing for new challenges*. Ottawa, CA. Retrieved from https://www.scienceadvice.ca/wp-content/uploads/2018/10/policing_fullreporten.pdf.

Fleming, J., & Scott, A. (2008). Performance measurement in Australian police organizations. *Policing, 2*(3), 322–330. https://doi.org/10.1093/police/pan038.

Goldstein, H. (1977). *Policing a free society*. Cambridge, MA: Ballinger Publishing. Retrieved from www.ssrn.com/abstract%3D2596883&usg=AOvVaw0GLKeOhXJHBxK_dykFLaW-.

Guilfoyle, S. (2015). Binary comparisons and police performance measurement: Good or bad? *Policing (Oxford), 9*(2), 195–209. https://doi.org/10.1093/police/pav004.

Guilfoyle, S. (2016). Getting police performance measurement under control. *Policing (Oxford), 10*(1), 71–87. https://doi.org/10.1093/police/pav027.

Kiedrowski, J., Petrunik, M., Macdonald, T., & Melchers, R. (2013). *Canadian police board views on the use of police performance metrics*. Ottawa, ON: Public Safety Canada.

Littleton, C. S. (1979). *Outline of a theory of practice*. Pierre Bourdieu, Richard Nice: American Anthropologist. https://doi.org/10.1525/aa.1979.81.1.02a00940.

Maslov, A. (2016). *Measuring the performance of the police: The perspective of the public*. Ottawa, ON: Sécuité publique Canada.

Moore, M. H., & Braga, A. (2003). *The "bottom line" of policing. Police executive research forum*. Washington, DC: Police Executive Research Forum. Retrieved from https://www.policeforum.org/assets/docs/Free_Online_Documents/Police_Evaluation/thebottomlineofpolicing2003.pdf.

Nolan, J., & Hinkle, J. C. (n.d.). Community dynamics, collective efficacy, and police reform. In *Policing in an age of reform: An agenda for research and practice*. London, UK: Palgrave Macmillan.

Rautiainen, A., Urquía-Grande, E., & Muñoz-Colomina, C. (2017). Institutional logics in police performance indicator development: A comparative case study of Spain and Finland. *European Accounting Review, 26*(2), 165–191. https://doi.org/10.1080/09638180.2015.1120412.

Ridgeway, V. F. (1956). Dysfunctional consequences of performance measurements. *Administrative Science Quarterly, 1*(2), 240–247. https://doi.org/10.2307/2390989.

Wisniewski, M., & Dickson, A. (2001). Measuring performance in Dumfries and Galloway constabulary with the balanced scorecard. *Journal of the Operational Research Society, 52*(10), 1057–1066. https://doi.org/10.1057/palgrave.jors.2601191.

10

Co-Operation Between the Police and Civil Society Organisations in the Field of Anti-Discrimination

Danijela Petković

Introduction

Discrimination always represents a violation of rights to equal treatment towards an individual or a group of people. A state needs to provide its citizens with the possibility of human rights and freedoms in line with the principles of the international community. The police in their turn are a part of the community, and their primary task is to secure public order, prevent crimes and provide the citizens with the feeling of safety. The most important task of the police is to provide for adequate protection of human rights and freedoms. The police and the society are interdependent and influence each other. Changes in one affect the other one. This is why the relationship between the police and civil society organisations are so important. Good relations between the police and civil society organisations contribute to security and

D. Petković (✉)
Police College, Police Academy, Zagreb, Croatia
e-mail: dpetkovic@fkz.hr

J. J. Nolan et al. (eds.), *Policing in an Age of Reform*,
Palgrave's Critical Policing Studies,
https://doi.org/10.1007/978-3-030-56765-1_10

efficient police work. Civil society organisations play a crucial role in the promotion of human rights and actively contribute to the functioning of democracy. To do their work, civil society actors involved in promoting fundamental rights need to be able to exercise their rights fully and without unnecessary or arbitrary restrictions (European Union Agency for Fundamental Rights, FRA, 2017). Often it is challenging and civil society organisations may, while engaging in their work for the community, encounter numerous obstacles, be they legislative or practical. Frequently, their activists are subjected to verbal and physical assaults and harassment. It is not unusual for discrepancies to arise between official police statistics and data on crime and anti-social behaviour reported directly to the civil society organisations. This is particularly the case with crimes that go unreported. The relationship of trust and co-operation may thus be of decisive significance. Benefits are immeasurable: the police reap enormous benefits from information obtained by civil society organisations, and their representatives can assist the police in carrying out investigations and detecting perpetrators of criminal acts. As they work with victims and offenders through their engagement and cooperativeness, the police can send a strong message about promoting the security of all citizens and making human rights a priority.

Why Are Police-Community Relationships Important?

Police officials rely on the co-operation of community members to provide information about crime in their neighbourhoods, and to work with the police to devise solutions to crime and disorder problems. Similarly, community members' willingness to trust the police depends on whether they believe that police actions reflect community values and incorporate the principles of procedural justice and legitimacy (United States Department of Justice Community Relations Service, 2016). In the short-term civil society organisations can function as mediators between the community and the police. This is a great confidence-building measure that allows the police to be seen as responding to concerns of citizens in all the communities (Marijan & Guzina, 2014).

NGOs are a source of expertise, specialist knowledge and advice in the area of human rights. The police can benefit from the opportunity to exchange knowledge on human rights issues, and to analyse, evaluate and revise their policy, procedures and operations accordingly. Co-operation with human rights NGOs can help the police target their policing at groups that are hard to reach. Co-operation sensitises the police to weaknesses in their human rights compliance and NGOs can assist the police with the development of a human right ethos (*Police and NGOs*, 2004).

Croatian Approach Towards Police Training and Co-Operation with Civil Society Organisations

Every society, including Croatia, has its own culture, its specificities and mentality, all of which reflects upon the cooperation between the police and citizens. In democratic societies, security is based on the protection of social values and the fundamental rights and freedoms of its citizens (Karlović & Sučić, 2017). Civil society plays an essential role in promoting the rule of law and accountability, empowering persons belonging to minorities and vulnerable groups, combating racism and racial discrimination, combating human trafficking, empowering women and youth, promoting the rights of the child and advancing social justice processes (European Union Agency for Fundamental Rights, FRA, 2017). Police training is the first and most significant step towards shaping more effective and professional policing in society. Human rights-based training helps the police to respect and protect fundamental rights proactively. It ensures and enables police officers to fulfil the role envisaged in the European Union's area of justice, freedom and security (FRA, 2013).

The area of human rights represents an integral part of the curriculum in police education conducted by the Police Academy of the Ministry of the Interior of the Republic of Croatia (MoI RC). The integration of normative parts with practical police procedures is imperative, as shown by the example of Standard operational procedures made for fourteen of the most frequently experienced situations in which police officers exercise police powers. The intention was to standardise the operation of police officers in their everyday work. The uniformity of the police operation at all levels is thus guaranteed. Consequently, the operation drilled at the Police Academy as a standard procedure is being equally applied in police work in the field. Standard operational procedures are flexible and updated in line with legislative changes and operational instructions. (Petković & Kozjak Mikić, 2015).

Police education focuses on situational teaching, simulations, case studies, problem-oriented teaching, and interdepartmental co-operation that presupposes co-operation with all relevant state bodies and other stakeholders, definitely including civil society organisations. Such an approach to police officers training proved itself as the most effective one. It is only through a real exchange of experience and interaction that we can build a culture of relations, communication, and strengthening that will create a relationship of partnership based on mutual respect and appreciation.

Hate Crime Training

The Republic of Croatia has an efficient system of monitoring hate crimes, often mentioned as an example of good practice in the member states of the Organization for Security and Co-operation in Europe (OSCE). Likewise, national policies and strategies supplement good legislation and institutional framework.

In particular, one has to single out the activities of the Hate Crimes Monitoring Working Group. The Working Group has been active since 2010, and its members include representatives of the bodies competent for dealing with this issue, representatives of the academic community and civil society organisations. The Working Group is responsible for coordinating the collection of data on hate crimes, monitoring and analysing the phenomenon of hate crime, coordinating interdepartmental co-operation in fighting hate crime and the drafting of recommendations for enhancing the system of fighting against hate crime. The Working Group issued a Protocol of procedure in the case of hate crimes, which clearly defines obligations of competent authorities involved in uncovering, acting on and monitoring prosecution of hate-motivated criminal acts and close co-operation of competent bodies for improving the system of monitoring hate crimes. Moreover, the Protocol clearly states: "In order to provide for the best possible prosecution of a specific case, co-operation shall be established with other stakeholders, who in a specific case of hate crime, may assist, for example, civil society organisations, religious communities, and experts dealing with this issue". More info is available at https://fra.europa.eu/en/promising-practices/hate-crimes-monitoring-working-group.

The Government Office for Human Rights and the Rights of National Minorities of the Republic of Croatia coordinates the activities of the Working Group, and it is also a national contact point for the collection of data and reporting on hate crime. The Office also organises joint education for police officers, state attorneys, judges and the representatives of civil society organisations on the phenomenon of hate crime and hate speech. The focus is placed on a substantive legal framework and manifestation in practice, the criteria for the identification of hate-motivated crimes and crimes committed on discriminatory grounds, victims' procedural rights, as well as on practical examples and observed challenges. The consistent practice of the European Court of Human Rights also plays a unique role regarding cases of discrimination and the question of the efficiency of investigation in cases versus the Republic of Croatia. There are continuous campaigns to raise awareness of the public and combat hate crime and hate speech, and to encourage reporting of their incidents.

The MoI RC was the first in Croatia but also in the region to launch the training in combating hate crime for its police officers in co-operation with the OSCE Office for Democratic Institutions and Human Rights (ODIHR) through a Law Enforcement Officer Programme on Combating Hate Crime—LEOP—CHC 2006, and later through a revised Training Against Hate Crimes for Law Enforcement (TAHCLE). The Police Academy adjusted the said programme and modified it in line with Croatian legislative and police practise and added some latest content like mediation in the community as a model of preventive police action. The intention was to train police officers for proactive operation and prevention of unwanted and security threatening situations employing mediation in the events of conflicts in the community and creating new and quality relations and communication between police officers and citizens (by developing social competencies). The training of trainers/multiplicators strengthened the police capacities in recognising and processing criminal acts committed out of hatred. All 20 national police administrations took part in the training. As the interinstitutional co-operation was imperative since the mere beginning of the education, also included were the representatives of relevant state bodies, especially State Attorney's Office, as well as the representatives of non-governmental LGBT associations Iskorak—Sexual and gender minorities rights centre, and the Lesbian Group Kontra. These two associations also initiated the amendments to the Criminal Code in order to introduce a legal qualification of "hate crime", which was accomplished on 1 October 2006 when the amendment to the Criminal Code entered into force. Croatia's hate crime laws are a combination of a general penalty-enhancement provision and penalty-enhancement provisions for specific offences. Therefore, Croatia's Criminal Code includes a statutory definition of hate crime[1] (Đaković & Senta, 2019). The Criminal Code identifies a person's race, colour, religion, national or ethnic origin, language, disability, sex, sexual orientation or gender identity as protected characteristics. Although the legislation is clear enough and enables protection, as expressly stated by the ECtHR in its decision Škorjanec v. RC (2017), legal standards are missing to clarify whether the exclusive motive for committing a crime is hatred or prejudice can suffice (Annual Report of the Ombudswoman of Croatia for 2018). Consequently, continuous training of the police and all other relevant stakeholders is necessary.

Police officer training was interactive, using practical exercises, group work, discussions and role-plays. It reached out for real examples from the police and judicial practice, and used examples of hate symbols specific to the Republic of Croatia and found throughout the world. Education materials were drafted, and international experts also extended their help and gave lectures on the experiences of American and British

[1]Criminal Code excerpts are available at https://www.legislationline.org/documents/id/21394.

police best practices. For the first time in any police training, the representatives of LGBT associations (Iskorak and Kontra) participated as trainers. Such a positive example grew into regular practice when it comes to activities conducted by the police in combating hate crimes. LGBT activists helped police officers to become aware of the importance of the role of non-governmental organisations in combating hate crimes that is possible at several levels: observational and investigative; in reporting criminal acts and misdemeanours (primarily through victim encouraging); in preserving and collecting evidence; at advisory level; in working with victims and through the rehabilitation of perpetrators. As to co-operation with the police, one needs to emphasise the establishment of communication with educated police officers, create a joint action platform aimed at preventing hate crimes and improve co-operation with civil society organisations in detecting and processing hate crimes by the police (Petković & Kozjak Mikić, 2015).

Good co-operation between activists from LGBT associations and the police continued through numerous joint projects, participating in conferences and round tables and permanent education carried out at the Police Academy and in police stations, as well as in the premises of civil society organisations. The example of a successful and well-designed co-operation between the police and LGBT associations is the project "Prevention and Combating Hate Crimes against LGBT persons" implemented in 2013 through the partnership between the Lesbian Group Kontra and Iskorak—sexual and gender minorities rights centre, and the General Police Directorate and the Police Academy, with the support and financial assistance of the Embassy of the Kingdom of the Netherlands to the Republic of Croatia. The Project's specific aims were as follows:

- Strengthening the capacities of police officers handling cases of hate crimes against LGBT persons.
- Informing LGBT persons of their rights and legal possibilities that protect them against hate crimes and encouraging LGBT persons to report hate crimes.
- Sensitising the broader public regarding hate crimes against LGBT persons.

- Promoting existing mechanisms and policies for combating hate crimes in Croatia.

The Minister of the Interior, the Dutch Ambassador to the RC and activists from the associations Iskorak and Kontra presented the Project at the media conference held in newly opened premises of LGBT Centre in Zagreb. The Ministry of the Interior sent a strong message about the significance of this problem area and the active involvement of the police in handling and preventing it. Project activities included the following:

1. Training held at the Police Academy. Included in this training were required content in LGBT terminology, challenging prejudices and stereotypes towards LGBT persons, reviewing hate crimes against LGBT persons, affirming psychological values of working with LGBT persons, and conducting sensitive procedures in working with victims of hate crimes that are motivated by sexual orientation or gender identity. The method used included interactive workshops and lectures held by the activists of the LGBT associations and their expert associates: lawyers and psychologists. Likewise, a leaflet for Police Academy students has been published.
2. Public campaign. Apart from the media conference, public actions took place at main city squares in the four biggest Croatian cities. LGBT activists used the occasion for passing out leaflets previously published within the campaign. The leaflets were also distributed across police stations. Furthermore, city lights and posters were created for the campaign purposes, containing the slogan directed to combat homophobic and transphobic hate crime, contact data of the Iskorak and Kontra Legal Team (for direct legal assistance to LGBT persons), as well as contact data of the police. Leaflets also contained real examples of hate crimes, instructions for behaviour in cases of violence, contact data of the Iskorak and Kontra Legal Team, the police and ambulance. All project partners mutually agreed on the visual identity and the campaign content.
3. Recommendations to state institutions. The purpose of the recommendations was to enhance the implementation of national and international regulations dealing with hate crimes and were submitted

to the competent institutions. The recommendations referred to the Council of Europe Recommendation on combating discrimination based on sexual orientation and gender identity and national legislation. The inclusion of LGBT civil society organisations to the Working Group for monitoring hate crimes was requested.
4. Workshops for the LGBT community. Informative workshops were organised for LGBT persons regarding hate crimes, the system of providing legal assistance and their rights should they become the victims of violence or discrimination.
5. Provision of direct legal assistance and support to the victims of homophobic and transphobic hate crimes. A direct phone line was introduced for providing support and the possibility for using legal assistance offered by lawyers, and monitoring of court proceedings. All cases of hate crimes were documented and included in an annual report on the situation regarding human rights of LGBT persons in Croatia (Petković & Kozjak Mikić, 2015).

The said activities contributed to strengthening the capacities of the institutions competent for combating homophobic and transphobic hate crime, the strengthening of trust between the competent state institutions and LGBT civil society organisations, encouraging LGBT persons to report hate crimes and raising the awareness about this issue in society in general.

A recent example of good practice is also the co-operation of the police and the Human Rights House Zagreb (a human rights organisation established in 2008 as a network of civil society organisations with a goal to protect and promote human rights and fundamental freedoms) at the V-START project (Victim Support Through Awareness Raising and neTworking).[2] Project activities include national research report on the support system for victims of hate crime in Croatia, training courses for CSOs, public services, legal practitioners and police officers, and information and awareness-raising campaigns, including the practical guide for real and potential victims of hate crimes.

[2]More information available at http://www.vstart.eu/about-the-project/.

Besides the fact that the thematic units of hate crime make an integral part of a compulsory police curriculum in basic police training and college police education, the mentioned contents are the part of the specialisation and professional training programme of police officers. The MoI RC continuously cooperates with relevant state bodies, especially the State Attorney's Office, the Government Office for Human Rights and the Rights of National Minorities, Ministry of Justice, courts, Public and specialised Ombudsmen, especially when data on hate crimes are collected, processed and exchanged. Police officers who are national trainers/multiplicators often are the experts included in the implementation of police officers training in other OSCE countries. Moreover, the police undertake numerous other measures to reinforce their administrative and operational capacities in the prevention and combating of all forms of violence and hate crimes. Guidelines and instructions issued by the General Police Director are binding for all police officers in the country and, along with the mentioned Protocol of procedure in the case of hate crimes, represent a necessary contextual framework for police operation in such cases. An efficient *track record* system for hate crimes, which requires for any new fact in any given case be updated, enables a situation review broken down by hate crimes beginning with the overall number of recorded incidents, the number of criminal acts and misdemeanours, motive and other indicators-based searching.

Ultimately, police departments play a significant role in the treatment of hate crimes. They are responsible not only for collecting statistics, but also for implementing hate crime legislation. They act as the primary liaison between victims and the legal system, as well as communities and the legal system. They have the opportunity to take actions to prevent such crimes from happening at all. Through their policies and procedures, but also the attitudes and behaviours of their officers, they influence the way the state and the public perceive and treat people in general (members of minority groups, especially). Therefore, the police response to hate crimes is a significant issue (Gerstenfeld, 2013).

Persons with Disabilities

In certain areas, all persons with disabilities face equal discrimination while in other areas, discrimination occurs only against some disability groups. In Croatia, service providers lack awareness that the inaccessibility of the services they provide to persons with disabilities is a denial of reasonable accommodation sanctioned by the Anti-Discrimination Act. The same lack of awareness and familiarity with the principle of reasonable accommodation is present among judges, lawyers and persons with disabilities themselves. Disability based discrimination cases at courts are few despite the widespread discriminatory practices. There have been only 17 judgements in 5 years following the entry into force of the Anti-Discrimination Act on 1 January 2009 (*Croatia-Parallel Report-Disability Ombudswoman*, 2014). In order to change stereotypes and prejudice about persons with disabilities in the general public, it would be important to include the education on human rights with a particular emphasis on disability, especially for law enforcement and public servants.

Over the past few years, the Police Academy of the MoI has intensified its efforts in the area involving persons with disabilities. In particular, the focus was on the quality and lawfulness of police operation. Among many undertaken activities, the Zagreb Red Cross City Society together with the Police School of the Police Academy as co-organiser organised a musical and stage piece entitled "Zapivala trišnja bila" *(The Song of a White Cherry Tree)*. Many performers included children, primary school pupils, pupils from the Centre for Rehabilitation, retired persons, beneficiaries of the Project of the Red Cross Society of the City of Zagreb, volunteers and participants of the basic police training course.

From 2014 to 2016, there was a series of two-hour workshops/talks with persons of various world-view profiles or political convictions called "Polic i Ja—razgovori o društvu" *(The Police and I—conversations about the society)*. Intended for Police Academy students and MoI employees, the focus was on cultural differences, universal values crucial for police operation and society expectations related to the protection of minority rights as the protection of rights and freedoms of every individual. Among the participants, there was also the Disability Ombudswomen who tackled, in particular, the issue regarding police procedures when intervening in cases including persons with disabilities. She presented proposals for improving the police work in cases in which persons with disabilities are victims of violence. To future police officers, she recommended seeking advice from associations active at the local level as these associations can be useful as the long arm of the police while executing sensitive tasks. The representative of the Centre for Rehabilitation of the Faculty of Education and Rehabilitation Sciences of the University of Zagreb acquainted the future police officers with the problem area of persons with autistic spectrum disorders, educating them further in terms of police procedures towards such persons.

A feature-length documentary on Ivan Jakovljević, a 25-years-old beneficiary of the Centre for Rehabilitation was made, telling the story about his visit to the Police Academy in January 2015. This documentary represents merely one part of the project activities undertaken by the Police Academy for including persons with intellectual disabilities into the life of the community. A young man with intellectual disabilities, whose life dream is to become a police officer, experiences first-hand the life at the Police Academy by spending time with basic police training participants and future police officers. His dream of becoming a police officer gets fulfilled for a day. He takes part in martial arts training, studies from criminal police officers, works with police dogs, impressed by how they accomplish every single task he gives them. He learns how to tie a person with police handcuffs, takes part in criminal investigations training, masters the fingerprinting technique and is given exposure to crime scene procedures. He drives in a police car and learns how to stop a person and ask for documents. The Police School exhibited his works of art, and during the time of the exhibition, lectures and workshops took place in co-operation with the Association for the promotion of inclusion, Alliance of autism associations and the Disability Ombudswomen. A particular emphasis was given to sensitising police officers to collaborating with persons with the so-called invisible disability.

Traditionally, students of the Programme of adult secondary education for the vocation of a police officer and other MoI employees and their guests participate in a humanitarian race "Wings for Life" every year. The race aims to promote the foundation bearing the same name and gather funds for further research and make the public aware of the problems of persons with spinal cord injuries.

In the Police Academy in Zagreb, CEPOL Course on Hate Crimes was delivered on two occasions, in 2016 and in 2018. Police officers from the EU Member States and other European countries had an opportunity to exchange best practice on hate crimes and hate speech, capacity building and procedures and how to improve police—NGO cooperation. Special attention was given to managing victims and witnesses of hate crimes, disability hate crimes, bias indicators and the significance of hate speech and online hate. Good balance of the participants coming from the police, prosecution, academia, government sector and civil society organisations enabled interactive engagement through lively discussions, case-based scenarios and role-play.

A comprehensive two-years project (December 2016–November 2018) "Education for raising the awareness on disability for police officers", with the Centre for Adult Education Validus as the project contractor, and the Police Academy as a partner, also needs to be mentioned. Its general aim was to educate and make the active and future police officers aware of a growing presence and participation of persons with intellectual and/or psycho-social disabilities in the community, intending to develop their communication skills in everyday interaction. In specific, the project aimed at:

- Educating future police officers on effective and appropriate communication with persons with intellectual and/or psycho-social disabilities.
- Educating the active police officers about a growing presence of persons with difficulties in a community in order to enable them to convey this knowledge and these values in individual police administrations.
- Educating Police College students on effective and appropriate communication with persons with intellectual and/or psycho-social disabilities.

Informative workshops/training were held for the Police School and Police College students, as well as for police officers from different police administrations. Leaflets and a Handbook for Communicating with Persons with Disabilities, with the emphasis on invisible disability, have been published for educational purposes, and video material was also produced. All of that was made available to all the participants of undertaken educational programmes.[3]

Difficulties associated with and experienced by police officers when confronted by people with disabilities pose a significant challenge for modern policing. Many negative attitudes, perceptions, beliefs and stereotypes exist around disabilities, stemming from limited knowledge, information and exposure to people with disabilities (Daruwalla & Darcy, 2005, Modell & Cropp, 2007). Nowadays persons with intellectual and/or psycho-social disabilities are ever more present in the community and their participation is more visible due to the process of deinstitutionalisation and transformation of social welfare institution and resettling of persons from institutions into the community. Public services employees, and particularly police officers, require specific knowledge and skills to be prepared for communicating with their fellow citizens. It is, therefore, crucial to have systematically ongoing measures and activities, leading to a better understanding of and communication with persons with disabilities. Consequently, such an approach would also lead to combating discrimination against the said persons.

Some Other Examples of Good Police-NGOs Co-Operation in Fighting Discrimination

A variety of factors can cause discriminatory behaviour by law enforcement officials. In some cases, a lack of adequate legislation or procedures certainly plays a role in how the police interact with members of minority groups. However, such legal or procedural gaps cannot justify discriminatory conduct (Amnesty International, 2016). Therefore, integrated strategies could be an efficient tool for dialogue, acceptance and closer co-operation.

[3] For more info visit: http://coovalidus.hr/edukacija-podizanja-svijesti-o-invaliditetu-za-policijske-djelatnike/.

Spain

Spanish society has over the last decades experienced one of the most significant transformations in its contemporary history, which makes diversity one of the essential features of its social system. The recognition of the rights of LGBT persons and persons with a disability thus represents remarkable progress. In 2010 a number of NGOs collaborated with an organisation of local police leaders to create a platform for police management of diversity. The aim was to bring about organisational change in police forces through improving their procedures for responding to the needs of a diverse society, with a strong focus on the most vulnerable minority groups including Roma, thereby ensuring that such groups would receive equal treatment from the police (Net-Kard Project NGOs, 2014). The Unión Nacional de Jefes y Directivos de Policía Local (Unijepol) and 9 NGOs make up the Platform. In 2016 the Platform published "Fair and Effective Police Stops Handbook" which exposes the Effective Police Identifications Programme—PIPE project and its procedures to avoid ethnic profiling by police forces. Main objectives of the Platform are to:

- raise the awareness of authorities in charge of public security and police services of the need for developing policies on social diversity management
- promote the improvement of police training regarding the management of diversity
- achieve a designated statistical register of hate crimes and discrimination cases and to establish operational protocols for the police on these issues by the competent institutions
- promote more significant relationships between public police services and minority communities as well as their participation in the development of citizen security policies
- encourage improved police service for people belonging to minority communities
- define criteria for police stop-and-search practices and establish preventive and oversight measures for the use of ethnic profiling

- promote positive measures to enable people belonging to minority communities to join the police and their auxiliary services
- publicise and acknowledge good practices and positive actions developed by the police relating to diversity.

The Netherlands

According to the ECRI (2007) General Policy Recommendation No. 11 on combating racism and discrimination in policing, the police have a major role to play in combating racism and discrimination by:

- being able to police a diverse society while respecting human rights;
- refraining from racial profiling and
- monitoring racist incidents and effectively investigating racist offences.

To combat racism and intolerance in order to make the police more accountable, a good community relationship between the police and minority groups is needed. The Dutch police introduced a code of practice together with civil society organisations which describes the four principles of a professional stop:

- a legitimate and justifiable selection of persons;
- explanation of the reason behind the stop and search;
- use of professional communication;
- officers to reflect on their practices and provide feedback to each other.

Police in Amsterdam has developed a bottom-up approach involving field officers (ambassadors) in the teams, assisted by their managers and trainers to raise awareness on proactive stops and to offer an alternative framework which is fair and effective (FRA, 2018).

Another interesting practice regarding racial profiling in the Netherlands is a cooperation between the police and Controle Alt Delete (a Dutch human rights organisation committed to end racial profiling) and Amnesty International. In a critical, constructive and creative way, together they address racial profiling by organising meetings and dialogue sessions, producing films, delivering trainings to improve the relationship with citizens and striving to provide solutions for a policy change. A Toolkit that makes police stops better (in Dutch: B.ET.E.R) has been acknowledged by the Dutch police and has been implemented in a national framework with regard to proactive police stops.[4]

Recommendations/Conclusions

Three core principles underpin democratic policing:

- the social contract
- public consent
- the balancing of rights.

International human rights standards refer to the relationship between policing and human rights as a means of assisting in maintaining order. Public order is maintained when the social contract, public consent and the balancing of rights are achieved (EPPHR, 2004). A right to non-discrimination is a universal human right guaranteed by a series of international instruments. In contrast, the principle of equal treatment stands for one of the fundamental values of the European Union. The Constitution of the Republic of Croatia enshrines it as one of the highest constitutional values.

Regardless of the type of discriminatory procedure or the grounds on which discrimination has been committed, it seriously endangers the rights and freedoms of individuals or a particular social group. Moreover, it influences the quality of the life of the entire community. The police and civil society organisations deal with the same area—discrimination, and share the same goal: respect for human rights and freedoms and creating a safe environment for all citizens. Civil society plays a significant role in effectuating positive change in police conduct (*Engaging with police reform: The role of NGOs and civil society in police reform*, 2006). Policing must be both effective and fair. From this comes the legitimacy

[4]For more info visit: https://controlealtdelete.nl/.

of policing, and from that, the protection of the human rights of all (The future of policing in Ireland, 2018).

The following includes some recommendations for good Police-NGO co-operation in fighting discrimination:

1. Partnerships: mutual relations among all interested parties: the police, government institutions and NGOs are necessary. Building a platform for joint activities at the national and regional level based on mutual trust, principles of fairness, legitimacy and accountability is essential.
2. Human Rights Protections: The overall aim of the engagement should be to produce relevant and genuine improvement in the level of human rights protection. Both parties must be realistic about what can be achieved in a given timeframe (*Police and NGOs*, 2004).
3. Monitoring and Reporting by Civil Society Organisations: Civil society organisations are a key stakeholder when it comes to the reporting and monitoring of any form of discrimination. By monitoring and reporting, NGOs can identify trends and take action on individual cases. They can also bring complaints about discriminatory action, including violence by the police. Accompanied by strong advocacy, this data collection and analysis can, in turn, help shape policy at the levels of the local or national government (Preventing and responding to hate crimes, OSCE/ODIHR, 2009).
4. Joint Education and Training. Training is crucial for all the professionals involved, but primarily for the police as the first responder. The most efficient way of fighting judgements and stereotypes is the possibility to have first-hand experiences of activists be heard because such "live testimonies" are always the most impressive ones. A discussion based on arguments and active listening helps in removing nonunderstanding and prejudices and in creating a mutual trust.
5. Share Resources and Initiatives: There are many different resources and initiatives to support training programmes and co-operation between the police and NGOs, such as:

- The European Union Agency for Law Enforcement Training (CEPOL) offers training activities (residential activities, webinars, online modules) and training material dedicated to human rights,

- ODIHR/OSCE provides specific training at the request of participating OSCE states and published several manuals providing guidance addressed to both the police and civil society,
- FRA can also contribute to the design and delivery of training courses and has Fundamental Rights Platform[5] as a channel for co-operation and information exchange with civil society organisations active in the field of fundamental rights at the national, grassroots, European or international level,
- The European Commission offers funding for projects by national authorities and civil society organisations in the field combating racism, xenophobia, and other forms of intolerance.

6. Media Support: Media attention helps to raise awareness among the general public on essential issues and good practices and spread a comprehensive and consistent message. The examples of good co-operation between the police and civil society organisations need to be "promoted" as it is essential that such cases do not go unnoticed but receive deserved attention.

The latest data from 2018 Eurobarometer survey on Democracy and Elections demonstrate the importance of civil society in protecting and promoting human rights and building democracy. In the EU, 76% of the respondents believe that civil society plays an essential role in promoting and protecting democracy and fundamental values, including encouraging an informed and pluralistic democratic debate. However, the FRA Report shows that it is becoming increasingly difficult for CSOs to fulfil their role and contribute to the protection, promotion, and fulfilment of human rights within the EU. Likewise, the CoE is repeatedly underlining the importance of civil society. Hence, in November 2018, the Committee of Ministers adopted the Recommendation CM/Rec (2018)11 on the need to strengthen the protection and promotion of civil society space in Europe, which, inter alia, recommends member states to provide a legal framework and an enabling environment for the

[5]For more info visit: https://fra.europa.eu/en/cooperation/civil-society/about-frp.

protection and promotion of space for civil society (Annual Report of the Ombudswoman of Croatia for 2018).

References

Annual Report of the Ombudswoman of Croatia. (2018). Retrieved from: https://www.ombudsman.hr/wp-content/uploads/2019/05/Annual-Report-2018-ENG.pdf.

Amnesty International. (2006). *Engaging with police reform: The role of NGOs and civil society in police reform* (Conference Report 2006). Amnesty International: Utrecht, The Netherlands. Retrieved from: http://amnesty-polizei.de/wp-content/uploads/2009/03/conferencereportengagingwithpolicereformdef1.pdf.

Amnesty International Dutch Section. (2016). *Police and human rights programme—Short paper series No.3: Police and minority groups* (Annual Report of the Ombudswoman of Croatia for 2018). Amnesty International: Amsterdam, The Netherlands. Retrieved from https://www.ombudsman.hr/wp-content/uploads/2019/05/Annual-Report-2018-ENG.pdf.

Commission on the Future of Policing in Ireland. (2018). *The future of policing in Ireland*. Retrieved from http://policereform.ie/en/POLREF/The%20Future%20of%20Policing%20in%20Ireland(web).pdf/Files/The%20Future%20of%20Policing%20in%20Ireland(web).pdf.

Community relations services toolkit for policing: Importance of police-community relationships and resources for further reading. Retrieved from https://www.justice.gov/crs/file/836486/download.

Daruwalla, P., & Darcy, S. (2005). Public sympathy: Private antipathy: Personal and societal attitudes towards people with disabilities. *Annals of Tourism Research, 32*(3), 549–570.

Đaković, T., & Senta, C. (2019). *Against hate: Guidebook of good practices in combating hate crimes and hate speech*. Zagreb, Croatia: ACT Printlab d.o.o.

ECRI. (2007). *General policy recommendation no.11 on combating racism and discrimination in policing*. Retrieved from https://rm.coe.int/ecri-general-policy-recommendation-no-11-key-topics-combating-racism-a/16808b7639.

European Platform for Policing and Human Rights. (2004). *Police and NGOs: Why and how human rights NGOs and police services can and should work together*. Retrieved from https://www.academia.edu/38118450/Police_

and_NGOs_Why_and_how_human_rights_NGOs_and_police_services_can_and_should_work_together_European_Platform_For_Policing_and_Human_Rights_EPPHR_.

FRA. (2013). *Fundamental rights-based police training: A manual for police trainers*. Luxembourg: Publications Office of the European Union. Retrieved from https://fra.europa.eu/sites/default/files/fra-2013-fundamental-rights-based-police-training_en_0.pdf.

FRA. (2017). *Challenges facing civil society organisations working on human rights in the EU*. Luxembourg: Publications Office of the European Union. Retrieved from https://fra.europa.eu/sites/default/files/fra_uploads/fra-2018-challenges-facing-civil-society_en.pdf.

FRA. (2018). *Preventing unlawful profiling today and in the future: A guide*. Luxembourg: Publications Office of the European Union. Retrieved from https://fra.europa.eu/sites/default/files/fra_uploads/fra-2018-preventing-unlawful-profiling-guide_en.pdf.

Gerstenfeld, P. (2013). *Hate crimes: Causes, controls, and controversies* (3rd ed.). Los Angeles, CA: Sage.

Karlović, R., & Sučić, I. (2017). Security as the basis behind community policing: Croatia's community policing approach. In P. S. Bayerl, R. Karlović, B. Akhgar, & G. Markarian (Eds.), *Community policing—A European perspective* (pp. 125–138). Cham, Switzerland: Springer.

Marijan, B., & Guzina, D. (2014). Police reform, civil society and everyday legitimacy: A lesson from Northern Ireland. *Journal of Regional Security, 9*(1), 51–66. https://scholars.wlu.ca/poli_faculty/35/,https://doi.org/10.11643/issn.2217-995x141spm38.

Modell, S. J., & Cropp, D. (2007). Police officers and disability: Perceptions and attitudes. *Intellectual and Development Disabilities, 45*(1), 60–63.

Net-Kard Project. (2014). *Practical guide for NGOs to prevent discrimination against the Roma communities*. Retrieved from http://www.crj.ro/userfiles/editor/files/Practical_guide_for_NGOs_to_prevent_discrimination_against_the_Roma_communities.pdf.

OSCE/ODIHR. (2009). *Preventing and responding to hate crimes: A resources guide for NGOs in the OSCE region*. Warsaw, Poland: OSCE/ODIHR. ISBN 978-92-9234-767-3.

Petković, D., & Kozjak Mikić, Z. (2015). Aktivnosti Ministarstva unutarnjih poslova Republike Hrvatske u suzbijanju diskriminacije LGBT osoba. *Kriminologija & socijalna integracija, 23*(2), 306–334. ISSN 1330–2604 (Print).

Republic of Croatia. (2014). *Parallel report on the implementation of the UN Convention on the rights of persons with disabilities in the Republic of Croatia.* Retrieved from https://posi.hr/disability-ombudsman-act-2/?lang=en.

Škorjanec v. RC. (2017). Retrieved from https://rm.coe.int/ecri-general-policy-recommendation-no-11-key-topics-combating-racism-a/16808b7639.

United States Department of Justice Community Relations Service. (2016). *Toolkit for policing: Importance of police-community relationships and resources for further reading*. Retrieved from https://www.justice.gov/crs/file/836486/download.

11

Digital Transformations in Forensic Science and Their Impact on Policing

Olivier Ribaux, Olivier Delémont, Simon Baechler, Claude Roux, and Frank Crispino

Introduction

The shift from a reactive approach to crime, to a pre-crime conception based on risk analysis, is a major direction in policing observed in criminology (Zedner, 2007). It relies on the analysis of accessible information to prevent new occurrences or mitigate the unpleasant effects of recurrent

O. Ribaux (✉) · O. Delémont · S. Baechler
School of Criminal Justice, University of Lausanne, Lausanne, Switzerland
e-mail: olivier.ribaux@unil.ch

O. Delémont
e-mail: olivier.delemont@unil.ch

S. Baechler
e-mail: simon.baechler@unil.ch

C. Roux
Centre for Forensic Science, University of Technology Sydney, Ultimo, NSW, Australia
e-mail: claude.roux@uts.edu.au

J. J. Nolan et al. (eds.), *Policing in an Age of Reform*, Palgrave's Critical Policing Studies,
https://doi.org/10.1007/978-3-030-56765-1_11

behaviours outside certain norms (e.g. problem-oriented, intelligence-led). It provides a new management style, and has led to structural reforms, changed recruitment and intensified networking between public and private actors.

As budget reductions can restrain the police role to traditional enforcement models, which are considered as "the real police work" (Keay & Kirby, 2018), services adopting this proactive policing approach should prioritise the most efficient action plans for preventing and disrupting crimes, or reducing harm it may cause. To this end, there is an evolution to make them more evidence-based (Ratcliffe, 2016; Weisburd & Majmundar, 2018).

Whatever the restrictive or proactive policing path followed, security systems are subjected to many tensions.

Forensic science has primarily positioned itself as a service provider to the criminal justice system, or is at least considered that way by many authors and even practitioners. Hence, the forensic science community seems relatively indifferent to evolutions in policing (Roux, Talbot-Wright, Robertson, Crispino, & Ribaux, 2015). Police managers, in general, do not perceive the potential and sufficient reasons for promoting an expanded use of forensic science in proactive policing models (see also Chapter 8—Crispino et al.).

As crime and security problems evolve in nature and scale (e.g. concentrations of crime and its seriality are better assessed), technologies are being used in a widespread and decentralised manner, enabling new levels of surveillance, the networking of police and forensic databases, and the intelligent processing of large data sets generated by widespread human traceability (Casey, 2019; Casey, Ribaux, & Roux, 2019). This trend is captured as digital transformations and requires a change of mentality.

F. Crispino
Département de Chimie, biochimie et physique, Laboratoire de recherche en criminalistique, Université du Québec à Trois-Rivières, Trois-Rivières, QC, Canada
e-mail: frank.crispino@uqtr.ca

While emphasising how forensic science remains locked into the reactive policing model imposed by the criminal justice system, we will first analyse the progressive extension of the use of DNA profiles using networked databases as an example of how digital transformations are changing the scale at which many forensic processes are applied. The ability of the standard law enforcement model, with its narrow view of forensic science, to absorb such expanding flows and together provide an added-value in policing will be questioned. We will then observe that digital forensics has progressively emerged within police organisations (Pollitt, 2010). Digital traces became so ubiquitous and new problems so varied that the digital forensics community has found itself at the centre of these tensions and pivotal to the reflection on policing models. Digital forensics, conceived firstly as a narrow technical support to forensic processes, has expanded to implement early applications of digital traces in investigations. These applications now include the rapid treatment of new volumes and varieties of traces in specific cases, and the development of new forms of intelligence and crime analysis processes for dealing with cyberfrauds or other forms of crimes exploiting digital infrastructures.

This unanticipated expansion of their role supports the view that forensic science, integrating physical and digital traces, is a solid foundation for reframing a science of policing, implementing new kinds of digital policing that balances the consideration of various relevant dimensions and perspectives. This requires cross-cutting and evidence-based attitudes (Weisburd & Neyroud, 2013), incorporating the basic principles and lessons learned from forensic science (Casey, 2019). Such an evolution is in opposition to the proliferation of specialisations, and the risks of fragmenting and complexifying the practice of policing in the digital age.

Forensic Science as a Service to the Criminal Justice System

Forensic science is currently under fire from critics. Its negative role in spectacular cases of miscarriages of justice has been repeatedly established. The FBI's false identification of Brandon Mayfield using a fingermark collected after the Madrid terrorist attack in 2004 served as a catalyst. This incredible mistake has largely initiated a strong movement over the past decade to challenge forensic science as a whole (NAS, 2009; PCAST, 2016).

One of the unintended effects of this movement is that it inhibits the development of a broader vision for forensic science. In a simplified way, the derived research in forensic science since largely focuses on how to strengthen forensic processes, mainly by re-enforcing quality controls. The evaluation of forensic information for supporting decisions of a Court of law attracts all the interest, because it is where miscarriages of justice are most dramatic. This movement insatiably leads forensic organisations to further specialisations defined around the use of sophisticated and rapidly changing technologies. The focus is on the means (technologies and separated processes), rather than on problems to be solved.

There are two changes here brought by digital transformations. Firstly, digital traces exacerbate the confusion about the positioning of forensic science as an integrated branch of the police or as an auxiliary to the justice system (Baechler et al., 2020). Traces extracted from electronic devices are used extensively early in investigations. In parallel with the movement of decentralisation and commoditisation of other types of more conventional analysis (e.g. rapid-DNA, live scan, breath-analyser), the investigative aspect is reinforced on a new scale (Casey et al., 2019). This situation makes the position of the traditional forensic laboratories more problematic, because they are supposed to operate independently and on request, mostly on an evaluative basis for the justice system. This is occasionally imposed by a specific law. Within their usual framework, they find it difficult to integrate the timely, collective and tacit nature of the investigation's reasoning.

Despite this changing context, policing models are still not really on the agenda of the normative forensic science community. This is in contradiction with real forensic practices undertaken at the level of the police, which are influenced by crime analysis models (e.g. understanding involved entities, modus operandi, hence, able to link crimes, bring knowledge on criminal networks) (Bradbury & Feist, 2005; Tilley & Ford, 1996).

An account of the evolution of DNA technologies will allow for further analysis of how forensic processes are designed from a law enforcement perspective, despite evidence that digitalisation requires integration with other policing strategies.

Digital Transformations: The Example of the Successive Evolutions of DNA Technologies

A specific area of development in forensic science has been the increasing use of so-called identification databases. Automated Fingerprint Identification Systems (AFIS), and then DNA databases (generally known as CODIS) serve as milestones in the digitalisation process. Their intensive use is expected to increase the volume of identifications of persons with a view of combating cross-border crimes and terrorism (Toom, 2018).[1] The implicit assumption is that increased identification possibilities would have a direct and obvious effect on the mitigation of all kinds of crime. However, it is far from being so simplistic in policing (Ratcliffe, 2016).

Beyond the important stage of database implementation, many other significant advances in the field of DNA technology have raised fundamental, often unexpected questions about the functioning of the criminal justice system and its relationship with forensic science.

We will divide the analysis of these developments into two parts. The first concerns the evolution of DNA processes from the early ages of technology to the present day. In the second part, we will examine how database networking is currently changing orders of magnitude in the number and nature of matches obtained and what these changes mean in terms of policing. This analysis will raise the general question of the adequacy of the law enforcement policing model to interpret forensic activities.

---

[1]See also the European Network of Forensic Science Institute's (ENFSI) strategy for 2017–2020, https://enfsi.eu/wp-content/uploads/2017/11/4.0-ENFSI-Strategic-Plan-2017-2020.pdf (accessed 3rd January 2019).

Successive Transformations from the Inception of the Technology

The use of DNA in forensic science originates from the mid-80s. The exploitation of new type of information extracted from biological traces expanded in an unprecedented way possibilities of investigating both serious crimes and high-volume crimes. This new technology was first used punctually to exclude or point to a possible suspect and to indicate the activity of serial perpetrators in high profile cases. It is since the mid-1990s that DNA profiles have been more widely exploited through the establishment of systematic, database-supported processes. These developments just followed the advent of Automated Fingerprint Identification Systems (AFIS). The two digitalised forensic identification processes (CODIS for DNA and AFIS) have enhanced the contribution of forensic science to investigations. However, at the same time, they have changed the volume of data flows in orders of magnitude, resulting in unanticipated problems and more fundamental changes in the criminal justice system as a whole.

Indeed, enthusiasm was rapidly tempered by the unanticipated consequences of the growth of databases. In the design of the first DNA databases in the 1990s, adventitious matches became statistically inevitable as the number of profiles submitted increased. The consequences were highlighted when Raymond Easton ran into difficulties in the United Kingdom in 1999. A profile extracted from one specimen collected from a burglary matched adventitiously his DNA profile stored in the database. Confidence in the DNA-process was so high, wrongly, that he was prosecuted for burglary. The responses were to improve the quantity and quality of the data stored on each DNA profile, as well as to strengthen the interpretation of matches using statistical and probabilistic approaches. In parallel, a new technological breakthrough has increased the sensitivity of DNA extraction techniques. This increased the proportion of DNA profiles extracted from difficult traces collected from the scene of crime (Castella & Mangin, 2008). These hard-to-interpret profiles (partial or mixture) now make up most of the data in some databases that have, moreover again grown. The difficulty of the interpretation process has added new levels of complexity in the use of DNA flows. However, these progresses came with greater specialisation and added a level of complexity to the entire criminal justice system. DNA specialists were in charge of collecting and extracting DNA profiles, as well as interpreting results. They developed their own methodologies and distributed roles and tasks in various forms of independent organisations across countries. In particular, specialisation has created greater divisions in the entire investigative process hindering communication of information and knowledge transfer. New failures due to this complexity started to emerge, for example, in the Jama case in Australia (Vincent, 2010). Farah Jama was wrongly convicted of rape on the basis of a (true) DNA match detected and misinterpreted in an incredible set of circumstances generated by fragmented DNA and investigative processes.

Other developments have allowed the expanded use of DNA and added a level of complexity, such as the so called familial searches, *i.e.* the way criminals are identified via relatives found by similarities in DNA profiles (Bieber, Brenner, & Lazer, 2006). This novelty brought many success stories, mainly in conjunction with the use of national DNA databases (Maguire, McCallum, Storey, & Whitaker, 2014; Pham-Hoai, Crispino, & Hampikian, 2014). More recently, publicly available genetic data have been used along the same lines, but with more complex data involving distant familial relatives. This investigative initiative led, inter alia, to the identification of the "Golden State Killer", Joseph James DeAngelo, having perpetrated a series of murders and assaults dating back more than 30 years, in California (Scudder, Robertson, Kelty, Walsh, & McNevin, 2018). Besides, the risks to human rights and privacy have become progressively more concrete with the scale of these forensic transformations and the impact of such spectacular illustrations (Erlich, Shor, Pe'er, & Carmi, 2018; Mc Cartney, 2006). This has also led to different legal frameworks and decision-making processes in the area of law enforcement, which explains why DNA-related processes take place very differently from one country to another.

At the same time, DNA processes quickly faced backlogs. For certain databases, results were delivered only in four to six months. This made the database inoperative in relation to the pace of investigations, and much DNA data was unexploited (Strom & Hickman, 2010). This led to two reactions. Firstly, the size of the infrastructures has been increased to absorb a larger flow, requiring new resources. Second, in parallel with budget concerns, a stronger triage process was also defined prior to submission to a DNA laboratory for the extraction of a profile. This has also led to new questions, such as defining the characteristics of a relevant trace to submit (Bitzer, Delémont, & Ribaux, 2016). Criteria chosen emphasised the typical influence of the law enforcement model. The severity of the cases involved as well as the quality of the specimen collected (for example, the quantity of biological material collected) are the main incentive to submit a trace. Pertinence and seriality are generally a much less important concern (Bitzer et al., 2016).

Another innovation disrupted the process: rapid DNA technologies can extract, in less than two hours, a profile taken from a person or from a specimen in a standalone manner. This makes it possible to decentralise the process, making it more systematic and timelier. It is a likely trend that challenges the infrastructures developed in the central laboratories to absorb the growing flows.

The second concern was to absorb a flow of data into an economically acceptable model. Choices are then obviously linked to what can be considered as the overall "efficiency" of these processes. This is generally measured in terms of proportions of cases investigated where a trace has led to identification. This is typically derived from a law enforcement model focused on resolution rates. In such evaluations, an attrition gives an embarrassing picture making it difficult to justify costs by a level of efficiency: from many traces collected at the scene, very few play a role in the ultimate decision-making in Court. Contrary to what was intuitively expected, end-to-end studies show that very few scenes attended concerning high-volume crimes lead to the identification of a suspect (1–2% for DNA traces and fingermarks) (Brown & Ross, 2012).

These kinds of analysis thus lead to further questions about the use and integration of DNA databases as a component of the whole criminal justice and security system. It was occasionally recognised that:

> A lack of integration between the DNA laboratories and the other components of the justice system responsible for following up on results

> is perhaps the biggest weakness, in that desirable outcomes have not been clearly defined or carefully researched. (Bieber, 2006, p. 231)

Surprisingly, instead of focusing on such fundamental issues, there seems to be a compelling trend towards full computerisation of DNA processes as part of the broader vision called Streamlined Forensic Reporting (SFR). This managerial vision, which does not require to challenge the law enforcement policing model, goes directly from the trace to its use by the justice, renouncing all intermediate investigations usually resulting from matches (Mc Cartney, 2019).[2]

Networking of Databases as a Further Expansion

Another wave of complexification is coming: DNA databases infrastructures are being networked at an international level. In particular, in Europe, the 2005 Prüm treaty was signed between seven European countries to combat global crimes, terrorism and deal with illegal immigration. It was then incorporated into a European Union law in 2008. It allows, in the European area, the automatic transmission of DNA traces and profiles of persons across the countries. The system is not yet fully operational, but many countries are already connected. The first results have been evaluated. Successful cases illustrate the value of the approach (Santos & Machado, 2017; Toom, 2018).

The process seems, however, much more difficult to implement than expected. Many disparities in the way processes are implemented in countries have also been highlighted. A trend emerges, indicating that only a very small part of matches obtained at an international level is finally integrated into a criminal procedure (Toom, 2018). This is due to their high number, difficulties of prosecuting internationally, as well as the definition of matches that creates significant probabilities of false positives. Scientists from traditional forensic science laboratories, who are part of the process, seem to have, in certain conditions, even unilaterally decided to retain information, when the police operate the DNA

[2] https://www.cps.gov.uk/legal-guidance/streamlined-forensic-reporting-guidance-and-toolkit (accessed 8th of February 2020).

database in the demanding country (Santos & Machado, 2017). This attitude typically results from the current forensic debate on risks of miscarriage of justice.

Regardless of how the process is implemented, it shows absolutely no connection with policing models. "Efficiency" goes implicitly hand in hand with the increase in the number of international identifications and prosecutions. However, simple statistical assessments and current experience show again changes of scale: when the network will be fully operational, criminal justice systems, already saturated, can be expected to become totally overwhelmed and ineffective to absorb DNA matches at the international level.

Priorities are required and they must balance the particularities of the case against other policing strategy guiding how the infrastructure should be used. In particular, in a proactive policing model, the importance of relying on targeting high concentrations of crimes and finding patterns will increase. Linking crimes will therefore be considered of utmost importance to detect the most relevant repetitive problems, help decipher their structure and implement effective responses. If such a view is adopted, beyond the identification of people, the links between crime and DNA will be much more ambitiously integrated into the analysis of crime. This application is currently largely ignored. Another advantage is that (unidentified) profile links significantly reduce legal issues, compared to the direct cross-border transmission of information about individuals. Such an approach has been successfully tested regionally (Rossy, Ioset, Dessimoz, & Ribaux, 2013).

Other Forensic Transformations

DNA is only one example, but ongoing transformations underlying forensic technologies go well beyond this area. The control of individuals (e.g. identity checks, alcohol control by means of a breath analyser, potentially illicit substances carried on by a person tested by NIR infrared tools and incoming Lab-on-Chip [LOC]) are also made much more immediate and easy to systematise in the field, blurring the previous investigative/evaluative dichotomy (Casey et al., 2019). Artificial intelligence systems eventually support decisions in the process, which go through the assessment of the risk presented by individuals, aspects of predictive policing or even lead to the implementation of so-called predictive justice (Nissan, 2017). Some of these technologies are only at the level of basic research, and the promises are sometimes higher than what they can actually deliver, while others are fully operational.

Regardless of the state of technology transfer in practice, the inclusion of powerful information processing in the criminal proceedings alters the scope and nature of surveillance, the rate of arrests, the detections of crimes or even the volume of punishment distributed. All these changes enhance the application of the traditional law enforcement paradigm on a scale that can create unintended and uncontrolled side-effects. For example, in addition to the many computerised biometric processes that have an impact on individual liberties, at the another end of the spectrum of the law enforcement model, automated licence plate recognition changes the order of magnitude of those sanctioned for speeding or parking. It is impossible to predict how society in general will react to these changes, and what moral values will emerge from such transformations.

Eventually, some commentators even consider that prosecuting large-scale global cybercrimes in the traditional way is too difficult, if not impossible (Dupont, 2017). Crime statistics have recently highlighted the extent of cyber-victimisation, as well as of their new pervasive forms such as online frauds (BCS, 2016). Police are changing their processes to integrate this new crime landscape and to develop the necessary investigative skills. There is, however, much hesitation about where to go from here (Rossy & Ribaux, 2020). It might be that the law enforcement reactive model, under its current traditions, will not resist to digital transformations.

The Rise of the Digital Forensics Community

The organisational movement to integrate computer specialists and new technical positions into police structures in the 1980s called for a change of police culture. This new digital forensics community has largely developed on the margins of the forensic and police professions (Pollitt, 2010). This community has gradually organised itself with rare academics to share knowledge and experiences. For a long time, this activity was carried out with relative indifference on the part of their organisation. Digitalisation created a radical change of scale in one of the most sensitive domain of crime investigation: paedophilia. This was one of the catalysts that led the police to examine the need to create an Internet investigative capacity within their own organisation. At the same time, mobile phone data began to be used progressively in a more systematic way until the emergence of the smart phone around 2007. This created major changes, as this information has provided quick insight into the relations between entities (persons, phones), locations and time, which are the main dimensions to exploit when investigating a crime. The flow of digital images to be processed has also increased considerably: it can be stated that, nowadays, each interesting event occurring in a public space is necessarily filmed, providing a new stream of traces to collect and exploit.

The activity of specialists extracting information from the device became more central and borderline between forensic science (how to extract and interpret data from multiple devices), the investigation (how to integrate this information with other sources of information) and criminal intelligence analysis (how to manage the large amount of information generated, how to structure knowledge around criminal networks). These changes impacted the traditional organisation of investigations and underlined tensions in applying combinations of policing models (law enforcement and intelligence-led). This community has also created new fragmentations (new skill profiles, new units, new roles, new silos). At the same time, it is struggling to keep pace with the dynamics behind the evolution of technologies. It is finally under higher pressure because quality control of forensic processes is rather weak in a police context, while legal developments considerably reinforce respect for fundamental rights and fair justice.

The traditional forensic laboratory can difficultly accommodate the new digital community, since the separation with the police has been a strategic goal to achieve in order to avoid any kind of biases (underlined by the quality management solution to forensic science critics). This contradicts the fact that it is especially at the beginning of the investigations that digital information is quickly used to conduct inquiries, with a high level of integration. In this context, where dynamic interactions among the various stakeholders in the investigation are required, the services of an external laboratory are not easy to set up and formalise clearly. Digital investigations require also attendance to crime scenes, which was largely deserted by most centralised forensic science laboratories.

The, de facto, central role taken by this community in police organisations causes tensions and anomalies that call for very deep reconfigurations in terms of policing strategies, as well as of delineating roles and tasks, relations with other private/public stakeholders or with the public in general.

Synthesis: Traceology at the Core of Proactive Policing in the New Age

As current digitalisation exacerbates existing tensions between traditional law enforcement and proactive forms of policing, we postulate that simple application of usual law enforcement strategies will not work in the coming era of digital transformations: the systematic application of innovative identification techniques produces already new volume of matches and hits that neither the police, nor the justice systems are able to deal with. Cybercrimes are global, requiring complex cross-jurisdictional investigations with low success rates; technologies are evolving at a high rate, making it impossible for organisations to keep pace and switch from one technology to another for conducting investigations. Hence, there is a trend to rely on the private sector, Big Tech and local IT providers, despite of all the organisational, economical and ethical problems ensuing. Investigations, in their current conception, are unlikely to succeed in the case of emerging so-called cyber-volume crimes (e.g. online fraud), which are ubiquitous, large-scale, etc.

Reforming policing models in the new context must consider the fact that everything changes in scale. Of particular importance is the volume and variety of traces generated by human and illicit activities, as well as the many methods and tools available to detect, collect and analyse them. One priority is therefore to create a framework for using these ubiquitous and basic pieces of information. Boullier (2017) considers traces as the atomic form of information for studying sociological, and hence criminological, phenomena in the digital age. The trace is, however, created on physical and computer substrates. It entirely depends on the immediate environment in which the activities of interest take place. Interpreting out of norms human activities through traces is exactly what forensic science is about (Margot, 2011). The term of traceology is increasingly used instead. This is to disconnect forensic science from its law enforcement connotation, and suggest a broader view (Margot, 2011). Whatever the terminology, a science of the trace has a pivotal role to play. A lot of basic principles, methods and tools elaborated in forensic science can serve as a fundamental framework. Adopting this view requires, however, mutations of the discipline and a more ambitious vision connected with policing aims: forensic science has to go beyond its well-established position as a service provider for the criminal justice system in a law enforcement perspective.

At its very bottom, the forensic science community should first integrate its different pieces. The digital forensics community has evolved until now too independently from the field of forensic science for supporting this vision. This is changing by a cross fertilisation movement, where the terms have been redefined and cover a broader and integrative view on the forensic contribution (Pollitt, Casey, Jaquet-Chiffelle, & Gladyshev, 2018). This is a step towards the creation in professional practices of an homogenous forensic ecosystem that makes the best use and account of the information available along evaluative, investigative and intelligence processes (Casey, 2019). This ecosystem must incorporate models of knowledge management and dissemination that adapt to the pace of change, the legal environment and the fact that highly specialised technologies tend to become commonplace rapidly. The sharing and reuse of experience through case-based reasoning and collaborative platforms complement this first proposal (Baechler et al., 2020; Casey, 2019).

On top of these bases, traces should be more actively and ambitiously integrated into crime analysis and forensic intelligence models for serving proactive policing models (Casey, 2019). There are many dimensions to explore, such as how traces can support the search for crime concentrations in new topological spaces and timescale, or how they help decipher the anatomy of certain frauds. This is accompanied by considerations about the nature of social interactions in virtual spaces and about new forms of organisations and implementation of crime processes, which generate traces in the form of patterns to be found (Dupont, 2017; Leukfeldt, Kleemans, & Stol, 2017).

This new forensic and crime analysis framework would then integrate knowledge brought by a new wave of research works around pervasive crime mechanisms of the digital age that together depend on communication infrastructures and have a strong physical component (Leukfeldt et al., 2017; Pazos, Giannasi, Rossy, & Esseiva, 2013; Rossy & Ribaux, 2020).

This new paradigm, based on the trace and taking into account policing experience and knowledge, integrates most of the cybersecurity concerns such as incident detection, incident response and forensic preparedness, infrastructure resilience, surveillance, protection and prevention (CMM, 2016). It brings much more by incorporating the many years of forensic, police and criminological experience that are poorly reflected in cybersecurity models. This joint effort will help draw the lines of a comprehensive model of policing in the digital age.

Conclusion

Digital transformations are requiring in-depth reforms in policing. The latter is currently shaken by the arrival of a new community of specialists that has grown-up in relation to digitalisation. It was, at first sight, supposed to deliver only technological services, and supporting traditional activities. However, this minimalist conception is not sustainable, as scales in human traceability and of crimes in many forms have changed dramatically, requiring new approaches to forensic science, investigation, crime analysis, intelligence and policing.

Elemental forensic science, or traceology, as well as theories behind proactive policing models consist of solid basis on which to build new frameworks. This requires that borders between the police professions and other stakeholders must be reshaped in a very ambitious and determined way. There is, however, still significant efforts to deploy so that managers and key decision-makers realise this potential (see also Chapter 8—Crispino et al.).

Bibliography

Baechler, S., Morelato, M., Gittelson, S., Walsh, S., Margot, P., Roux, C., & Ribaux, O. (2020). Breaking the barriers between intelligence, investigation and evaluation: A continuous approach to define the contribution and scope of forensic science. *Forensic Science International*, 110213. https://doi.org/10.1016/j.forsciint.2020.110213.

BCS. (2016). *Crime in England and Wales-year ending March 2016*. Office for National Statistics. https://www.ons.gov.uk/peoplepopulationandcommunity/crimeandjustice/bulletins/crimeinenglandandwales/yearendingmar2016. Accessed 26th September 2020.

Bieber, F. R. (2006). Turning base hits into earned runs: Improving the effectiveness of forensic DNA data bank programs. *The Journal of Law, Medicine & Ethics, 34*(2), 222–233. https://doi.org/10.1111/j.1748-720X.2006.00029.x.

Bieber, F. R., Brenner, C. H., & Lazer, D. (2006). Finding criminals through DNA of their relatives. *Science, 312*(5778), 1315–1316. https://doi.org/10.1126/science.1122655.

Bitzer, S., Delémont, O., & Ribaux, O. (2016). To analyse a trace or not? Evaluating the decision-making process in the criminal investigation. *Forensic Science International, 262,* 1–10. https://doi.org/10.1016/j.forsciint.2016.02.022.

Boullier, D. (2017). Big data challenge for social sciences and market research: From society and opinion to replication. In F. Cochoy, J. Hagberg, M. Petersson McIntyre, & N. Sörum (Eds.), *Digitalizing consumption, tracing how devices shape consumer culture*. London and New York: Routledge.

Bradbury, S.-A., & Feist, A. (2005). *The use of forensic science in volume crime investigations: A review of the research literature* (43/05). London: Home Office.

Brown, C., & Ross, A. (2012). *End-to-end forensic identification process project: Volume crime*. Australia New Zealand Policing Advisory Agency—National Institute of Forensic Science.

Casey, E. (2019). The checkered past and risky future of digital forensics. *Autralian Journal of Forensic Sciences, 51*(6), 649–664. https://doi.org/10.1080/00450618.2018.1554090.

Casey, E., Ribaux, O., & Roux, C. (2019). The Kodak syndrome: Risks and opportunities created by decentralization of forensic capabilities. *Journal of Forensic Sciences, 64*(1), 127–136. https://doi.org/10.1111/1556-4029.13849.

Castella, V., & Mangin, P. (2008). DNA profiling success and relevance of 1739 contact stains from caseworks. *Forensic Science International: Genetics, 1*(1), 405–407. https://doi.org/10.1016/j.fsigss.2007.10.071.

CMM. (2016). *Cybersecurity capacity maturity model for nations (CMM)*. Oxford: Global Cyber Security Capacity Centre, University of Oxford.

Dupont, B. (2017). Bots, cops, and corporations: On the limits of enforcement and the promise of polycentric regulation as a way to control large-scale cybercrime. *Crime, Law and Social Change, 67*(1), 97–116. https://doi.org/10.1007/s10611-016-9649-z.

Erlich, Y., Shor, T., Pe'er, I., & Carmi, S. (2018). Identity inference of genomic data using long-range familial searches. *Science, 362*(6415), 690–694. https://doi.org/10.1126/science.aau4832.

Keay, S., & Kirby, S. (2018). The evolution of the police analyst and the influence of evidence-based policing. *Policing: A Journal of Policy and Practice, 12*(3), 265–276. https://doi.org/10.1093/police/pax065.

Leukfeldt, E. R., Kleemans, E. R., & Stol, W. P. (2017). Cybercriminal networks, social ties and online forums: Social ties versus digital ties within phishing and malware networks. *The British Journal of Criminology, 57*(3), 704–722. https://doi.org/10.1093/bjc/azw009.

Maguire, C. N., McCallum, L. A., Storey, C., & Whitaker, J. P. (2014). Familial searching: A specialist forensic DNA profiling service utilising the national DNA database® to identify unknown offenders via their relatives—The UK experience. *Forensic Science International: Genetics, 8*(1), 1–9. https://doi.org/10.1016/j.fsigen.2013.07.004.

Margot, P. (2011). Commentary on the need for a research culture in the forensic sciences. *UCLA Law Review, 58*(3), 795–801.

Mc Cartney, C. (2006). *Forensic identification and criminal justice*. London: Willan.

Mc Cartney, C. (2019). Streamlined forensic reporting: Rhetoric and reality. *Forensic Science International: Synergy, 1,* 83–85. https://doi.org/10.1016/j.fsisyn.2019.04.004.

NAS. (2009). *Strengthening forensic science in the United States: A path forward*. Washington, DC: National Research Council of the National Academies.

Nissan, E. (2017). Digital technologies and artificial intelligence's present and foreseeable impact on lawyering, judging, policing and law enforcement. *AI & Society, 32*(3), 441–464. https://doi.org/10.1007/s00146-015-0596-5.

Pazos, D., Giannasi, P., Rossy, Q., & Esseiva, P. (2013). Combining Internet monitoring processes, packaging and isotopic analyses to determine the market structure: The example of Gamma Butyrolactone. *Forensic Science International, 230*(1–3), 29–36. https://doi.org/10.1016/j.forsciint.2013.02.033

PCAST. (2016). *Forensic science in criminal courts: Ensuring scientific validity of feature-comparison methods*. Washington: Executive Office of the President President's Council of Advisors on Science and Technology Committee.

Pham-Hoai, E., Crispino, F., & Hampikian, G. (2014). The first successful use of a low stringency familial match in a french criminal investigation. *Journal of Forensic Sciences, 9*(3). https://doi.org/10.1111/1556-4029.12372.

Pollitt, M. (2010). *A history of digital forensics*. Paper presented at the Advances in Digital Forensics VI, Berlin, Heidelberg.

Pollitt, M., Casey, E., Jaquet-Chiffelle, D.-O., & Gladyshev, P. (2018). *A Framework for harmonizing forensic science practices and digital/multimedia evidence*. OSAC Task Group on Digital/Multimedia Science.

Ratcliffe, J. (2016). *Intelligence-led policing* (2nd ed.). Cullompton, UK: Willan.

Rossy, Q., Ioset, S., Dessimoz, D., & Ribaux, O. (2013). Integrating forensic information in a crime intelligence database. *Forensic Science International, 230,* 137–146. https://doi.org/10.1016/j.forsciint.2012.10.010.

Rossy, Q., & Ribaux, O. (2020). Orienting the development of crime analysis processes in police organisations covering the digital transformations of fraud mechanisms. *European Journal on Criminal Policy and Research*. https://doi.org/10.1007/s10610-020-09438-3.

Roux, C., Talbot-Wright, B., Robertson, J., Crispino, F., & Ribaux, O. (2015). The end of the (forensic science) world as we know it? The Example of Trace Evidence. *Philosophical Transactions of the Royal Society B, 370*(1674), 20140260. https://doi.org/10.1098/rstb.2014.0260.

Santos, F., & Machado, H. (2017). Patterns of exchange of forensic DNA data in the European Union through the Prüm system. *Science and Justice, 57*, 307–313. https://doi.org/10.1016/j.scijus.2017.04.001.

Scudder, N., Robertson, J., Kelty, S. F., Walsh, S. J., & McNevin, D. (2018). Crowdsourced and crowdfunded: The future of forensic DNA? *Australian Journal of Forensic Sciences*, 1–7. https://doi.org/10.1080/00450618.2018.1486456.

Strom, K. J., & Hickman, M. J. (2010). Unanalyzed evidence in law enforcement agencies. *Criminology & Public Policy, 9*, 381–404. https://doi.org/10.1111/j.1745-9133.2010.00635.x.

Tilley, N., & Ford, A. (1996). *Forensic science and crime investigation* (73). Police Research Group. London: Home Office.

Toom, V. (2018). *Cross-border exchanges and comparison of forensic DNA data in the context of the Prüm decision*. Bruxelles: Policy Department for Citizens' Rights and Constitutional Affairs, European Parliament.

Vincent, F. (2010). Inquiry into the circumstances that led to the conviction of Mr. Farah Abdulkadir Jama (PP no. 301, Session 2006–10). Melbourne: Victorian Government.

Weisburd, D., & Majmundar, M. K. (2018). *Proactive policing: Effects on crime and communities (2018)*. National Academies of Sciences, Engineering, and Medicine, Division of Behavioral and Social Sciences and Education; Committee on Law and Justice; Committee on Proactive Policing: Effects on Crime, Communities, and Civil Liberties.

Weisburd, D., & Neyroud, P. (2013). *Police science: Toward a new paradigm*. National Institute of Justice.

Zedner, L. (2007). Pre-crime and post-criminology? *Theoretical Criminology, 11*(2), 261–281. https://doi.org/10.1177/1362480607075851.

12

Tools for a New *Situational* Policing

James J. Nolan and Joshua C. Hinkle

Introduction

In Chapter 2 we described the status quo in American policing using the metaphor of a football game. Behaviour on a football field is influenced heavily by the game's logic. For instance, the game identifies various positions on the field and provides rules of engagement. It also specifies what counts as good or bad plays and how to score points for the

This work was supported in part by The Office of Community Oriented Policing [Cooperative Agreement Number 2007-CK-WX-K009 to James Nolan].

J. J. Nolan (✉)
Department of Sociology & Anthropology, West Virginia University, Morgantown, WV, USA
e-mail: jim.nolan@mail.wvu.edu

J. C. Hinkle
Department of Criminal Justice and Criminology, Georgia State University, Atlanta, GA, USA
e-mail: jhinkle@gsu.edu

J. J. Nolan et al. (eds.), *Policing in an Age of Reform*,
Palgrave's Critical Policing Studies,
https://doi.org/10.1007/978-3-030-56765-1_12

team. In addition, the game also provides rewards and recognition to skilled players who regularly do the right things. Then we showed how the game of American policing identifies law enforcement as its core purpose—i.e., an end in itself. The heavy focus on such things as arrests and the seizure of guns and drugs shapes the reward structure and guides behaviour on the field. It also produces a disposition and world view in officers that is counterproductive to public safety. When the primary goal is to find and arrest criminals, officers leave the station house with a mindset to sort good people from bad. When officers arrive in communities, the residents may appear to them as criminals or potential criminals that can be converted to capital (status in the organisation) by way of arrest. This mindset—which originates in the logic of the game and not in the person—keeps officers suspicious of strangers, overly cautious and fearful, and unable to see how the lack of trust in the police contributes to crime and violence in the community. Finally, we showed that by misrecognising the law enforcement game as the natural way to "do" policing, the false assumptions about causes of crime and criminality are never challenged. Rather, the game is accepted *as is* and the notion that crime begins and ends with the criminal offender leads police reformers searching for better ways to identify and arrest them.

This is why evidence-based strategies are so highly valued today among reformers. They begin with the question "What works in policing?" And then they test various strategies to see what works best. However, the phrasing of this question implies the *field* of policing (and its game of law enforcement) is appropriate, but in need of more effective strategies. It never gives up the false assumptions about the causes of crime and criminality. When criminal offenders are viewed as the source of a problem such as gun violence, an evidence-based policing strategy may seek to find the best ways to identify, arrest or deter serial offenders. Doing this may reduce gun violence significantly, albeit temporarily. As long as conditions remain the same in neighbourhoods more shooters from the same places are likely to emerge. Therefore, we do not believe that better law enforcement strategies—even those based on scientific evidence—will reform policing. The reason being is that source of the problem in policing today is the game itself! In recognising this fact, we changed the core question for reformers from "What works in policing?" to "What makes places safe?".

In Chapter 5 we attempted to answer this question through the study of latent psychodynamic process in neighbourhoods. We showed how the safety of small places in a community, such as neighbourhoods or segments of neighbourhoods, is related to these psychodynamic processes. In addition, we showed that by shifting the focus of policing from law enforcement outputs to strong community outcomes, we might actually transform the field of policing in ways that make communities and the police safer. The purpose of the present chapter, then, is to show how this can be done.

A New Game: Situational Policing

The idea of situational policing was first introduced in 2004 and 2005 in articles that appeared in the FBI *Law Enforcement Bulletin*, the journal *Policing and Society*, and the National Institute of Justice (NIJ) publication *Geography and Crime* (Markovic, 2009; Nolan, Conti, & McDevitt, 2004, 2005). In these early publications, situational policing was presented as a "conceptual framework" for police reform that articulated a desired end for the work of the police—i.e., the Strong neighbourhood. We argued that by having an end-in-mind that relates to the safety of the community, the police and community were better able to collaborate and evaluate progress towards this desired end.

The situational policing approach is inextricably connected to the concept of neighbourhood dynamics described in Chapter 5. The psychodynamic processes in neighbourhoods and communities create an atmosphere for crime prevention and related behaviours. By considering both the neighbourhood atmosphere and the level of neighbourhood crime, we create four main neighbourhood types: Anomic, Responsive, Vulnerable, and Strong. We then recommend general strategies for each neighbourhood type: *secure then organise* in Anomic neighbourhoods, *systems planning and coordination* in Responsive neighbourhoods, *substitute and sell* in Vulnerable neighbourhoods, and *support and recognise* in Strong neighbourhoods. Figure 12.1 presents a graphical depiction of the situational policing framework.

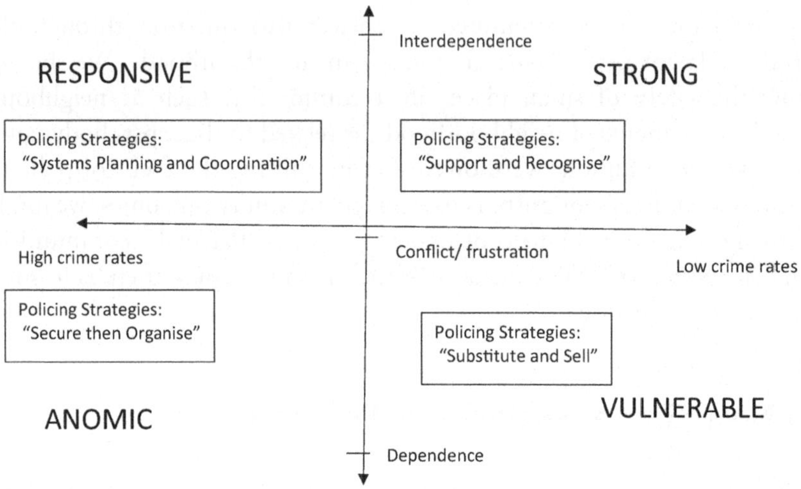

Fig. 12.1 The situational policing framework: four neighbourhood types and suggested policing strategies

The neighbourhood types are constructed as follows: The vertical line in Fig. 12.1 presents the neighbourhood atmosphere as a linear progression from dependence at the bottom, through states of frustration and conflict in the middle, and towards interdependence at the top. The horizontal axis represents the level of crime or disorder from high to low. A Strong neighbourhood is one where crime rates are low and interdependence among community members and with the police is high. Like Strong neighbourhoods, Vulnerable neighbourhoods have low crime rates, but residents don't know each other well and must depend on the police to keep the neighbourhood safe. Anomic neighbourhoods have high crime rates and residents are dependent on the police to solve the crime problem. Finally, Responsive neighbourhoods are places that have high rates of crime and disorder, but residents are generally integrated and know and trust each other. Residents are willing to pitch in and help, but their efforts lack organisation or leadership.

The framework provided in Fig. 12.1 serves as a conceptual map. It can be used to establish starting and desired ending points for collaborative action and for assessing progress along the way. From a situational policing perspective, high technology tools, such as real-time data centres, should include metrics of neighbourhood atmosphere in its "dashboard" of tools for assessing police progress. For transformational reform[1] to occur, rewards and recognition (sources of capital—see Chapter 2) must be aligned with this new goals of building and maintaining Strong neighbourhoods. Additionally, we believe that research and programme evaluations in policing must take into account the neighbourhood type as the context for any evidence-based evaluation. For example, foot patrols may work well in Responsive neighbourhoods, but not in Anomic ones. Current evidence-based evaluations do not include these neighbourhood contexts, which we believe is a limitation. In the next section we introduce concepts, tools, and methods for the new situational policing.

Concepts, Tools, and Methods for Situational Policing

In this section we move from theory to practice and describe how to "do" situational policing. In the following pages, we will walk through the process of implementing situational policing, showing how the police might consider using new tools and methods aimed at making communities safer and stronger. Situational policing is complimentary to earlier versions of community and problem-oriented policing. However, it provides important enhancements and refinements which will be discussed in this chapter.

[1]Transformational reform was identified in Chapter 2 of this volume as one of four types of reform. It implies that the game on the field has changed along with methods for achieving the new goals.

Situational Policing Concepts: Neighbourhood Types and Situational Strategies

As described previously, the term situational policing means matching policing style to the neighbourhood type (see Fig. 12.1). Although there are many activities that could be employed in each neighbourhood type, we recommend the following general strategies.

In the Anomic neighbourhood, we suggest policing strategies that involve *securing then organising*. Foot patrols or other high visibility police deployment methods may be ways to offer security while officers make connections with residents and existing community organisations. In the Responsive neighbourhood type, we recommend *systems planning and coordination.* In these types of places, residents are generally ready to participate with police to reduce crime, but they need a vision for change and the coordination of activities to accomplish it. In Vulnerable neighbourhoods we suggest strategies that *substitute and sell.* By this we mean the police should find out what matters most to the people who live in the community. If crime is not a major concern because it is so low, officers should try to find what does concern residents and *substitute* this issue for crime. The term *selling* refers to advocating the benefits of substituting crime for more relevant issues as a way to create Strong neighbourhoods. Finally, in Strong neighbourhoods we recommend *supporting and recognising* the efforts currently underway to keep the neighbourhood safe. From the logic of the law enforcement game, activities not directly related to crime may seem unnecessary or outside the responsibility of the police. However, from a situational policing perspective, it is necessary to remain fully engaged in ALL neighbourhoods and communities because the relationships that are formed between the police and the community that can help keep a neighbourhood safe.

Situational Policing Tools

The practice of situational policing requires tools and methods for establishing baseline measures and for assessing progress towards the Strong neighbourhood goal. We present three instruments below that are specifically designed for this purpose. The Neighbourhood Dynamics Instrument (NDI) provides a measure of the neighbourhood atmosphere depicted by the vertical axis of Fig. 12.1. Location Quotients and Systematic Social Observations (SSO) can be used to assess levels of crime, disorder, and crime clearance rates along the horizontal axis. We will start with a brief description of each instrument.

Neighbourhood Dynamics Instrument (NDI). The Neighbourhood Dynamics Instrument (NDI) is useful for assessing the atmosphere in a community at a particular time.[2] It is a twenty-item tool that can be used by police, community members or researchers to assess levels of interdependence, frustration and conflict, and dependence. Its self-scoring page makes it easy to use at meetings in the community to do quick assessments of the neighbourhood atmosphere. The NDI is also useful as a research tool for a neighbourhood survey as it can provide baseline measures of neighbourhood atmosphere that guide measures of progress. The NDI is included in the Appendix of this chapter.

Location quotients. During the mid-1990s Canadian criminologists Patricia and Paul Brantingham introduced location quotients as a way to compare crime rates in particular places with the average rates in larger area, such as in cities or towns (Brantingham & Brantingham, 1995). Location quotients can help us see how the crime rate of one small geographic location—like a neighbourhood—compares with the city in which it is located. They are calculated according to Eq. 12.1:

$$\frac{\text{Neighborhood Crime Rate}}{\text{City Crime Rate}} = \text{Location Quotient} \qquad (12.1)$$

[2]The concepts of neighbourhood dynamics and neighbourhood atmosphere are described fully in Chapter 5 of this volume and so will not be repeated here.

Location quotients are interpreted as follows: If the neighbourhood crime rate is the same as the city's rate, the location quotient will be 1. If it is smaller than the city rate, the location quotient will be less than 1. Conversely, if the neighbourhood rate is larger than the city rate, it will be greater than 1. We think this method provides a handy tool for police to determine whether a neighbourhood has a high or low crime rate compared with the average rate for the entire city.

Location quotients are also useful for depicting variation in crime clearance rates by neighbourhood. We believe it is useful to think of crime clearance rates as a measure of police-community relations. In places where residents do not know or trust each other or the police it is likely that crime clearance rates will be extremely low. The opposite is true where residents of a neighbourhood are fully engaged in community life and have a trust in the police to do the right things. In such places victims and witness are more likely to report crimes and cooperate with police investigations. In any event, just as rates of crime can be considered on the horizontal axis of Fig. 12.1, it is also useful to consider crime clearance rates in this way. In fact, any particular problem that will energise collective action can be the issue measured on the horizontal axis, from the least desirable on the far left to the most desirable on the far right (see Fig. 12.1).

Systematic social observations. In addition to measuring crime and crime clearance rates in neighbourhoods, levels of social and physical disorder can also be measured in useful ways by the police and community. Again, the level of disorder can be recorded from high (to the left on the horizontal axis of Fig. 12.1) to low (far right). In this section we discuss how to conduct systematic observations of disorder in neighbourhoods as a baseline measure in order to assess progress over time.

The Systematic Social Observation (SSO) methodology is a standardised approach for making direct observations of physical, social, and economic conditions in neighbourhoods. Physical disorder means visible evidence of deteriorating conditions in a community, such as dilapidated buildings, overgrown lots, excessive litter, and graffiti/tagging. Social disorder is commonly measured through the presence of minor crimes and nuisance behaviours such as public consumption of alcohol, noise complaints, panhandling, and loitering problems. A disorderly environment can lead residents to view the area with indifference, or even become afraid or fed up and move away. This, in turn, affects the behaviour of individuals who live in, move to, or travel through such neighbourhoods. It has been argued that signs of disorder erode social control and leave areas more vulnerable to crime increases (Hinkle, 2013; Kelling & Coles, 1996; Mayer & Jencks, 1989; Skogan, 1990; Wilson & Kelling, 1982).

Typically, SSO measures of neighbourhood disorder are observed and documented by individuals who do not reside in the neighbourhood (for examples, see Sampson & Raudenbush, 1999; Weisburd & Braga, 2006). These researchers claim that outsiders can be objective because they do not have a personal stake in the community. In addition, residents who are fearful of crime may report higher levels of disorder in their community, which presents a skewed view of reality (Sampson & Raudenbush, 1999). From a situational policing perspective, we disagree with these researchers. Residents' perceptions of physical and social disorder are useful to initiate conversations with police about strategies to build Strong neighbourhoods. In addition, recent research has also suggested that there is a major disconnect between researcher-collected SSO measures of disorder and the perceptions of disorder among residents of the observed areas (Hinkle & Yang, 2014; Yang, Hinkle, & Wyckoff, 2018) and that police may define scenes as disorderly or not differently than citizens (Yang & Pao, 2015). As such, police conducting SSOs of neighbourhoods may lead to data (which is used to drive police actions) that does not match the perceptions of residents who live there. Given this, a possible solution is to have residents and police officers team up and walk through neighbourhoods block by block to document physical and social disorder. The collaborative efforts of residents and police can be used to identify strategies that focus on curbing the harmful effects of disorder on crime rates and community quality of life. Such teamwork between police and community members can also help build and enhance the relationships needed to create and maintain Strong neighbourhoods.

The SSO instrument included in the Appendix of this chapter is a one-page worksheet that can be expanded as needed. It is designed to document specific forms of social and physical disorder while walking (or driving) through a neighbourhood. Travelling by foot through the neighbourhoods in teams allows reviewers to more accurately count and record the multiple elements of disorder evidenced on each face block. It may also be useful for each team member to record a score and later assess interrater reliability in scores. For example, given the research reviewed above, it may be the case that police and residents evaluate the disorder on certain blocks differently. Both from a research and evaluation perspective—and from the perspective of building Strong neighbourhoods—the differences may provide important insights. Our SSO worksheet contains nine items, but more can be added as needed depending on the issues that are most important in each particular neighbourhood.

Information on physical and social disorder should be recorded for each face block in a defined neighbourhood. We typically use a street map of the neighbourhoods to assign a number to each face block, defined as the block segment on one side of the street. Numbering the face block in this way provides a systematic method to keep track of the SSO data. Ideally, each face block in a neighbourhood will be numbered. While numbering face blocks is the most precise method to implement SSOs, this strategy may not be practical for all residents or police officers. Alternatively, one might keep track of the block levels (100 block of Main Street, 200 block, etc.) when recording signs of disorder (see Fig. 12.2).

The benefit of obtaining detailed information at the face-block level is that it can highlight how the incidence of disorder in a community can vary drastically in undefined patterns. Evidence of dilapidated conditions may be present on one street or one side of a street, but non-existent on an adjacent parallel street or on the other side of the street. The level of disorder can also differ across the length of one street. Physical disorder is represented by visual cues of dilapidation in the neighbourhood and can be recorded using SSOs at any time of the day, though visibility is often

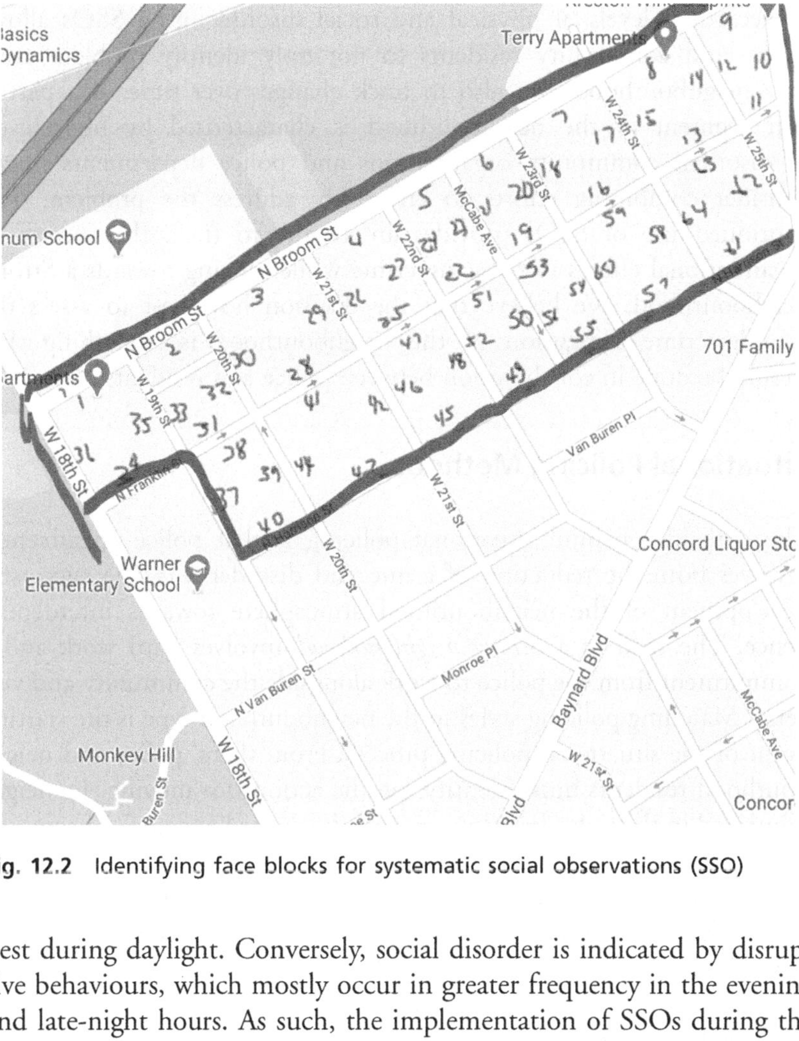

Fig. 12.2 Identifying face blocks for systematic social observations (SSO)

best during daylight. Conversely, social disorder is indicated by disruptive behaviours, which mostly occur in greater frequency in the evening and late-night hours. As such, the implementation of SSOs during the evening and nighttime hours will present a more accurate reflection of disorder in the social neighbourhood. The challenge of safely conducting observations of socially disruptive behaviours emphasises the role police can play in assessing neighbourhood disorder, as officers maintain a level of protection due to their status.

Recording levels of physical and social disorder using SSOs allows police and community residents to not only identify problem areas in a neighbourhood, but also to track changes over time. If a particular segment of the neighbourhood is characterised by high levels of disorder, community organisations and police departments might consider combining efforts to effectively address the problem. The continued use of SSOs provides an avenue to track the success of organisational efforts in reducing crime while moving towards a Strong neighbourhood. We believe that the decision how best to assess the disorder/crime dimension of the neighbourhood is something that should be done in collaboration between police and residents.

Situational Policing Methods

The core idea behind situational policing is that police effectiveness involves both the reduction of crime and disorder *and* the successful development of the neighbourhood atmosphere towards interdependence. The road to a *Strong neighbourhood* involves hard work and a commitment from the police to work alongside the community and vice versa. Matching policing styles to the neighbourhood type is the starting point of the situational policing process. From there, police and neighbourhood residents must identify specific actions for moving the neighbourhood in the right direction towards the desired end goal—becoming and remaining a *Strong neighbourhood* (see Fig. 12.1).

There are a few more things to consider when implementing a situational policing approach which we will discuss in the section below: (1) representative samples, and (2) establishing an educational process that includes dialogue, action, and reflection.

Probability sampling. The first issue involves getting a probability sample of the NDI, SSO metrics described above. It is often easy for the police to ask questions of residents who regularly come to meetings. However, when we talk about the neighbourhood atmosphere we are really talking about the neighbourhood-as-a-whole and what residents throughout the neighbourhood are willing to do to help. Those residents who regularly attend community meetings and/or who are actively involved in community activism may not represent the views of all (or even the majority) of residents. Importantly, this may vary across neighbourhood types. For instance, in Anomic or Vulnerable neighbourhoods those who lack faith, trust, or confidence in the police may be the least likely to attend meetings. This would be a challenge to situational policing efforts as their voices and opinions are perhaps the most important if police are going to gain the understanding needed to build and repair relationships.

The situational policing approach requires methods to obtain a representative sample of the neighbourhood-as-a-whole to avoid the potential biases in measuring community sentiment discussed above. We have used two main methods for obtaining an unbiased sample of neighbourhoods. The first approach involves face-to-face surveys that are conducted by the community with the police. We start by obtaining a map of the neighbourhood such as the one depicted in Fig. 12.2. Once the boundaries of the neighbourhood are defined, then each block or face block can be numbered. With a list of numbers, the police and community can randomly select certain face blocks to survey. Once a face block is selected, repeated attempts to get responses from *every* house on the block should be made. For example, 20 blocks from the map in Fig. 12.2 may translate to a total of 120 homes to survey. The police and community together may want to strategize on how best to get a high response rate from these homes. This strategy is scalable so as to get a large enough sample size that is representative of the neighbourhood.

Another method, which is much simpler, involves the use of social media to contact residents with a link to an online survey. We have used a number of online applications including Messenger and Facebook, but there are many others created specifically for communicating confidentially with neighbourhood residents (e.g., Nextdoor). An initial step in this process may involve getting residents to join in on social media before sending the survey to everyone. Our neighbourhood surveys have included the NDI questions as well as questions about crime victimisation, community crime and disorder, as well as open-ended responses to questions about major concerns or suggestions. We also include items in the survey that help us compare the survey results with known population parameters, such as race, gender, employment, and housing that are easily obtained via the U.S. Census Bureau or the city planning department. Comparing the sample results with known population parameters will help validate the survey responses and ensure the sample is not biased in some unintentional way.

Dialogue, action, and reflection. The second item that must be considered relates to the educational process of change and involves three main steps: dialogue, action, and reflection. These are explained in more detail below.

The desired neighbourhood outcome at which all police activity is aimed in the situational policing approach is the Strong neighbourhood. For this to happen, the police and community residents must engage in dialogue, collective action, and then reflect on these actions to see if they work. If they are not effective or if they produce unintended negative consequences, the dialogue should consider new strategies. This process should continue to be repeated while the group continues to grow with more participation from residents and with increasing resources from government and outside sources.

The initial police-community dialogue should involve a presentation of the situational policing framework so that everyone involved knows how it works. Once residents understand what the horizontal and vertical dimensions of the framework mean, they can describe their own neighbourhood location on this conceptual map. We have found that once residents explain why they think their neighbourhood fits in a particular place on the conceptual map, they generally understand the basic idea of the framework and how it could work to guide dialogue and action.

From here, the core group of residents might want to begin collecting baseline data via survey research methods. This should include the NDI and questions related to current neighbourhood problems. It should also include police-community teams collecting SSO data. Both instruments (NDI and SSO) are included in the Appendix. It is also helpful to assess neighbourhood crime rates *vis a vis* the city crime rate using the location quotient. It is also useful at this point to compare crime clearance rates in this way. Again, all of this is to get some local residents involved in gathering baseline information before collective action can begin.

Once the baseline data is gathered, the police with residents should present the findings to a wider range of people from the neighbourhood. The findings presented within the situational policing framework help participants see how various strategies may be implemented concurrently or consecutively in order to move the neighbourhood to the Strong neighbourhood ideal. The framework prevents residents from demanding the police do it alone and the police from arguing that they can do it alone.

We have found that it is helpful at the early stages of collaboration to address problems that are important enough, but not too complex. For instance, during a situational policing project in Wilmington, Delaware, police-community teams had collected SSO data by walking together block by block. During this process the police became aware of several houses in which drug dealing was suspected. The residents were fearful and wanted the police to enforce drug laws to solve the problem. But, it was important to remember that the situational policing approach requires that law enforcement activities be part of a larger strategy to make the neighbourhood safer through the building of strong relationships. From the logic of the law enforcement game (Chapter 2), the typical response to a complaint from neighbours about drug dealing is a referral to the drug task force or similar unit that specialises in drug investigations. These special investigative units typically operate on information they already have via informants and undercover work. As such, referrals from neighbourhood groups about suspected drug dealing rarely reach the level of importance necessary for immediate action. So, although it is logical to refer a suspected drug house to the law enforcement efforts, they generally go unaddressed which causes frustration and conflict between the police and community.

In this particular case a prosecutor from the state Office of the Attorney General helped the local neighbourhood group draft a letter to the suspected drug dealers. In the letter, it informed the residents that neighbours suspected that drug dealing was going on and that the police had been made aware of it. The police delivered the letter and the problem stopped immediately! When the police work with residents to solve problems creatively and quickly, as they did in this case, it builds momentum and encourages others to join in. When the goal shifts from the big lockup and large drug seizure to the strong neighbourhood outcome, relationships can change for the better making the community safer. Through the educational process of dialogue, action and reflection, the social networks in neighbourhoods grow and relationships in the community and between the police and community grow stronger.

Conclusions

The police and community co-produce public safety outcomes whether they plan to or not (Duffee, Renauer, Scott, Chermak, & McGarrell, 2006). The situational policing framework, with its concepts, tools, and methods provides a way to systematically collect data, engage in dialogue and action, evaluate what works, and make modifications as needed to improve public safety in local neighbourhood and community places.

Appendix

The appendix of this chapter includes the following tools for Situational Policing: Neighbourhood Dynamics Instrument (NDI), Systematic Social Observation Worksheet.

Neighbourhood Development Instrument (NDI)

FOR EACH OF THE FOLLOWING STATEMENTS ABOUT YOUR NEIGHBOURHOOD & THE POLICE, PLEASE RATE HOW STRONGLY YOU FEEL BY CIRCLING A NUMBER ON THE SCALE FROM 1 TO 9, WHERE 1 IS VERY STRONGLY DISAGREE AND 9 IS VERY STRONGLY AGREE. WHEN YOU FINISH, PLEASE PUT YOUR SCORE IN THE TABLE AND ADD THE COLUMNS FOR A TOTAL SCORE IN EACH NEIGHBOURHOOD DYNAMICS CATEGORY.

Generally speaking, people in my neighbourhood…	Very Strongly DISAGREE → Very Strongly AGREE
a. Know how to work together to prevent crime.	1 2 3 4 5 6 7 8 9
b. Don't get along with one another.	1 2 3 4 5 6 7 8 9
c. Know how to deal with minor community problems.	1 2 3 4 5 6 7 8 9
d. Are willing to help one another.	1 2 3 4 5 6 7 8 9
e. Watch out for each other's property.	1 2 3 4 5 6 7 8 9
f. Feel frustrated with each other.	1 2 3 4 5 6 7 8 9
g. Tell each other what is going on.	1 2 3 4 5 6 7 8 9
h. Do not work well together to prevent crime.	1 2 3 4 5 6 7 8 9
i. Trust each other.	1 2 3 4 5 6 7 8 9
j. Rely heavily on each other.	1 2 3 4 5 6 7 8 9

Generally speaking, people in my neighbourhood…	Very Strongly DISAGREE → Very Strongly AGREE
k. Are frustrated with the police.	1 2 3 4 5 6 7 8 9
l. Call the police for most community problems.	1 2 3 4 5 6 7 8 9
m. Think the police don't seem to care.	1 2 3 4 5 6 7 8 9
n. Think the police do very little to prevent crime.	1 2 3 4 5 6 7 8 9
o. Trust the police to be highly effective crime fighters.	1 2 3 4 5 6 7 8 9
p. Assume the police know what is going on.	1 2 3 4 5 6 7 8 9
q. Rely heavily on the police.	1 2 3 4 5 6 7 8 9
r. Think the local police are ineffective.	1 2 3 4 5 6 7 8 9
s. Have confidence that the police alone are capable of preventing crime.	1 2 3 4 5 6 7 8 9
t. Want more police protection	1 2 3 4 5 6 7 8 9

NDI SCORING SHEET

When finished scoring the twenty items on the Neighbourhood Dynamics Instrument, please transfer your scores to the table below and add the columns.

DEPENDENCE	FRUSTRATION/ CONFLICT WITH POLICE	FRUSTRATION/ CONFLICT IN COMMUNITY	INTERDEPENDENCE
l.	k.	b.	a.
o.	m.	f.	c.
p.	n.	h.	d.
q.	r.		e.
s.			g.
t.			i.
			j.
TOTAL #/54	TOTAL #/36	TOTAL #/27	TOTAL #/63

Systematic Social Observation (SSO) Worksheet

Street Name	FACE BLOCK Number	ABANDONED PROPERTY	EXCESSIVE TRASH	VACANT HOUSES	ABANDONED LOTS	EXCESSIVE GRAFITTI	LOUD GROUPS	LOUD MUSIC	DRUGS BEING USED	ALCOHOL CONSUMPTION	ADD MORE
Street name	1										
	2										
	3										
	4										
	5										
	.										
	.										
	.										
TOTALS											

References

Brantingham, P. L., & Brantingham, P. J. (1995). Location quotients and crime hot spots in the city. In C. R. Block, M. Dabdoub, & S. Fregly (Eds.), *Crime analysis through computer mapping* (pp. 129–149). Washington, DC: Police Executive Research Forum.

Duffee, D., Renauer, B. C., Scott, J. D., Chermak, S., & McGarrell, E. F. (2006). *Community building measures: How police and neighbourhood groups can measure their collaboration.* National Institute of Justice. Retrieved from https://www.ncjrs.gov/pdffiles1/nij/grants/213134.pdf.

Hinkle, J. C. (2013). The relationship between disorder, perceived risk, and collective efficacy: A look into the indirect pathways of the broken windows thesis. *Criminal Justice Studies, 26*(4), 408–432.

Hinkle, J. C., & Yang, S. M. (2014). A new look into broken windows: What shapes individuals' perceptions of social disorder? *Journal of Criminal Justice, 42*(1), 26–35.

Kelling, G., & Coles, C. (1996). *Fixing broken windows: Restoring order and reducing crime in our communities.* New York: Free Press.

Markovic, J. (2009). Neighbourhoods matter: A situational policing perspective. *Geography and Public Safety, 2*(2). Washington, DC: National Institute of Justice. Retrieved from https://nij.ojp.gov/library/publications/neighbourhoods-matter-situational-policing-perspective.

Mayer, S. E., & Jencks, C. (1989). Poverty and the distribution of material hardship. *Journal of Human Resources, 24*(1), 88–114.

Nolan, J., Conti, N., & McDevitt, J. (2004). Situational policing: Neighbourhood development and crime control. *Policing & Society, 14*(2), 99–117.

Nolan, J., Conti, N., & McDevitt, J. (2005). Situational policing. *Law Enforcement Bulletin.* Federal Bureau of Investigation.

Sampson, R. J., & Raudenbush, S. (1999). Systematic social observation in public spaces: A new look at disorder in urban neighbourhoods. *American Journal of Sociology, 105*(3), 603–651.

Skogan, W. (1990). *Disorder and decline: Crime and the spatial decay in American cities.* Berkeley: University of California Press.

Weisburd, D., & Braga, A. (2006). *Police innovation: Contrasting perspectives.* Cambridge, UK: Cambridge University Press.

Wilson, J. Q., & Kelling, G. L. (1982). Broken windows: Police and neighbourhood safety. *The Atlantic Monthly, 249,* 29–38.

Yang, S., Hinkle, J. C., & Wyckoff, L. A. (2018). Using multitrait-multimethod (MTMM) techniques to examine the convergent and discriminant validity of social disorder. *Journal of Research in Crime and Delinquency, 55*(5), 571–608.
Yang, S. M., & Pao, C. C. (2015). Do we "see" the same thing? An experimental look into the black box of disorder perception. *Journal of Research in Crime and Delinquency, 52*(4), 534–566.

13

The Use of Social Media in Intelligence and Its Impact on Police Work

Francis Fortin, Julie Delle Donne, and Justine Knop

Introduction

Adaptation to and integration of science and technology are cultural in police organisations, and traced back to the nineteenth century, from fingerprints identification to present digital transformations (see Chapter 11), including adapting and upgrading communications and transport means (Dupont, 2004; Leman-Langlois, 2013; Purenne & Wuilleumier, 2011; Renard, 2011). One of the most recent innovations to draw the attention of researchers is the adoption and integration of social media platforms into intelligence activities. The growing interest

We have no conflicts of interest to declare.

F. Fortin (✉) · J. Delle Donne · J. Knop
School of Criminology, Université de Montréal, Montreal, QC, Canada
e-mail: Francis.fortin@umontreal.ca

J. Delle Donne
e-mail: julie.delle.donne@umontreal.ca

J. J. Nolan et al. (eds.), *Policing in an Age of Reform*,
Palgrave's Critical Policing Studies,
https://doi.org/10.1007/978-3-030-56765-1_13

in the subject is not surprising when one looks at the increasing use of social media by citizens.

This chapter presents a summary of studies that have addressed the topic of social media and its effect on police practices, particularly for criminal intelligence. It should be noted that some of these studies are not directly concerned with the applications of social media to police work but still provide information that is relevant to meeting police objectives. A summary of the impact of social media on police work is discussed, pointing out challenges and opportunities. Studies that present specific cases of how social media can be used to produce criminal intelligence are then described. The chapter ends with a discussion of ethical, legal, and technological issues.

Social Media as a New Technological Challenge and Opportunity for Police Work

Social media are Web platforms that encourage and facilitate communication, interaction, and the creation and circulation of content within virtual communities (Boyd & Ellison, 2008). Whether used for social networking (Facebook), sharing photos and videos (Instagram, YouTube), or microblogging (Twitter), social media have transformed media systems, irrevocably changing the production, consumption, and dissemination of information (Walsh & O'Connor, 2019). When combined with other technological advances, such as the development of smart phones, geolocation systems, and powerful computer servers that can hold a large amount of data, these platforms have redefined several dimensions of daily life (Bennett, Haggerty, Lyon, & Steeves, 2014; Rainie & Wellman, 2012) and are creating a new space for individuals to connect with each other, share information, and publish their opinions on various topics (Rainie & Wellman, 2012). More than a simple change in habits, these new places to share are part of what Rainie and Wellman (2012) describe as a new social system. This new social system is the result of three revolutions: a change in the form of interactions between individuals, the evolution of the Internet, and the advent of technological mobility. All three of these components mean that the places where individuals meet have moved beyond homes, schools, parks, or places of worship. Meeting places are now virtual and exist on blogs or other platforms for exchange. Geography is becoming less important in the choice of relationships, replaced by common interests. Moreover, meetings, which used to be highly structured (for example, during working hours, communications took place mainly between colleagues in the same office), now take place sporadically throughout the day. Work can be carried out from home with employees communicating with each other by conversation on a personal cell phone, exchanging e-mails or sending instant messages, or using digital meeting places. A business meeting can be followed by a general discussion with colleagues and planning an activity with a family member without changing location. However, this new place for interaction provides new visibility and traceability for each individual's interactions and activities (Trottier, 2012, 2016).

Adoption of social media by law enforcement agencies seems to be a global phenomenon. Surveys and interviews with stakeholders show significant levels of adoption in the United States (IACP, 2017), Europe (Denef, Kaptein, Bayerl, & Ramirez, 2012), and Canada (Delle Donne & Fortin, 2018; Frank & Cheng, 2011). Social media are now indispensable tools in police work, especially for surveillance and intelligence gathering (Martin, 2018; Scassa, 2017). Police agencies use the media to conduct investigations (Fallik, Deuchar, Crichlow, & Hodges, 2020), often monitoring individuals, identifying a suspect, locating missing persons, and tracking police officers, suspects, witnesses, and victims (Fallik et al., 2020; Hofmann & Feltes, 2020). Social media provides information that can assist investigations both prospectively (i.e., identifying networks or indications of criminal intentions, etc.) and retrospectively (i.e., tracing what a person did on the day of the crime) (Estellés-Arolas, 2020; Fallik et al., 2020). Social media can help the justice system find evidence about the planning, commission, or consequences of a crime, aid in identifying suspects, victims, or witnesses, and reveal the motive for the crime (Lane, Ramirez, & Pearce, 2018). The use of social media may lead criminals to post pictures of themselves with weapons and drugs or committing crimes and offenses, allowing police to gather evidence and information about criminal networks. In addition, it is possible to analyse relationships between individuals through their contacts on various media, identification in publications, online conversations, and associations between individuals. Social media can thus be used to corroborate physical evidence (Lane et al., 2018).

Social Media as a New Intelligence Source (SOCMINT)

There is no consensus on the definition of intelligence in policing (Brodeur, 2006; Coyne, 2014). There are, however, certain concepts that help delineate its meaning. First, criminal intelligence assists police organisations in carrying out their law enforcement and crime prevention activities (Lemieux, 2008). Intelligence is gathered in these agencies at several organisational levels: tactical, operational, and strategic (Ratcliffe, 2009). Intelligence produced at a tactical level helps front-line actors make decisions about a specific case. The information being sought relates directly to the suspects or criminal group being investigated (Lemieux, 2008). Strategic intelligence is intended for senior managers and allows them to plan long-term operations and implement crime prevention and reduction strategies (Ratcliffe, 2009). Between these two levels is operational intelligence, generally used by managers who work closely with those on the front lines in planning crime reduction strategies and deploying resources to achieve operational objectives (Coyne & Bell, 2011; Ratcliffe, 2009).

Social media have been studied to assess their relevance in the production of operational, tactical, or strategic intelligence. For example, many individuals, before committing a criminal act, indicate their intentions on social media (Frank & Cheng, 2011). Similarly, some members of criminal groups clearly display their affiliations and share their ideas about the use of violence and endorsement of criminal acts to achieve their ends (Frank & Cheng, 2011; Trottier, 2012, 2016). Suspects who are the target of a police investigation may not publish incriminating material but still provide information that is of interest to anyone who would like to know more about an individual or a group of individuals (Antonius & Rich, 2013; Rodriguez, 2014).

The use of social media as a source of information is commonly referred to as Social Media Intelligence (SOCMINT) (Omand, Bartlett, & Miller, 2012a) and is part of the broader context of intelligence-led policing, which relies on the collection and analysis of information in making decisions at the tactical, operational, and strategic levels. SOCMINT is not unique to policing; social media analysis is used in many other disciplines. For example, marketing agencies have developed programs that allow them to survey the public to learn their opinion of a product. SOCMINT might also be useful as a way to use crowds to provide information and understand specific events. For instance, at the operational level, analysing media traffic and looking for sudden increases in tweeting from particular areas could provide a picture of events that allows more rapid detection of emergencies, making a more rapid response by authorities. Finally, SOCMINT can be used to monitor the behavior of interest groups and analyse their reaction to certain events as well as detecting information about intentions to commit crimes (Carter, 2009).

Given the wealth of information available on social media platforms, such as photos, geolocation data, and written material, looking at the history of SOCMINT reveals that the most important problem is how to target relevant information and make links between suspects. The product of such intelligence also has to meet several quality criteria, including accuracy, objectivity, usefulness, relevance, availability, timeliness, and impact (Krizan, 1999) and has to be understandable, added value and evaluated in its context (ONUDD, 2010) like any intelligence.

Obtaining Information on Crimes

In the United States, since 2005, college and university investigators have been among the first to use social media to ask for the public's help in identifying suspects involved in various events for which they had photos or videos (Marsico, 2009). Social media have also become a "place" where law enforcement agencies communicate with the public to obtain information that contributes to the production of criminal intelligence. Law enforcement agencies also publish photos of suspects and videos of events and then solicit the public's help in identifying suspects (Brainard & Edlins, 2015). For example, on several occasions and in several countries, citizens have taken pictures of looters during riots and then posted them on social media, allowing police to identify at least some of the individuals involved (Denef et al., 2012; Panagiotopoulos, Bigdeli, & Sams, 2014; Procter, Crump, Karstedt, Voss, & Cantijoch, 2013; Trottier, 2012). Requests can be disseminated in particular social networks but are later often shared between users, which considerably increases public access to police publications (Denef et al., 2012).

The relevance of information found on social media does not end with the content of publications. Other data, such as the links between individuals, the places they frequent, and their geolocation can become equally relevant sources of information. Publications also lead to interactions between individuals on various media platforms. These interactions provide information on the links between various topics of interest and make it possible to analyse the material to create graphs of various networks (Antonius & Rich, 2013). Similarly, the geolocation of publications combined with their content can be used to verify the effect of terrorist groups on different populations (Rodriguez, 2014).

Social media can help the police increase public involvement in the fight against crime and production of public safety by involving them in the collection of evidence. For example, police forces have created a "#shopalooter" hashtag that allows citizens to comment on publications they consider compromising and directs police officers to the identified content. The same strategy was used during riots in 2011 when citizens created the hashtag "#riotcleanup" and used it to help police find those involved in the riots. This co-production of security can also be part of anti-terrorist policies (Bartlett et al., 2013).

The Detection of Criminal or Anti-Social Behavior

Social media can help in the detection of criminal or anti-social behavior and is particularly relevant for dealing with the under-researched themes of cyberhate and Islamophobia (Awan, 2014). Online racism, especially in the context of jokes, is rooted in stereotypes (Weaver, 2013) and tweets including such portrayals can be extracted from large datasets based on clusters of identities as well as other parameters (Joseph, Wei, & Carley, 2017). Some researchers have focused on hateful messages posted online after a particular event (Bérubé et al., in press). The Cardiff Online Social Media ObServatory (COSMOS) has developed tools to help researchers collect and analyse such online data (Berube et al., in press; Edwards, Housley, Williams, Sloan, & Williams, 2013). By using tools that detect social tension, researchers were able to construct a typology of tweets that contained aggression or provided information or opinion (Burnap et al., 2015). Models that classify cyber speech, particularly when developed after specific events, such as a terrorist attack, can help in developing proactive policies while also reducing victimisation (Burnap & Williams, 2016). However, it is difficult to be completely accurate in designating a tweet as involving antagonistic content as the material may involve sarcasm or semantic structures unrecognised by the researcher. Despite this, developing classifiers for contents of tweets, including hashtags, has the potential to be of use to police (Burnap & Williams, 2015). In cases of cyberhate, criminological studies paired with police actions could have a real-world impact for online victims.

Tweet content has also been studied in the context of radicalised youth. Researchers found that concepts related to the Islamic State, punishment, and Western countries were associated with a list of terms that identified female teenage supporters of ISIS (Ghajar-Khosravi, Kwantes, Derbentseva, & Huey, 2016). The frequency of certain concepts in tweets in a dataset gathered from radicalised teenagers differed from those in control groups. For instance, the idea of violence was found in 3.33% of tweets by ISIS supporters but in fewer than 1% of the tweets of the sample of "regular" teenagers. Controls are important when considering tweets related to sensitive topics to take account for irony, which is often part of textual features (hashtags included) (Reyes, Rosso, & Veale, 2012). The absence of such controls can lead to misclassifications, affecting results.

Cohen, Johansson, Kaati, and Mork (2014) focus on the problem of detecting "lone wolf" terrorists. They suggest that traditional investigative methods are ineffective for detecting and preventing this type of crime and suggest that social media and other Internet sites might be used for text analysis that would make it possible to detect certain precursor manifestations by such individuals. They present a research that has identified and categorised precursor behaviours in individuals who have carried out this type of attacks and conclude that certain types of manifestations can be detected using text analysis markers. They note, however, that this analysis cannot be done completely automatically but should always involve analysts who can distinguish the real threats among identified individuals and messages from false positives. Any police intervention is likely to involve a large number of such red-flag-oriented tools that, while pointing in the right direction, still need additional police work to determine the contextual and legal value of the information.

The Internet in general, not just social media, has been studied as a place where racist cultures can emerge (Back, 2002) as it is easy for extremist ideologies to be widely spread, reaching large groups. The case of far-right Dutch politician Geert Wilders, who constantly tweets inflammatory content about Islam, is one example (Blanquart & Cook, 2013). While white supremacists, including those encouraging terrorism, make up a small proportion of Twitter users, the strategies they use have influenced large numbers of individuals (Graham, 2016). As such ideologies spread, police can track the source, using an inductive approach based on analysing followers, liked content, and retweets (Berger & Strathearn, 2013). Such methods are important for law enforcement agencies, as the spread of extreme ideas has become an important concern during the last decade.

Several studies focus on whether it is possible to use automatic methods to detect publications whose content poses a threat (Kumar & Singh, 2013; Oostdijk & Van Halteren, 2013; Rasheed, Khan, Bashir, & Fatima, 2019) and conclude that technologies and intelligent software that can categorise content can help detect messages that pose a potential security threat.

Uncovering Systems of Connections that Promote or Help in Committing Illegal Activities

Social network analysis can help law enforcement and governmental agencies uncover systems of connections that promote illegal activities. Berger and Strathearn (2013) assessed the level of engagement with white supremacy ideology on Twitter by measuring influence (a tweet leads to a reaction), exposure (reaction is communicated to others), and interactivity (influence and exposure combined, indicative of high engagement). This information might make it possible to disrupt such networks by targeting those who appear to be most influential. The principle of homophily applies on Twitter: users tend to follow accounts that express opinions similar to their own. This has been demonstrated in studies of the accounts of celebrities and bloggers, who are distinguished by the content they produce, the accounts they follow, and the Twitter lists they appear on (Wu, Hofman, Mason, & Watts, 2011). Such findings suggest that there are divergent realities on Twitter, allowing users to interact without leaving their bubble to confront ideas or situations different from their own. Identifying such instances of homophily can be useful once a researcher has located some members of a criminal population through hashtags or other tools, following a procedure that resembles a snowball sampling approach. For instance, looking at followers, followees, and retweets has been used in research on gangs and helped discover gang members (Balasuriya, Wijeratne, Doran, & Sheth, 2016).

Crisis Response

Content analysis of social media data has other implications for public safety. For instance, Twitter has been used in the provision of security, making it possible for criminologists and police to construct maps of activity by targeted groups or individuals that are useful for prevention and intervention by law enforcement agencies and also in managing real-time events (Camargo, Torres, Martinez, & Gomez, 2016). In times of crisis, social networks are an important source of information for citizens and the police (Moore, 2020). Information provided by the public can help the police to better target where interventions should take place. However, the amount of information available is a considerable challenge, as police services do not have the manpower to analyse all the content provided online (Reuter, Kaufhold, Spahr, Spielhofer, & Hahne, 2020). Police have had difficulty adapting to new technologies (Fallik et al., 2020). The rapid change in social media has been difficult for law enforcement as knowledge in policing has not evolved at the same speed. The lack of specialised resources and formal training, as well as ineffective online training, are factors in the delay in effective police activity in dealing with cybercrime (Hadlington, Lumsden, Black, & Ferra, 2018).

The independent body responsible for monitoring and reporting on law enforcement in England, Her Majesty's Inspectorate of the Constabulary (HMIC), analysed police work during several riots that occurred over a four-day period in 2011 in response to the death of Mark Duggan, a 29-year-old man shot by a police officer. The report found that, even before the riots began, hostile comments and threats to police officers had been appearing on social media (HMIC, 2011). As the riots developed, citizens who saw their property and businesses threatened used social media to send information to police officers to help them identify attackers and the locations of the riots. While the information transmitted on various communication platforms should have helped the police, instead they found themselves overwhelmed by the large amount of information provided. The report's conclusions are unequivocal: police officers, unlike those in the commercial sector, are not sufficiently equipped to analyse information provided to them on social media. To alleviate these difficulties, the authors of the report suggest creating a central organisation to collect and analyse information in order to anticipate disorders related to riots and other major events (HMIC, 2011; Omand et al., 2012a).

Newnham and Bell (2012) look at how both demonstrators and governments used Facebook, Twitter, and YouTube during political uprisings in Iran, the United Kingdom, and Egypt from 2009 to 2011. Information available on social media has been used to produce intelligence on activities and the creation of false accounts, has been used to obtaining further information on specific targets. They conclude that governments, and especially law enforcement and intelligence agencies, cannot ignore the opportunities and threats emanating from this new reality but must address the use of social media in developing their strategies and policies.

Discussion

Social media are a part of everyday life for most individuals and their use does not appear to be decreasing. As society faces the fact that criminals have adapted to this online environment, the police, who are playing catch-up, have become more and more proactive. Law enforcement agencies that have taken the time to adapt to new technologies are now using them to fight crime more efficiently (Faith & Bekir, 2015). In this chapter, we discuss many studies that focus on the use of social media by law enforcement agencies. Our findings suggest that social media intelligence (SOCMINT) has become a new source of useful information for intelligence production in several ways. First, it is used on the tactical level. Whether obtained from what criminals reveal on social media or from information sent by the public, such data are an important way to increase knowledge about crime. Second, proactive detection of crime can be useful not only tactically (e.g., detecting specific threats), but also operationally (e.g., for crisis response) and strategically (e.g., identifying criminal environments and obtaining information on organised crime). This study also supports the idea that social media provides socio-behavioral signals that can be used in crime prediction (Aghababaei & Makrehchi, 2016) and that improve knowledge about actual crimes. In other words, using OSINT, including SOCMINT, "can often provide an efficient, effective, and fast insight into the issue that may often validate the need for further inquiry" (Carter, 2009, p. 286).

There are, however, legal and ethical issues in using social media in intelligence gathering and in dealing with criminal activities. Scholars have suggested that using social media data raises legal issues in terms of prosecution and jurisdiction (Horsman, Ginty, & Cranner, 2017; Murphy & Fontecilla, 2013). One of the difficulties identified by several researchers concerns the ability to find online profiles of the individual for whom information is sought (Frank, Cheng, & Pun, 2011; Marsico, 2009). This difficulty arises both because criminals do not always use their real names and because several individuals, including some not being targeted in the investigation, may have the same name. As well, prosecution requires that the law enforcement agency locate the offender, which can be much more difficult than identifying their online identity.

Another issue arises when it comes to the use of information that is available but not accessible to the public. Police organisations, which operate in particular jurisdictions, may find that their work is hindered by the presence of international users and the discrepancies between laws in different jurisdictions. Requests for authorisations and warrants may have to be obtained and such requests require the collaboration of social media platforms that are not necessarily located in the country where the request originates, which can considerably complicate procedures (Denef et al., 2012). In a study by Frank et al., (2011) conducted in Canada, respondents reported difficulty in obtaining information from these platforms and difficulty in complying with the technical aspects of online evidence collection. A number of studies point out that there is no legislative framework specific to the use of social media by the police. Police officers therefore have to use the standards created to govern their general activities in dealing with social media (Denef et al., 2012). This means that there may be a lack of previous decisions regarding whether particular evidence is relevant, appropriate, and has been gathered while respecting legal procedures.

Working with data derived from social media has influenced how investigations are conducted and a lack of standards in acquiring this data has been observed. McKeown, Maxweel, Azzopardi, and Glisson (2014) conducted interviews with analysts assigned to criminal intelligence and responsible for identifying persons of interest regarding the tools they use in conducting research using open source intelligence (OSINT). They conclude that analysts do not use new specific tools but custom usual general ones available to any other analyst. As well, there was no standard approach, with each analyst using a separately chosen method. While one analyst might include false accounts in the data being analysed, another would categorically refuse to use this approach to obtain information.

It points out, as claimed by Omand, Bartlett, and Miller (2012b), that techniques used to ensure public safety must be accepted by citizens. However, this democratic legitimacy is and will be difficult to achieve as long as the use is not well standardised.

Finally, obvious ethical issues are levered though getting information from social media (Omand et al., 2012b; Bartlett et al., 2013). For instance, using a created false account, deceiving a target to infiltrate its social network is usually controlled by other rules or through requests for transmission of information addressed to platform managers (Omand et al., 2012b; Frank et al., 2011). Besides, the demarcation between what is private and public in this new social reality is sometimes ambiguous (Omand et al., 2012b), questioning the need and the nature of warrants.

References

Aghababaei, S., & Makrehchi, M. (2016, October). Mining social media content for crime prediction. In *2016 IEEE/WIC/ACM International Conference on Web Intelligence (WI)* (pp. 526–531). IEEE.

Antonius, N., & Rich, L. (2013). Discovering collection and analysis techniques for social media to improve public safety. *The International Technology Management Review, 3*(1), 42–53. https://doi.org/10.2991/itmr.2013.3.1.4.

Awan, I. (2014). Islamophobia and Twitter: A typology of online hate against Muslims on social media. *Policy & Internet, 6*(2), 133–150.

Back, L. (2002). Aryans reading Adorno: Cyber-culture and twenty-first century racism. *Ethnic and Racial Studies, 25*(4), 628–651.

Balasuriya, L., Wijeratne, S., Doran, D., & Sheth, A. (2016, August). *Finding street gang members on Twitter.* Article presented at the 2016 IEEE/ACM International Conference on Advances in Social Networks Analysis and Mining, San Francisco, USA. Retrieved from https://arxiv.org/pdf/1610.09516.pdf.

Bartlett, J., Miller, C., Crump, J. et Middleton, L. (2013). Policing in an Information Age. *Demos*, 1–42.

Bennett, C. J., Haggerty, K. D., Lyon, D., & Steeves, V. (2014). *Vivre à nu : La surveillance au Canada.* Athabasca University Press.

Berger, J. M., & Strathearn, B. (2013, March). *Developments in radicalisation and political violence. who matters online: Measuring influence, evaluating content and countering violent extremism in online social networks*. Retrieved from http://icsr.info/wp-content/uploads/2013/03/ICSR_Berger-and-Strathearn.pdf.

Bérubé, M., Tang, U, Fortin, F., Ozalp, Williams, M., & Burnap, P. (in press). Social media forensics applied to assessment of post–critical incident social reaction: The case of the 2017 Manchester Arena bombing. *Forensic Science International, 0,0*.

Blanquart, G., & Cook, D. M. (2013, December). *Twitter influence and cumulative perceptions of extremist support: A case study of geert wilders*. Article presented at the 4th Australian Counter Terrorism Conference, Perth, Australia. Retrieved from http://ro.ecu.edu.au/cgi/viewcontent.cgi?article=1021&context=act.

Boyd, D., & Ellison, N. B. (2008). Social network sites: Definition, history, and scholarship. *Journal of Computer-Mediated Communication, 13*, 210–230.

Brainard, L., & Edlins, M. (2015). Top 10 U.S. municipal police departments and their social media usage. *The American Review of Public Administration, 45*(6), 728–745. https://doi.org/10.1177/0275074014524478.

Brodeur, J.-P. (2006). Le renseignement: Distinctions préliminaires. *Canadian Journal of Criminology and Criminal Justice*. https://doi.org/10.3138/cjccj.47.1.15.

Burnap, P., Rana, O. F., Avis, N., Williams, M., Housley, W., Edwards, A., et al. (2015). Detecting tension in online communities with computational Twitter analysis. *Technological Forecasting and Social Change, 95*, 96–108.

Burnap, P., & Williams, M. L. (2015). Cyber hate speech on Twitter: An application for machine classification and statistical modeling for policy and decision making. *Policy & Internet, 7*(2), 233–242.

Burnap, P., & Williams, M. L. (2016). Us and them: Identifying cyber hate on Twitter across multiple protected characteristics. *EPJ Data Science, 5*(11), 1–15.

Camargo, J. E., Torres, C. A., Martinez, O. H., & Gomez, F. A. (2016, September). *A big data analytics citizens' perception of security*. Article presented at the 2016 IEEE International Smart Cities Conferences (ISC2), Trento, Italy. Retrieved from http://ieeexplore.ieee.org/document/7580846/.

Carter, D. L. (2009). *Law enforcement intelligence: A guide for state, local, and tribal law enforcement agencies* (2nd ed.). Retrieved from: https://fas.org/irp/agency/doj/lei.pdf.

Cohen, K., Johansson, F., Kaati, L., & Mork, J. C. (2014). Detecting linguistic markers for radical violence in social media. *Terrorism and Political Violence, 26*(1), 246–256.

Coyne, J. (2014). *The role of strategic intelligence in law enforcement: Policing transnational organized crime in Canada, the United Kingdom and Australia*. New York: Springer.

Coyne, J. W., & Bell, P. (2011). The role of strategic intelligence in anticipating transnational organised crime: A literary review. *International Journal of Law, Crime and Justice, 39*(1), 60–78.

Delle Donne, J., & Fortin, F. (2018). Innovation and policing: Factors influencing the adoption of social medias by members of Quebec police organizations. *Policing: A Journal of Policy and Practice*. https://doi.org/10.1093/police/pay079.

Denef, S., Kaptein, N., Bayerl, P. S., & Ramirez, L. (2012). *Best practice in police social media adaptation. EU Project COMPOSITE*.

Dupont, B. (2004). La technicisation du travail policier: Ambivalences et contradictions internes. *Criminologie, 37*(1), 107–126. https://doi.org/10.7202/008719ar.

Edwards, A., Housley, W., Williams, M., Sloan, L., & Williams, M. (2013). Digital social research, social media and the sociological imagination: Surrogacy, augmentation and re-orientation. *International Journal of Research Methodology, 16*(3), 245–260.

Estellés-Arolas, E. (2020). Using crowdsourcing for a safer society: When the crowd rules. *European Journal of Criminology*, First Published April 23, https://doi.org/10.1177/1477370820916439.

Faith, T., & Bekir, C. (2015). Police use of technology to fight against crime. *European Scientific Journal, 11*(10), 286–296.

Fallik, S. W., Deuchar, R., Crichlow, V. J., & Hodges, H. (2020). Policing through social media: A qualitative exploration. *International Journal of Police Science & Management*, 146135572091194. https://doi.org/10.1177/1461355720911948.

Frank, R. G., & Cheng, C. (2011). *Social media sites: New fora for criminal, communication, and investigation opportunities*. https://www.semanticscholar.org/paper/Social-Media-Sites%3A-New-Fora-for-Criminal%2C-and-Frank-Cheng/ba46587e7f21b726a92aae47eed216d50462d0c0.

Frank, R., Cheng, C., & Pun, V. (2011). *Social media sites: New fora for criminal, communication, and investigation opportunities*. Ottawa, ON: Public Safety Canada.

Ghajar-Khosravi, S., Kwantes, P., Derbentseva, N., & Huey, L. (2016). Quantifying salient concepts discussed in social media content: A case study using Twitter content written by radicalized youth. *Journal of Terrorism Research, 7*(2), 79–90.

Graham, R. (2016). Inter-ideological mingling: White extremist ideology entering the mainstream on Twitter. *Sociological Spectrum, 36*(1), 24–36.

Hadlington, L., Lumsden, K., Black, A., & Ferra, F. (2018). A qualitative exploration of police officers' experiences, challenges, and perceptions of cybercrime. *Policing: A Journal of Policy and Practice*. https://doi.org/10.1093/police/pay090.

HMIC. (2011). *The rules of engagement: A review of the August 2011 disorders*. London: HMIC.

Hofmann, R., & Feltes, T. (2020). Social media for community oriented policing: Best practices from around the world and future challenges. *European Law Enforcement Research Bulletin* Nr. 18 (Winter 2019).

Horsman, G., Ginty, K., & Cranner, P. (2017). Identifying offenders on Twitter: A law enforcement practitioner guide. *Digital Investigation, 23*, 63–74.

International Association of Chiefs of Police. (2017). *2016 Law enforcement use of social media survey*. From: http://www.theiacp.org/Portals/0/documents/pdfs/2016-law-enforcement-use-of-social-media-survey.pdf.

Joseph, K., Wei, W., & Carley, K. M. (2017, February). Girls rule, boys drool: Extracting semantic and affective stereotypes from Twitter. In *Proceedings of the 2017 ACM Conference on Computer Supported Cooperative Work and Social Computing* (pp. 1362–1374).

Krizan, L. (1999). *Intelligence essentials for everyone*. Washington, DC: Joint Military Intelligence College.

Kumar, A. S., & Singh, S. (2013). *Detection of user cluster with suspicious activity in online social networking sites*. 2013 2nd International Conference on Advanced Computing, Networking and Security, 220–225. https://doi.org/10.1109/ADCONS.2013.17.

Lane, J., Ramirez, F. A., & Pearce, K. E. (2018). Guilty by visible association: Socially mediated visibility in gang prosecutions. *Journal of Computer-Mediated Communication, 23*(6), 354–369. https://doi.org/10.1093/jcmc/zmy019.

Leman-Langlois, S. (2013). *Technocrime : technology, crime and social control*. New York: Routledge.

Lemieux, F. (2008). Vers un renseignement criminel de qualité. *Traité de sécurité intérieure*, 290–299.

Marsico, E. M., Jr. (2009). Social networking websites: Are MySpace and Facebook the fingerprints of the twenty-first century? *Widener LJ, 19,* 967.

Martin, G. (2018). *Crime, media and culture*. New York, NY: Routledge.

McKeown, S., Maxwell, D., Azzopardi, L., & Glisson, W. B. (2014, August). Investigating people: A qualitative analysis of the search behaviours of open-source intelligence analysts. In *Proceedings of the 5th Information Interaction in Context Symposium* (pp. 175–184).

Moore, K. (2020). *The use and effectiveness of law enforcement social media sites.* Master: University of Oklahoma.

Murphy, J. P., & Fontecilla, A. (2013). Social media evidence in government investigations and criminal proceedings: A frontier of new legal issues. *Richmond Journal of Law and Technology, 19*(3), 1–30.

Newnham, J., & Bell, P. (2012). Social network media and political activism: A growing challenge for law enforcement. *Journal of Policing, Intelligence and Counter Terrorism, 7*(1), 36–50.

Omand, D., Bartlett, J., & Miller, C. (2012a). Introducing social media intelligence (SOCMINT). *Intelligence and National Security, 27*(6), 801–823. https://doi.org/10.1080/02684527.2012.716965.

Omand, D., Bartlett, J., & Miller, C. (2012b). *A balance between security and privacy online must be stuck (Demos).* London.

ONUDD. (2010). *Criminal intelligence. Manual for front-line law enforcement.* 1–58. Available : http://www.unodc.org/documents/organized-crime/Law-Enforcement/Criminal_Intelligence_for_Front_Line_Law_Enforcement.pdf.

Oostdijk, N., & Van Halteren, H. (2013). *Shallow parsing for recognizing threats in Dutch tweets.* Proceedings of the 2013 IEEE/ACM International Conference on Advances in Social Networks Analysis and Mining, 1034–1041. https://doi.org/10.1145/2492517.2500271.

Panagiotopoulos, P., Bigdeli, A. Z., & Sams, S. (2014). Citizen–government collaboration on social media: The case of Twitter in the 2011 riots in England. *Government Information Quarterly, 31*(3), 349–357.

Procter, R., Crump, J., Karstedt, S., Voss, A., & Cantijoch, M. (2013). Reading the riots: What were the police doing on Twitter? *Policing and Society, 23*(4), 413–436.

Purenne, A., & Wuilleumier, A. (2011). L'introduction des technologies de surveillance dans le travail policier. Facteur de changement ou de réassurance ? *Droit et Cultures. Revue Internationale Interdisciplinaire, 61,* 119–130.

Rainie, H., & Wellman, B. (2012). *Networked: The new social operating system* (Vol. 419). Cambridge, MA: Mit Press.

Rasheed, H., Khan, F. H., Bashir, S., & Fatima, I. (2019). Detecting suspicious discussion on online forums using data mining. In Dans I. S. Bajwa, F. Kamareddine, & A. Costa (Éds.), *Intelligent technologies and applications* (pp. 262–273). Springer. https://doi.org/10.1007/978-981-13-6052-7_23.

Ratcliffe, J. (2009). *Strategic thinking in criminal intelligence: 2nd edition.* Sydney, Australia: Federation Press.

Renard, B. (2011). La technologie ADN dans la justice pénale : Une illustration de la recomposition de l'action de la justice par la science, la technique et l'expertise ? *Droit et cultures. Revue internationale interdisciplinaire, 61*, Article 61. http://journals.openedition.org/droitcultures/2467.

Reuter, C., Kaufhold, M. A., Spahr, F., Spielhofer, T., & Hahne, A. S. (2020). Emergency service staff and social media—A comparative empirical study of the attitude by emergency services staff in Europe in 2014 and 2017. *International Journal of Disaster Risk Reduction, 46* (October 2018). https://doi.org/10.1016/j.ijdrr.2020.101516.

Reyes, A., Rosso, P., & Veale, T. (2012). A multidimensional approach for detecting irony in Twitter. *Language Resources & Evaluation, 47*(1), 239–268.

Rodriguez, R. M. J. (2014). *A spatial analysis of Boko Haram and Al-Shabaab references in social media in Sub-Saharan Africa* [Thesis]. http://mars.gmu.edu/handle/1920/9110.

Scassa, T. (2017). Law enforcement in the age of big data and surveillance intermediaries: Transparency challenges. *SCRIPT-Ed, 14*(2), 239–284. https://doi.org/10.2966/scrip.140217.239.

Trottier, D. (2012). Policing social media. *Canadian Review of Sociology/Revue Canadienne de Sociologie, 49*(4), 411–425. https://doi.org/10.1111/j.1755-618X.2012.01302.x.

Trottier, D. (2016). *Social media as surveillance: Rethinking visibility in a converging world*. Farnham: Ashgate Press.

Walsh, J. P., & O'Connor, C. (2019). Social media and policing: A review of recent research. *Sociology Compass, 13*(1), 1–14. https://doi.org/10.1111/soc4.12648.

Weaver, S. (2013). A rhetorical discourse analysis of online anti-muslim and anti-semitic jokes. *Ethnic and Racial Studies, 36*(3), 483–499.

Wei, W., Joseph, K., Liu, H., & Carley, K. (2016). Exploring characteristics of suspended users and network stability on Twitter. *Social Network Analysis and Mining, 6*(51), 1–18.

Wu, S., Hofman, J. M., Mason, W. A. & Watts, D. J. (2011, March). *Who says what to whom on Twitter.* Article presented at the International World Wide Web Conference, Hyderabad, India. Retrieved from http://www.wwwconference.org/proceedings/www2011/proceedings/p705.pdf.

14

"Doing Right": Police Ethics in an Age of Reform

James J. Nolan, Timothy Parsons, and Frank Crispino

Introduction

The rule of law is the cornerstone of democracy, and the police are tasked with preserving it even in difficult circumstances. In many places today, there are growing concerns about the police for a variety of reasons. For

J. J. Nolan (✉)
Department of Sociology & Anthropology, West Virginia University, Morgantown, WV, USA
e-mail: jim.nolan@mail.wvu.edu

T. Parsons
Centre for Advanced Policing, School of Justice Studies, Liverpool John Moores University, Liverpool, UK
e-mail: T.F.Parsons@ljmu.ac.uk

F. Crispino
Université Du Québec à Trois-Rivières (UQTR), Trois-Rivières, QC, Canada
e-mail: frank.crispino@uqtr.ca

J. J. Nolan et al. (eds.), *Policing in an Age of Reform*, Palgrave's Critical Policing Studies,
https://doi.org/10.1007/978-3-030-56765-1_14

example, the police in the United Kingdom are under increasing strain due to deep funding cuts that have diminished the forces by nearly 20 percent. These cuts have likely contributed to rising violent crime rates, such as knife attacks and gun violence, at a time when crime overall in the UK is in decline. There seems to be a huge disconnect in what citizens, MPs and the Home Office expect from the police (Syal, 2018).

In France the police and gendarmerie are responsible for internal security. In recent years, a growing frustration with the national government has sparked violent protests over issues like high taxes, pension reform, a soaring cost of living and a popular view that the government seems out of touch with the average person (Samuel, 2018). In their efforts to quell these protests and restore the rule of law, the police in France have increasingly been accused of using excessive force.

Similarly, excessive force by the police is a growing concern in the United States. Each year, about 1000 citizens are shot and killed by the police.[1] Although the American police have had a long history of violence and conflict that includes the enforcement of slavery and whites-only segregation laws, the recent shooting deaths of unarmed African American men have fuelled the Black Lives Matter[2] movement and ignited widespread protests and calls for police reform. In each of these countries—the UK, France and the USA—the police struggle to do the right things in the right ways. But, in times of change such as these, how do the police navigate the competing demands and expectations in order to know clearly what the right things are and why they are right? In this chapter, we try to answer this two-pronged question in a way that extends beyond intuition and habit. We begin with a look at the ethical principles and moral standards that currently guide the police in these three

[1]The source of information on police shootings is the *Washington Post*, https://www.washingtonpost.com/graphics/investigations/police-shootings-database/.

[2]The Black Lives Matter (BLM) movement initially formed in 2013 in response to the acquittal of George Zimmerman in the shooting death of Trayvon Martin. BLM was the epicenter of protest following the police killing of Michael Brown in Ferguson, Missouri and Eric Garner in New York City. It has helped organize street protests in these and many other US cities following the deaths of unarmed African American men at the hands of the police. The message from BLM reformers easily connected to the chronic discontent many people felt about the police due to decades of aggressive enforcement in their local communities (Levin & Nolan, 2017).

countries. We then explore the strengths and limitations of these ethical codes from a philosophical perspective. We then move beyond philosophy to find empirical measures of ethics that may be more effective as a guide for police in these changing times.

We think it is important to note at the beginning of this chapter that the recorded history of moral philosophy extends nearly 3000 years. Each generation of philosophers has attempted to find ways, beyond hunch or tradition, to know what is "right". Out of necessity, we draw only on a small fragment of this rich history and must ignore the rest. In doing so, we acknowledge that our analysis has limits. But, the importance of this chapter is that it begins to untangle some of the philosophical knots in ethical codes that can hide opportunities for growth and change in a profession that is both essential and constantly evolving.

Police Codes of Ethics

In order to prepare police officers for their challenging careers, they are generally provided with a code of ethics to help them make the right decisions and behave morally, both on and off duty. But do these codes really help the police officers do the right things? Let's first take a look at the police codes of ethics in three countries considered here to see if we can gain more insights into the strengths and limitations of each.

Policing principle 2.1 of the Code of Ethics published by the College of Policing in the United Kingdom is simply this: Do the right thing in the right way (College of Policing, 2014). In the UK, ethical behaviour is believed to come from "…values, beliefs, attitudes and knowledge that guide the judgements of each individual" (College of Policing, 2014, p. iv). Doing the right thing in the right way is tied closely to Sir Robert Peel's notion that the police are working on behalf of the community as "a citizen in uniform" in order to "secure and maintain public respect (College of Policing, 2014, p. v). The expectations of the police were codified in 1995 in the "Principles of Public Life" (Committee on Standards in Public Life, 1995). From these codes the UK constructed nine principles that were intended to guide police behaviour and influence police culture. These nine principles are: accountability, fairness, honesty, integrity, leadership, objectivity, openness, respect and selflessness. The nine policing principles, then, form ten standards of professional behaviour which are written in the form of an oath, such as "I will be honest and act with integrity at all times and will not compromise my position" and "I will act with fairness and impartiality. I will not discriminate unlawfully or unfairly" (p. 4). The full list of ethical policing principles and moral standards are described in Table 14.1.

France: The Police and Gendarmerie Code of Ethics

The code of ethics for the police and gendarmerie in France is slightly different from the UK code. Ethical principles in France are presented as rules that align with Constitution and international treaties, such as the European Convention for the protection of Human Rights and Fundamental Freedoms, and in the nation's laws and regulations. The police and gendarmerie, both in the Ministry of the Interior, are security forces tasked with "...defending national institutions and the national interest, upholding the rule of law, maintaining law and order, safeguarding people and property" (Ministry of the Interior, France, 2014, p. 1). The police as the civil force and the gendarmerie a military force both share a common code of ethics in carrying out their law enforcement missions (p. 2). Essential to this mission are the ethical principles to obedience within a chain of command, professional secrecy and confidentiality, integrity, sound judgement, impartiality, dignified behaviour on and off duty and the avoidance of conflicts of interest. With regard to their relationships with the public, the code requires the police and gendarmerie to be courteous and respectful. They should carry out their duties in uniform; conduct identity checks without harming the dignity of those being checked; show respect for those who are arrested; use only the amount of force necessary; assist people in danger, including victims of crime; show respect for people's privacy; and treat informants respectfully. In addition, officers of both forces must keep their philosophic, religious and political beliefs confidential while performing

Table 14.1 Summary of nine police principles and ten standards of professional behaviour for the police in England and Wales

Policing principle	Ethical requirement	Standards of professional behaviour	Moral oath
Accountability	You are answerable for your decisions, actions and omissions	Honesty and integrity	I will be honest and act with integrity at all times and will not compromise or abuse my position
Fairness	You treat people fairly	Authority, respect and courtesy	I will act with self-control and tolerance... I will use my powers and authority lawfully and proportionately... respect the rights of all individuals
Honesty	You are truthful and trustworthy	Equality and diversity	I will act with fairness and impartiality. I will not discriminate unlawfully or unfairly
Integrity	You always do the right thing	Use of force	I will only use force... to the extent that it is necessary, proportionate and reasonable in all the circumstances
Leadership	You lead by example	Orders and instructions	I will ... give and carry out lawful orders only and will abide by Police Regulations

(continued)

Table 14.1 (continued)

Policing principle	Ethical requirement	Standards of professional behaviour	Moral oath
Objectivity	You make choices on evidence and your best professional judgement	Duties and responsibilities	I will be diligent in the exercise of my duties and responsibilities
Openness	You are open and transparent	Confidentiality	I will treat information with respect and access or disclose it only in the proper course of my duties
Respect	You treat everyone with respect	Fitness for work	I will ensure, when on duty or at work, that I am fit to carry out my responsibilities
Selflessness	You act in the public interest	Conduct	I will behave in a manner…which does not bring discredit on the police service or undermine public confidence in policing
		Challenging and reporting improper behaviour	I will report, challenge or take action against the conduct of colleagues which has fallen below the standards of professional behaviour

Source College of Policing (2014)

official duties. These requirements extend off-duty to the gendarmerie due to its military status.

Although the first title in this code of ethics is "General Principles", they are actually presented as statutory obligations. For example, the first guiding principle under the subtitle Chain of Command states the following: "The duly empowered commanding officer makes decisions, gives orders, and sees that they are carried out" (p. 2). Further, it instructs commanding officers to "...create and implement suitable training for personnel, in particular as regards respect for people's physical integrity and dignity and concerning civil liberties" (p. 3). With respect to general ethical principles such as the requirement to use "sound judgement" it is tied closely to legal rather than ethical standards. For example, the police and gendarmerie are "...to take into account in all circumstances the nature of the risks and threats of every situation that they have to face and the time they have to react, to choose the best *legal* solution to resolve it" (p. 4, emphasis added).

United States: The Police Code of Ethics

There are more than 18,000 state and local police agencies in the United States, many whose codes of ethics were modelled after the International Association of Chiefs of Police (IACP) code of ethics which was adopted by that organisation in 1957 at its annual conference. Essentially, the code of ethics is written in the form of an oath of office. It begins with the following sentence:

> As a law enforcement officer, my fundamental duty is to serve the community; to safeguard lives and properly protect the innocent against deception, the weak against oppression or intimidation and the peaceful against violence or disorder; and to respect the constitutional rights of all to liberty, equality, and justice. (IACP, 1957)[3]

This code of ethics continues with a series of personal pledges intended to guide officers in making ethical decisions while on and off duty. Examples of this include the promise not to bring discredit to the police agency, to always maintain a "courageous calm", to be mindful of the

---

[3]Notice how the first line of the code recasts the police officer as a law enforcement officer. This may seem like a small shift, but this is, in significant part, why policing in the United States has become so focused on enforcement as its raison d'etre (see Chapter 2).

welfare of others, to be honest in thought and deed, to be obedient to laws and rules of department and to be unbiased and relentless in the prosecution of criminals (IACP, 1957). The final line in the code of ethics is this: "I will constantly strive to achieve these objectives and ideals, dedicating myself before God to my chosen profession …law enforcement" (IACP, 1957).

In all three of these codes of ethics, whether presented as a guiding principle or behavioural standard, as in the UK, a rule or obligation, as in France or as a professional oath, as in the United States, the "rightness" of behaviour is located in the principle or obligation itself rather than in the consequences of action it promotes. Focusing on the rightness of an ethical principle without attention to the circumstances in which it occurs or the consequences of action can quickly lead to self-contradictory knots as Plato describes in *Republic* by way of a dialogue between Socrates and Cephalus.

> Socrates to Cephalus: "But what about this thing you mentioned, doing right? Shall we say it is, without qualification, truthfulness and giving back anything one has borrowed from someone? Or might the performance of precisely these actions sometimes be right, but sometimes wrong? This is the kind of thing I mean. I'm sure everyone would agree that if you'd borrowed weapons from a friend who was perfectly sane, but he went insane and asked for the weapons back, you shouldn't give them back, and if you give them back you wouldn't be doing right, and neither would someone who was ready to tell the whole truth to someone like that". (Plato, 1993, p. 8)

An ethics that obliges action based on a rule or principle without regard to the circumstances or consequences is sometimes referred to as deontological ethics.[4] In the dialogue between Socrates and Cephalus truthfulness and returning something one has borrowed are ethical principles against which we might judge a person's behaviour. If they don't tell the truth or they don't return borrowed items to the rightful owner,

[4] The term deontological is derived from the Greek word "deon" for duty and "logos" for science. From this perspective the moral goodness of an action is found in a characteristic of the act itself rather than in its consequences.

would we judge them as immoral? The ten commandments are also examples of a deontological ethics, where morality is judged by compliance to these rules. But, as Plato demonstrates, this type of ethics can quickly lead to problems when we modify the circumstances in which it occurs. For example, the standards of professional behaviour in the UK include honesty at all times, but what about in situations in which an officer is trying to infiltrate a suspected terrorist organisation? Would lying be unethical for officers trying to conceal their identity in order to protect the country? The ethical code in the UK also requires officers to follow lawful orders and to never discriminate, but suppose the policies and practices of the government or of the police department themselves are discriminatory? Should officers follow lawful orders that discriminate? These same dilemmas arise in France where the police code of ethics requires officers to follow orders yet use sound judgement. How should they decide what is morally right when they know the orders are lawful, but don't believe they are sound? Similar problems arise in the US where the code of ethics promotes intense law enforcement and the "...relentless prosecution of criminals". But what should the police do when they discover that their tactics are counterproductive and can actually make places less safe?

Moral philosophers sometimes avoid these traps by broadening the focus of ethics from the rule or act itself to the outcomes of those rules and acts, sometimes referred to as utilitarianism, consequentialism or teleological ethics. These ethical codes look at the outcomes of behaviours and search for empirical evidence of right and good rather than simply rely on the actor's state of mind or what "feels right". The concept of *summum bonum*, or life's greatest good, is sometimes used to refer to the desired end, i.e. the ultimate good, which would help an actor or observer determine if the act or rule was actually good. Once the "greatest good" is defined, a moral action is one that leads to its realisation. An immoral act leads us away from it. Ethics, then, is the theory of right conduct and the good life and morals is the practice of these things (Sahakain & Sahakain, 1966, p. 31).

As demands on the police are continually changing, we find ourselves searching for an ethics to guide the practice of policing in this era of reform, one that is unburdened by changing circumstances or evolving social conditions. What is the ultimate good for the person or the community or the nation at which we should aim? What is the philosophical and empirical evidence of its goodness? Once these questions can be answered, then acts which achieve these desired ends—or which align with rules aimed at achieving it—can now be viewed as "doing right". But, there are difficulties and dangers inherent in this approach as well as we shall see below.

Plato's Cave

Our total immersion in a culture that shapes the way we see things makes us unwitting prisoners as Plato described in his allegory of the cave. Again, in the form of a dialogue, he asks us to imagine people born into captivity and living deep inside an underground cave. Since birth, these prisoners have been physically restrained in such a way that they cannot move their heads. All they can see is the wall directly in front of them. Behind the prisoners, a huge fire burns. The light from the fire casts shadows of their captors and the artefacts they carry on the wall. The prisoners can hear their captors talking and they attribute these sounds to the shadows they see on the wall. The shadows are the only reality the prisoners know and have ever known. Since they have always been in captivity, they do not realise they are imprisoned and that the shadows are distorted representations of reality rather than reality itself. Plato asks us to imagine that one day a prisoner is suddenly set free. As he is released and led away from his position among the other prisoners, he turns around and sees the fire and objects that cast the shadow for the first time. The light hurts his eyes and he has difficulty comprehending what is in front of him. He is told that all the images he thought were real actually had no substance, and what he is seeing now for the first time is *reality*. As he is led out of the cave, his eyes slowly adjust to the light and the objects now in front of him slowly come into focus. Now seeing things as they actually are, the freed prisoner looks to the heavenly bodies and theorises that the sun is the source of the seasons and all that exists. As he takes all of this in, the enlightened prisoner thinks back on what used to pass for knowledge in the cave and reflects on the activities and skills that brought prestige and credit among the prisoners. These things are meaningless now in light of what he has just discovered.

Then, Plato asks us to imagine that the prisoner is eventually returned to his place in the cave where he can no longer interpret things as quickly and efficiently as he once had. He makes a fool of himself in completing tasks that would have previously earned him praise. The other prisoners recognise this change and see that he has been damaged. They are outraged at what has happened to this poor person and swear that they would kill anyone who tried to force them "up there" (Plato, 1993, pp. 240–243).

The Policing Cave

There are many lessons from the allegory of the cave that apply to the ethics of policing. Plato suggests that we are all born into captivity. We are imprisoned in a place on a planet by a culture and social structure, and yet we are barely aware we are captives. We were all born on a rotating earth and so the sun appears to rise. In everyday life, no one thinks to question the reality of a rising sun, even though it does not actually rise as it appears. Similarly, our social world appears so natural to us that we would never question—or think to question—the reality of the images and labels we see and use daily. But, as Plato suggests, we may be living an illusion. If we don't know what is real or true, how do the police know what is ultimately right?

"Doing right" as a police officer generally means acting in ways that align with the purpose of policing. But, when the purpose of policing is mistaken as natural rather than socially constructed, its underlying assumptions are rarely questioned. For example, in the United States the police code of ethics cast the profession of policing as "law enforcement" with a moral duty for the "relentless prosecution of criminals" (IACP, 1957). But, just as the prisoners in the cave never thought to ask if the shadows were real, the assumptions about criminals that provide the logic for the law enforcement focus are never challenged—or even thought to be challenged. Who are the criminals the police should pursue, especially if the word itself is a label imposed on some violators of the law and not others?

Outside the cave we also notice that crime rates are not randomly distributed. There are places where crime rates are extremely high and local places where criminality is virtually non-existent. There is also diversity in crime types that seem to follow social conditions of local areas. From a sociological view we can see that things like population density, racial and economic inequality, abject poverty, mixed land use,[5] and degree of urbanisation are among the structural conditions related to the variation in crime rates. In this volume (Chapter 5), Nolan and Hinkle showed how local community dynamics affect the risk of crime. Community dynamics refer to the expectations local residents have of each other and the police relating to safety in public places. Whether the police and residents meet—or fail to meet—these expectations, an atmosphere in the neighbourhood or community is created that is tightly linked to the crime rate and the risk of personal victimisation. In places where there are high levels of cohesion and trust, crime is almost non-existent. In places where residents are frustrated or in conflict with each other or with the police, crime tends to thrive. Crime and fear of crime also seem to thrive in places where residents do not know each other well but depend on the police for protection.

In the United States the police profession is recast as law enforcement. This confuses means for ends in a way that prioritises one tool among many that could be used to change the conditions associated with crime. Think about it this way: Professional carpenters would never consider themselves professional "nail hammerers". And, we would never consider paying a carpenter for hammering a thousand nails if he did not build something. The work of the police should be the same, i.e., it should build something. Criminal offenders may be actual people, but the criminal shadow cast on them in our cultural cave conceals their human identity and practical logic (Bourdieu, 1977). In the same way that our view on this spinning planet makes the sun appear to rise, our view from a spinning social world makes criminals appear to rise. The conditions

[5]Mixed land use refers to private residences co-located in neighborhoods with business establishments, government buildings, storage facilities, bus depots and other types of non-residential homes.

in local places most associated with high crime rates are unwittingly maintained, with no incentives for the police to change them. In fact, crime rates will remain relatively stable in these places until conditions change regardless of the number of people arrested.

A Consequentialist View of Police Ethics

From a consequentialist perspective, we must broaden the police code of ethics by connecting ethical principles and moral behaviours to some desired outcome. At the outset of this chapter, we briefly described the conditions that put the police in the United Kingdom, France and United States at odds with the government, the community or segments of the community. These conditions are the impetus for police reform. We have also shown how difficult it can be to define the ultimate good, i.e. the consequences at which police might aim. As prisoners inside a cultural tradition, we must first free ourselves from intuition and habit and look for empirical evidence of what is good.

Nolan and Hinkle (Chapter 5) argued that the Strong community should be the desired end of all police activity. Strong communities were defined as having low levels of crime, high levels of cohesion and trust among residents and trusting relations with police. If the Strong neighbourhood is the preferred outcome, i.e., the *summum bonum*, the greatest good, at which all police work is aimed, then the probability of a police officer doing the right thing is now a function of an ethical principle and moral behaviour that is conditioned by this desired end. For clarity, this can be expressed symbolically as the conditional probability $P(AB|C)$, where

P = Probability
A = Ethical principle
B = Moral standard
AB = Ethical principle AND Moral standard = doing the right thing
C = *Summum Bonum*, the greatest good, the desired outcome of policing.

Although we are not actually trying to calculate the probability of a police officer doing the right thing, we are using these symbols to express the probability of doing right as the product of an ethical principle (A) and a moral standard (B) that are conditioned by a desired end, i.e. the *summon bonum*, i.e. the greatest good. An ethical principle alone (A) or moral standards of behaviours alone (B) may not help the police officers do the right things, particularly in times of change when the right things are cast as obligations with no consideration for circumstances or consequences. There are many examples of law enforcement initiatives, such as stop and frisk, broken windows policing and the war on drugs that align with ethical codes and moral standards of police behaviour, but whose consequences weakened community relations and trust in the police, and thus overall safety (Hinkle & Weisburd, 2008). The claim by Kevin Davis, the police commissioner in the city of Baltimore, following the release of a United States Department of Justice investigation of widespread abuse that the majority of the police do the right things, relied only on his observation that most behaviours conform to ethical standards but with no consideration to the consequences of those behaviours (Davis, 2016). In an age of conflict and controversy over police behaviour, obligations to a deontological code of ethics that ignore outcomes in its moral calculus are bound to exacerbate problems both for the police and the community. On the other hand, a consequentialist code of ethics as we suggest would render law enforcement activities immoral if they weaken community ties, appear widely unjust and destroy trust in the police.

P(AB|C) in Practice: An Example from Wilmington, Delaware, USA

In 2014, the police in Wilmington, Delaware in the United States had assigned several officers to a particular neighbourhood for the purpose of reducing crime (Nolan, 2016). The neighbourhood had a small organisation of residents who were concerned about rising crime rates. They were especially concerned about gun violence, since a popular corner store had recently been robbed and the owner shot and killed. The officers assigned to the project had an end in mind for the work they were doing. They wanted to build strong relationships in a community that had become fearful and isolated because of rising crime. The "strong neighbourhood" ideal (Chapter 5) was the goal they had in mind.

Interest in the project among residents had grown over the first few months as the police were highly visible in the community and were reaching out to residents to ask them about local problems. Over a short period of time, a growing number of people from the neighbourhood began showing up at monthly meetings to get involved. At one meeting, several long-time residents of the neighbourhood reported minor illegal drug activity at an apartment house that had become a major nuisance to the community. The residents in one apartment in the building were regularly smoking marijuana inside and the odour of the drug penetrated the walls and was recognisable throughout the building. From a police perspective this was a very minor drug violation especially in light of the major drug sales and gun violence that was going on in the community. There had been repeated complaints to police from residents in the community for more than a year, but they were never addressed. This created a great deal of frustration for residents as the police didn't seem to care. So, at this public meeting in the neighbourhood the police were asked to take action immediately. It is likely that the problem was presented at a public meeting in this way to test the will of the police to see if they were serious about helping the community solve problems and build relationships.

As a backdrop to this, the mission of the Wilmington Police Department and its code of police ethics cast the police first and foremost as "law enforcement officers". The expressed mission of the Wilmington Police Department, which appears on its website (https://www.wilmingtonde.gov/government/city-departments/department-of-police) is "…to raise the level of public safety through law enforcement and thereby reduce the fear and incidence of crime". The police in Wilmington also pledge a code of ethics "(w)ith no compromise for crime and with relentless prosecution of criminals, I will enforce the law…" (IACP, 1957). Given these factors, the right thing to do is clearly to enforce the law. But, conducting an investigation of a crime that occurs inside a residence takes time. Typically, these kinds of investigations are referred to special drug investigations units for follow up. But, minor crimes like the use of marijuana or even the sale of marijuana fail to reach the level of importance that would ever result in an actual investigation. In the minds of the police, there is a hierarchy of criminal conduct where the most serious crimes get the most attention. So these kinds of minor nuisance violations are really never addressed satisfactorily by the police even when they are viewed as the most problematic by the residents.

Doing the right thing was still related to the law enforcement ethical principles and moral standards (A & B), but it was now conditioned by the strong neighbourhood ideal, *the summon bonum*, the greatest good (C). With the strong neighbourhood end in mind, the police decided on a different tactic. They worked with the community organisation and a state prosecutor to write a letter to the occupants of the apartment. The letter advised the residents that there had been complaints of marijuana use in the building. In the interest of community health and safety the use of illegal drugs must stop or the police would be notified. Further, the letter invited the residents to join the community organisation and apologised in advance if they were mistaken about the source of the odour. The police delivered the letter to the residents on behalf of the community group, and the nuisance behaviour ended immediately, which is really all the neighbours wanted anyway. A law enforcement investigation and criminal prosecution is not necessary to solve the day-to-day problems in the community even if they involve illegal activity. In this case, and many like it, the deontological ethics can lead the police astray. Notice that they did not abandon the law enforcement principles and standards, but these were conditioned by the strong neighbourhood outcome at which all of their work was now aimed.

Conclusion

The police generally follow a deontological code of ethics in which behaviours are good or bad based on adherence to general ethical principles and moral standards without regard for the consequences of these behaviours. In times of change such as these, where the actions of the police are often challenged, we offer a consequentialist view in which ethical principles and moral standards of behaviour are conditioned by the desired end at which the police are aiming. In a case example in the United States, we defined the ultimate good, the *summum bonum* of policing, as the strong neighbourhood. But, we recognise that in democratic societies, the desired ends, i.e., the ultimate good of policing—whether it be a strong nation, strong community, strong neighbourhood or something altogether different—must be carefully defined, thoughtfully operationalised and fully capable of being measured rather than based solely on intuition and habits in thinking.

References

Bourdieu, P. (1977). *Outline of a theory of practice*. UK: Cambridge University Press.

College of Policing. (2014). *Code of ethics: A code of practice for the principles and standards of professional behaviour for the policing profession of England and Wales*. Retrieved from https://assets.publishing.service.gov.uk/government/uploads/system/uploads/attachment_data/file/341650/Code_of_Ethics_2014_FINAL_July14.pdf.

Committee on Standards in Public Life. (1995). *The 7 principles of public life*. Retrieved online at https://www.gov.uk/government/publications/the-7-principles-of-public-life.

Davis, K. (2016, August 17). Baltimore police commissioner: Changes are underway. *USA Today*. Retrieved from https://www.usatoday.com/story/opinion/2016/08/17/baltimore-police-commissioner-kevin-davis-editorials-debates/88911038/.

Hinkle, J. C., & Weisburd, D. (2008). The irony of broken windows policing: A micro-place study of the relationship between disorder, focused police crackdowns and fear of crime. *Journal of Criminal Justice, 36*, 503–512.

International Association of Chiefs of Police. (1957). *Law enforcement code of ethics*. Retrieved at https://www.theiacp.org/resources/law-enforcement-code-of-ethics.

Levin, J., & Nolan, J. (2017). *The violence of hate: Understanding harmful forms of bias and bigotry*, 4th edition. New York: Rowman & Littlefield.

Ministry of the Interior, France. (2014). *Code of ethics of the police and gendarmerie in France*. Retrieved at https://www.interieur.gouv.fr/…/code-deontologie-police-gendarmeie-version-anglaise.pdf.

Nolan, J. (2016). How American policing fails neighborhoods—And cops. *The Conversation*. Retrieved at https://theconversation.com/how-american-policing-fails-neighborhoods-and-cops-63302.

Plato. (1993). *Republic* (R. Waterfield, Trans.). UK: Oxford University Press.

Sahakain, W. S., & Sahakain, M. L. (1966). *Ideas of great philosophers*. New York: Barnes & Noble.

Samuel, H. (2018, December 3). French police call for army to help quell riots amid warnings of "pre revolutionary" unrest. *The Telegraph*. Retrieved at https://www.telegraph.co.uk/news/2018/12/03/french-government-holds-crisis-talks-yellow-vest-rioters-wreak/.

Syal, R. (2018, November 6). Public confidence in police damaged by cuts, report warns. *The Guardian*. Retrieved at https://www.theguardian.com/uk-news/2018/nov/07/police-public-confidence-damaged-cuts-report-warns-mps.

15

The Allegory of the Dangerous Intersection: A Structural View of Law Enforcement and Social Problems

James J. Nolan

Introduction

In May 2020 a video of Minneapolis police making an arrest went viral allowing millions of people to witness the horrifying death of George Floyd (Levenson & Cooper, 2020). Floyd, a black man, handcuffed and lying face down on the street with a white Minneapolis police officer kneeling on his neck, was struggling to stay alive. He said he couldn't breathe. He begged officers not to kill him. He called out for his mother. He died.

This incident ignited a powder keg of anger and frustration centering on police violence in general, but especially against people of colour. Demonstrations and rioting erupted in cities and towns throughout the United States and abroad. George Floyd was another casualty of

J. J. Nolan (✉)
Department of Sociology & Anthropology, West Virginia University, Morgantown, WV, USA
e-mail: jim.nolan@mail.wvu.edu

J. J. Nolan et al. (eds.), *Policing in an Age of Reform*, Palgrave's Critical Policing Studies,
https://doi.org/10.1007/978-3-030-56765-1_15

this racially charged violence, which in recent years included the high profile cases of Eric Garner[1] in New York City, Tamir Rice[2] in Cleveland, Freddy Gray[3] in Baltimore, LaQuan McDonald[4] in Chicago, Antwon Rose[5] in East Pittsburgh, Michael Brown[6] in Ferguson, Philando Castille[7] in Minnesota, Walter Scott[8] in South Carolina, Elijah McClain[9] in Colorado, and many more.

The death of George Floyd was particularly alarming and resulted in widespread calls to defund the police. Based on arguments made by Alex Vitale (2017), reformers now called to cut police budgets so that resources and services could be redirected to those better prepared to deal with social problems like homelessness, drug addiction, mental illness, and the myriad of non-crime issues that regularly come to the attention of the police. It is often assumed that these problems have roots in the decisions and failings of individuals. Although it is true that individuals are involved, it is rarely the case that they are the *root cause* of the problem. We know this because these problems arise at high rates in certain places and low rates in others. For example, mass shootings do not happen at the same rate around the world as they do in the United States. Does this mean that the most violent people in the world just happen to live in the United States? Suicide is also found more often in some places rather than others. It is not likely that the most depressed people end up living together in certain towns, cities, or countries. Rather, it is

---

[1] https://time.com/3618279/eric-garner-chokehold-crime-staten-island-daniel-pantaleo/.

[2] https://www.usatoday.com/in-depth/news/2020/06/22/tamir-rices-mother-fights-racism-america-and-police-brutality/3116710001/.

[3] https://www.cbsnews.com/news/arrest-to-death-what-happened-to-freddie-gray/.

[4] https://www.cnn.com/2019/10/10/us/chicago-inspector-general-laquan-mcdonald-shooting/index.html.

[5] https://www.cbsnews.com/news/antwon-rose-shooting-michael-rosfeld-not-guilty-criminal-homicide-live-updates-today-2019-03-22/.

[6] https://www.independent.co.uk/news/world/americas/michael-brown-shooting-what-happened-in-ferguson-10450257.html.

[7] https://www.aclu.org/blog/racial-justice/two-years-after-police-killing-philando-castile-justice-continues-be-denied.

[8] https://www.theguardian.com/us-news/2017/dec/07/michael-slager-walter-scott-second-degree-murder.

[9] https://abcnews.go.com/US/wireStory/thousands-gather-denver-protest-elijah-mcclains-death-71495180.

more likely that there is something going on in the particular place that explains these high rates. Now, this does not mean that individuals are not responsible for their actions. Rather, the *source* of these problems is more likely located in the social context. As long as things stay the same in a given context, the social problems will likely continue at the same rate.

Crime and violence are "structured." This means they happen in regular patterns that are predictable. Society is also structured. Poor neighbourhoods tend to stay poor and wealthy neighbourhoods tend to thrive in regular ways. Our interaction patterns are also structured in that we meet each other in public (or online) in predictable ways. Social institutions such as governments, legal systems, economies, and criminal justice systems also have stable patterns in the way they are organised and work. They appear natural, and so their underlying beliefs and assumptions are never challenged even when outcomes contradict those beliefs. For example, the assumption that "criminals" are the source of the crime problem is embedded in the law enforcement approach to policing (Chapter 2). The belief that 10% of the people cause 90% of the crimes supports an effort by the police to catch and arrest this 10%. But, law enforcement efforts can tend to make people feel less safe. When the police come into neighbourhoods on a regular basis as law enforcers, residents may resent them and despise their presence. Still, regardless of this outcome the basic beliefs that sustain the system tend to hold. In this sense it is sacred (Chapter 2). Efforts to challenge these sacred beliefs are often met with vigorous resistance. Therefore, the allegory of the dangerous intersection provides a way to explore sacred beliefs about causes of crime and appropriate responses based on these beliefs. It highlights the structured nature of social problems. The traffic accident at the intersection itself is a metaphor for many types of social problems, including crime, violence, drug abuse, domestic violence, among others. Figure 15.1 is a typical police drawing of a traffic accident at an intersection. The focus of police attention at the accident scene is the point of impact and the circumstances found at the intersection itself. Decisions about right and wrong occur there. The police are law enforcers and so they apply their understanding of the law to their observations at the

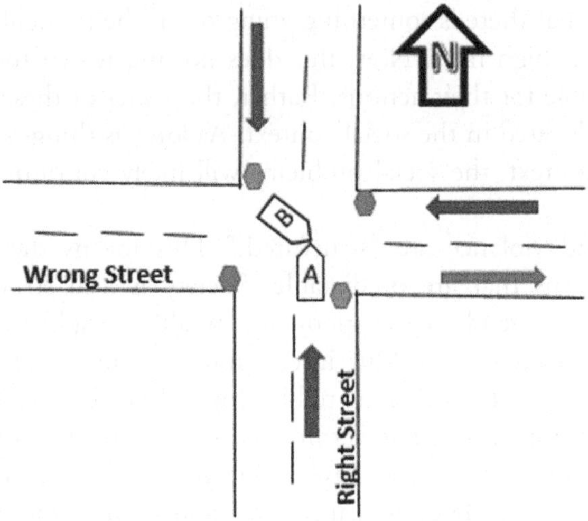

Fig. 15.1 Officer Hume's depiction of the traffic accident

intersection. However, as the reader will see, the sum of seemingly unbiased decisions at the intersection can lead to discriminatory results and serve to exacerbate other structural problems. In this allegory, three levels of structure are considered: (1) structured inequality (wealthy and poor), (2) structured patterns of interactions shaped by inequality (including advantages and disadvantages), and (3) the structured nature of the law enforcement approach to policing and the way this is internalized in officers as "common sense."

The Allegory of the Dangerous Intersection[10]

On June 20, 1995, Officer David Hume, a young police officer with 5 years on the job, is assigned to work in a new police district. He has heard a lot about this new assignment from other officers in the department and he hopes to be able to contribute to making this district safer. He knows there are "hot spots" in certain neighbourhoods in the district

[10]The idea of an allegory to explore the sociological problems in American policing was first introduced earlier by this author in Levin and Nolan (2017).

where crime and violence thrive. Residents in these places hate the police and "stop snitching" is the message from the streets. These are places where the heroics of policing happen. They are the front line in the war on drugs and crime where the image of the thin blue line between order and chaos becomes reality. Officer Hume also realises there are "good" neighbourhoods in this new district where little crime exists and where the residents really like the police. Although he is not racist in any way, he notices that the good neighbourhoods are predominately white and the bad neighbourhoods are primarily black. People in the good neighbourhoods are fearful because of the high levels of crime and violence that occur in their district. They know that the violence is mostly located in the bad neighbourhoods where gun violence is high and where "black on black" violence is the norm, but they are still afraid.

At 4:00 p.m., as he enters the boundaries of his district for the first time, the dispatcher sends Officer Hume to the intersection of Right and Wrong Streets to investigate a traffic accident.

Insights from Officer David Hume

Upon his arrival to the accident scene, Officer Hume observes two cars in the middle of the intersection. He learns from witnesses that both vehicles, vehicle A heading north and vehicle B heading south but turning eastbound, had a green light as they entered the intersection. Officer Hume easily determines that vehicle B, which was making a left onto Wrong Street, caused the collision. In his police report, he wrote the following: "While turning eastbound on Wrong Street, vehicle B failed to yield the right of way to Vehicle A which was traveling northbound on Right Street. The driver of vehicle B was issued traffic citation B9580192 for this violation of the state traffic code." Officer Hume submitted a diagram of the accident scene which is presented here as Fig. 15.1.

As a standard practice in law enforcement, Officer Hume had the name of driver B run through national and local criminal databases. Central dispatch advised him that the driver of vehicle B was wanted on a court-issued warrant for failure to appear. Driver B had been issued a traffic citation several months ago for the exact same offense, "failure to yield to oncoming traffic." When he failed to show up for court, the judge issued a warrant for his arrest. Officer Hume placed the driver of vehicle B in handcuffs and transported him to police headquarters for booking. During a search of vehicle B, Officer Hume found a small quantity of marijuana in the glove compartment. He booked driver B for possession of marijuana, the court-issued warrant, and the new traffic charge.

After booking driver B, Officer Hume, whose new patrol assignment includes the intersection of Right and Wrong streets, was curious about the quantity of traffic accidents that normally occur there. He checked the call-center database and learned there are many accidents at this intersection. He could see that it was a real problem in the district. He decided he would be "proactive" and do something to prevent the accidents. For an hour or so each day, Officer Hume sat at the intersection and watched several "near misses" inside the intersection. He stopped the drivers and issued summonses. To his surprise, Officer Hume found that many of the drivers were wanted for previous offenses, but mostly for failure to appear in court or failure to pay fines. He noticed that many of these aggressive drivers lived in the same neighbourhood, a notoriously bad neighbourhood, just northwest of the intersection.

Officer Hume was a welcome addition in the new police district. His supervisors regularly commended him for the quantity and quality of his law enforcement activity. His innovative thinking, analytical skills, ability to capture wanted persons and make many arrests made him one of the top officers in the district. He received ribbons and commendations for getting guns and drugs off the street too. All of this success was due to his insight about enforcing traffic laws at the dangerous intersection.

Years go by, and now Captain Hume has passed on his lessons to many other law enforcement officers. Throughout his career, he has always taken time to show junior officers how to do *good* policing. First, he shows them how to find problems by looking at the database. He calls this "data-driven policing." He also shows them how to be proactive by using a variety of law enforcement strategies to deal with problems. Further, he tells them how relatively mundane tasks like car stops for traffic violations can lead to *quality* arrests and the seizure of illegal guns and drugs. In his new role as patrol captain, he tells the new patrol officer

John Rousseau that working on problems this way will provide many opportunities to make good arrests, locate wanted people, and prevent dangerous crimes from occurring. He expresses great pride in the law enforcement profession and its role in protecting the public! Although confident in his approach and proud of his profession, Captain Hume remains vaguely aware that accidents are still occurring at high rates at the intersection.

Insights from Officer John Rousseau

One day, Officer Rousseau presented his report of an accident investigation at the intersection of Right and Wrong Streets. His drawing is slightly more expansive than those normally used to depict a traffic accident in the intersection. Instead, the drawing provides a little more detail about the conditions that lead to the accident (see Fig. 15.2).

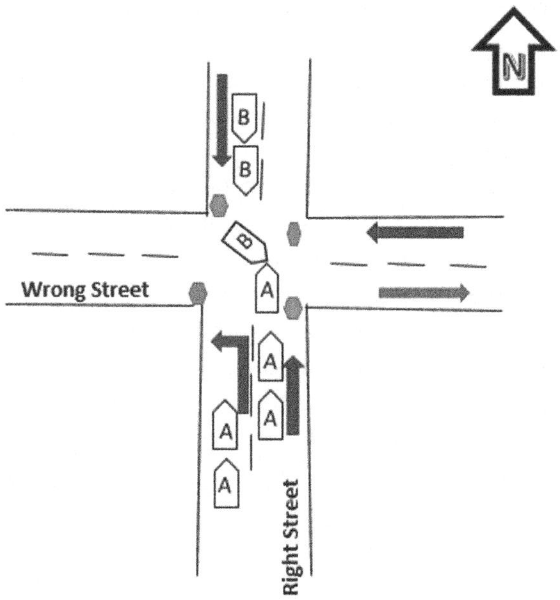

Fig. 15.2 Expanded depiction of traffic accident

Officer Rousseau had scheduled an appointment to meet with Captain Hume. He wanted to explain that traffic accidents were not simply the result of bad driving or bad choices, but they were better understood by looking at the conditions in and around the intersection. In his drawing (Fig. 15.2), Officer Rousseau showed how the one-way section of Right Street just south of the intersection forced vehicles to either turn left (westbound) or right (eastbound) on Wrong Street. Since there are no shopping areas west of this intersection, most vehicles going south on Right Street were bound to turn left—eastbound toward the shopping areas. Officer Rousseau also showed how making Right Street a two-way street south of the intersection might alleviate some of the traffic congestion. He then offered a more significant suggestion. Installing a turn arrow for vehicles entering the intersection southbound on Right Street and turning eastbound on Wrong Street would surely eliminate the number of traffic accidents that occur there.

Hume's Resistance and Rousseau's Persistence

Captain Hume agreed that Officer Rousseau's suggestions might fix the problem of traffic accidents at the dangerous intersection. However, deep down he believed that leaving things as they are would be better for law enforcement purposes. Captain Hume had personally witnessed the benefit of stopping people for violating traffic laws. Yes, these were minor offenses, but the offenders were often involved in serious criminal behavior. Some of those he had stopped for traffic violations were in possession of guns and drugs. Many were simply thugs from the bad neighbourhoods in the district. Although Officer Rousseau's suggestions would probably work to prevent traffic accidents in the intersection, they might inhibit good law enforcement practices that have worked well for capturing wanted people, taking guns and drugs off the street, and putting criminals away.

Officer Rousseau was undeterred by Captain Hume's decision to continue law enforcement practices at the intersection rather than address the underlying conditions that cause traffic accidents. Prior to becoming police officer, he had studied sociology in college. He understood how social problems like those experienced at the intersection were structured. He could see how Captain Hume's law enforcement efforts worked to "score points" and gain status in the police organisation. But, he also realised how ineffective they were for deterring traffic accidents which was the task he was trying to accomplish. While he was considering what he should do next, Officer Rousseau was dispatched once again to the intersection of Right and Wrong Streets to investigate another traffic accident. This time, he decided to make a more expansive drawing of the intersection to see if this would provide new insights. His drawing is presented as Fig. 15.3.

In the center of the intersection is a traffic accident. This scene has occurred many times over the past several decades. Vehicle B turns left onto Wrong Street in front of Vehicle A and a collision occurs. Captain Hume regularly requires a patrol car to sit at the intersection to enforce the law. He believes that poor choices and bad driving are the cause of the

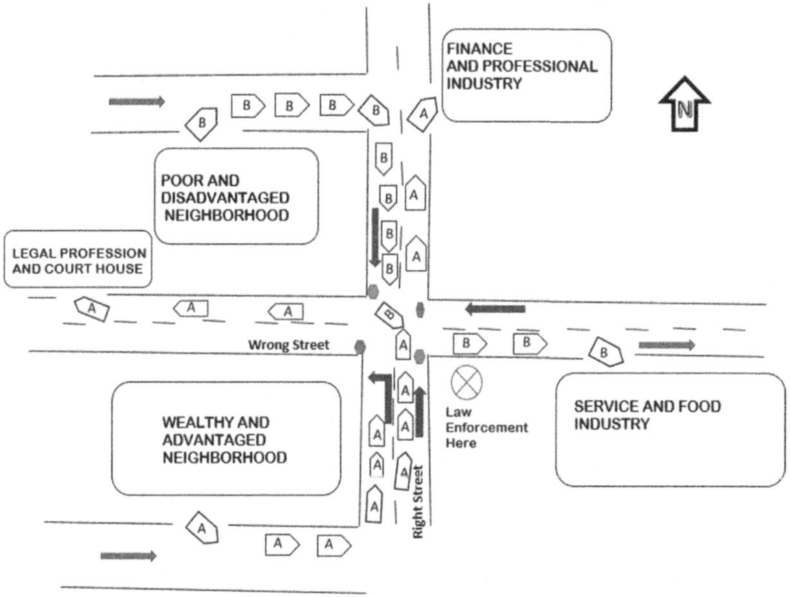

Fig. 15.3 Officer Rousseau's expanded depiction of the dangerous intersection

accidents. He also believes he can deter these bad decisions by aggressive law enforcement at the intersection. Although, the enforcement of traffic laws has not resulted in significantly fewer accidents, it has benefitted officers over the years in making more arrests.

Officer Rousseau can see clearly that the law enforcement practices at the intersection are ineffective in reducing accidents, and they also create expanded harms to the community. Police officers throughout the department know that the residents of Poor Neighbourhood distrust the police. They post "Stop Snitching" signs all around, and it is dangerous for residents to talk to the police. In addition, many people from Poor Neighbourhood are wanted on court-issued warrants because they were unable to pay the fines for traffic violations in the intersection. Many of these residents do not even go to court on the day of trial because they know they are unable to pay a fine. Over the years, the widespread inability of residents from Poor Neighbourhood to contact the police for fear of arrest on warrants or harassment has led to the emergence of a violent "code of the street" whereby residents settle disputes on their own—sometimes with guns. In addition, the people of Wealthy Neighbourhood, just southwest of the intersection, dislike the people from Poor Neighbourhood. They think of them as criminals and horrible drivers who are always in a hurry and who carelessly create accidents. In addition, many people in Poor Neighbourhood do not have insurance and a good number of drivers flee the scene of the accident before the police arrive. Regularly the police have to use physical force to take residents from Poor Neighbourhood into custody. They resist because they are angry and frustrated and completely over burdened by fines and legal expenses related to their arrests. They claim the police are racists and that they feel harassed by them. The residents of Poor Neighbourhood despise the legal system. What the police are doing does not keep them safe or secure. The police are simply not trustworthy.

Officer Rousseau met once again with Captain Hume and used his drawing to discuss the efficacy of the law enforcement efforts at this dangerous intersection. He described how the police culture, with a heavy emphasis on law enforcement, has been ineffective in preventing traffic accidents. Moreover, it has contributed to bigger problems of strained relations between the police and residents of Poor Neighbourhood and between Poor Neighbourhood and other neighbourhoods in the district, especially Wealthy Neighbourhood. Officer Rousseau described how drivers from Wealthy Neighbourhood and Poor Neighbourhood meet at the intersection in a structured way. Most of the drivers from Wealthy neighbourhood are traveling northbound on Right Street through the intersection because they work in the finance and other professional industries. The drivers from Poor Neighbourhood are turning left at the intersection and heading east on Wrong Street because they are heading to the food and service industries. These regular patterns are associated with their disparate social and economic realities in each of these two neighbourhoods. This means that the drivers from these two neighbourhoods will meet at the intersection in predictable ways, drivers from Wealthy Neighbourhood going northbound and straight through the light and drivers from Poor Neighbourhood heading southbound and turning left at the light. These patterns also affect the circumstances in which the drivers from these two neighbourhoods come to the attention of the police.

Upon hearing this information, Captain Hume's instinct was to argue that the residents of Poor Neighbourhood are careless drivers. They disobey the law and, therefore, they deserve what they get. Instead of saying this to Officer Rousseau, he thanked him for his insights, and assured him that the residents of Poor Neighbourhood had free will and could conform if they wanted to. He insisted that the law enforcement efforts would continue at the intersection.

Still undeterred, Officer Rousseau decided to conduct a survey of residents in Wealthy and Poor Neighbourhoods about their driving habits. Surprisingly, the respondents in both neighbourhoods reported committing traffic violations at similar rates. Therefore, Officer Rousseau responded to the courthouse, just one block west of the dangerous intersection, to see if he could view the traffic citation database. With the permission of court administrators, he analyzed ten years of traffic citation data. Officer Rousseau found that residents of Poor Neighbourhood were vastly overrepresented in the court system. He wondered if this discriminatory outcome was the result of *implicit bias* on the part of the police officers in the district or something else. He looked once more at the database and found that 95% of citations issued at the intersection of Right and Wrong Streets went to residents from Poor Neighbourhood. This analysis helped Officer Rousseau notice something he had not seen before. When cars collide in this intersection, the drivers from Poor Neighbourhood are always wrong and the drivers from Wealthy neighbourhood are always right. He could see more clearly how Captain Hume's law enforcement approach to the problem was not only ineffective, but actually the cause of the disparity in arrests. It also served to reinforced biases against the people in Poor Neighbourhood. Officer Rousseau recognised how his own negative view of people from Poor Neighbourhood had been influenced by the way he normally meets them in the intersection—i.e., as bad drivers and suspected criminals.

Officer Rousseau is still young and looking forward to a long, successful career in law enforcement. Unlike many of his peers, he has read much of the evidence-based research in policing. He knows the strengths and limitations of all policing strategies, particularly those aimed at deterring criminals. This was Captain Hume's original idea in the intersection many years ago. He believed he could deter accidents through aggressive law enforcement. Even though this did not actually work as imagined, the law enforcement strategy enabled good, aggressive cops to stop cars and issue citations. During these vehicle stops, the police officers were also able to run the names of drivers and passengers through the database. This often resulted in the identification of wanted persons. It also authorised them to search the vehicles for illegal contraband. This procedure enabled officers to make good lock ups. These officers were good cops and held in high regard in the department. They were often the ones chosen as recipients for departmental awards. And, they were the ones most often selected for special assignments and transfers to high-prestige units such as detectives and the drug task force.

Officer Rousseau was somewhat bewildered by this. The law enforcement strategy worked for the cops, but it did not seem to work for the community. The dangerous intersection was still dangerous and he could see the harmful effect of this strategy on the lives of residents in Poor Neighbourhood. He could also see how this strategy reinforced biases and stereotypes which exacerbated already poor circumstances. So, he committed himself to finding out what really makes places safe.

Officer Rousseau read as much as he could of the research on neighbourhood safety. He spent hours and hours on his days off, perusing library databases for articles about the dynamics of safe places. This body of work clearly showed that *trust and cohesion among residents along with trust in the police* are strong defenses against crime. He could see now why the aggressive law enforcement had had such a harmful affect in Poor Neighbourhood.

Officer Rousseau had an idea. He would use the problem intersection as a reason to bring people from various groups together. He had to convince Captain Hume that this was a worthwhile commitment of resources. After all, there were shootings, robberies, burglaries, and other serious crimes throughout the district. Law enforcement agencies tend to prioritise crimes based on seriousness. Violent crimes are the most serious, followed by certain property crimes such as burglary. Traffic violations and traffic accidents are always a low priority. They are only important as a law enforcement tool, because they helped catch criminals who would otherwise go undetected.

Officer Rousseau was able to convince Captain Hume to try this approach. The police department hosted several meetings of representatives from the neighbourhoods and businesses surrounding the intersection. Officer Rousseau invited residents from Wealthy and Poor neighbourhoods and representatives from the finance, fast food, and service industries to meet and work together to define and solve the problem at the intersection. He also invited other city departments who had resources that might help, such as a traffic engineer. By all accounts, the group had a positive experience developing a plan to prevent traffic accidents. The plan included changing street directions and installing traffic arrows so that traffic no longer backed up when trying to turn eastbound on Wrong Street from Right Street. The plan was implemented immediately and it worked. It significantly reduced accidents at the intersection and it fostered stronger relationships across neighbourhoods. In addition, it connected residents of both neighbourhoods with the economic institutions in the area. It was clear during these meetings that the participants had mutual concerns and interests.

They were interdependent parts of a whole community whose well being was impacted by the success and failure of each part. They could see this more clearly as they worked on this common problem together.

New Insights from Captain David Hume

When Captain Hume discusses the plan for the intersection developed by the community group, he admits the following: "The enforcement strategy I employed for many years was really ineffective in solving the traffic accident problem at the intersection. When someone proposed a way to fix the problem by installing a green arrow, I thought this was a great idea. However, I resisted this solution because I could see how it would limit law enforcement in the intersection. Law enforcement had become an end in itself rather than a means to an end."

Captain Hume would continue: "Officer Rousseau helped me realise that the problems were deeper than the light at the intersection. Our law enforcement efforts had destroyed trust in the institution of policing and pitted residents against each other. I now recognise that public safety problems can be reasons to bring people together for the dual purpose of fixing the problems they are most concerned about and building relationships."

Officer Rousseau had helped Captain Hume see the structured nature of the problems in the intersection. Issuing a ticket to the driver of Vehicle B was not, in itself, a bias-motivated act. Officers were simply enforcing the law. However, over time, the patterned way residents of Poor Neighbourhood met with residents of Wealthy Neighbourhood in the intersection led to bias. It reinforced negative stereotypes about poverty and carelessness and thoughtlessness and individual responsibility (or lack thereof). Interestingly, Captain Hume could now see more clearly how the sum of unbiased traffic citations in a single intersection could lead to discriminatory results. Over his career, Captain Hume had been a good law enforcer. He had always dutifully complied with the policies and practices of the law enforcement profession. He was ethical in this regard and was simply doing his job. However, now Captain Hume was reflecting more critically on the law enforcement approach at the intersection and the harmful consequences it had had. Individually, the police officers were not to blame. It was the game they were playing that caused the problems. Using a sports analogy, Captain Hume would explain it this way: "If you were to ask a group of NFL executives how to reduce concussions in professional football, the responses might include things like better helmets, new procedures for kickoffs, better training and more thorough statistics. All of these things combined may lead to slight declines in the number of concussions, but they will never significantly reduce the problem. This is because the source of the problem is the game itself!" "Think about it," he would say. "The game's logic and reward structure requires aggressive hard-hitting collisions between supersized and super-strong individuals." Captain Hume would then compare this to the game of policing, with its heavy law enforcement focus, as a source of the harm. He would say, "Notice that I am not blaming police officers for the crime problem nor am I blaming the NFL players for the number of concussions. I am focusing specifically on the game they are playing." Captain Hume would say that the law enforcement game provides a logic for action and offers rewards and recognition for those who play the right way. The law enforcement game requires repeated hard-hitting collisions between people with great power disparities. These collisions create long lasting economic and social harm to individuals, families, and communities. And, it increases violence by the police and against them.

Now Captain Hume could clearly see how distrust between the police and Poor Neighbourhood exacerbated problems. Violence soared as residents settled disputes on their own. A high percentage of people in Poor Neighbourhood had warrants pending from the courts. This seemed in influence rates of hit and run accidents. It also allowed the police to search cars and to take a closer look for more violations. This served Captain Hume well over the years as a law enforcement officer, but he now could see how he had unwittingly contributed to the problem of violence and poverty in Poor Neighbourhood. With this new understanding, Captain Hume is teaching officers how to notice structural problems that are often the root of violence. He encourages officers to bring community members together to find solutions to these problems. This has resulted in stronger relationships in the community, increased safety for the police, and reduced levels of crime. He now recognises and rewards officers for creating these community outcomes rather than for simply police officer outputs, in terms of numbers of arrests and guns seized. His real-time crime center and CompStats meetings prioritise new metrics for success, including levels of trust and cohesion in the community, the resident's willingness to intervene to help other neighbours, and trust in the police. The police are now much safer and their careers seem to be far more rewarding.

Closing Comments

The allegory of the dangerous intersection provides a way to explore sacred beliefs that underlie the law enforcement approach to policing. The law enforcement approach often assumes the social problems originate with the individual. People make bad decisions when they violate the law and this causes harm to innocent people. The police often believe they can deter these bad decisions through detection, apprehension, and punishment. This, in significant part, is the *common sense* of the law enforcement approach. The depiction of the traffic accident in Fig. 15.1 shows what the police believe is most important. It is simply the two vehicles, A & B and the traffic lights. There is no need for more information than this, because this figure explains it all. It was a bad decision.

The allegory presents more information to demonstrate the actual nature of the problem. Since there are many accidents at this intersection, the "bad decision" explanation has limited utility. Here we begin to see the nature of social structure. Economic inequality places people in different situations. At the intersection, the drivers from Wealthy Neighbourhood have an advantage. Their life position sends them straight through the intersection. When a collision occurs, they are frequently in the right. It is just the opposite for drivers from Poor Neighbourhood. They have limited options, the best choice is often to turn left at the intersection. The reason for turning left is likely to be for economic opportunities in the food or service industries. Without an arrow to direct traffic, and with traffic backing up behind them, and with concerns for being late for work, the right decision appears to be to hurry through the intersection. This results in many traffic accidents.

The law enforcement approach, albeit with good intentions, does not alleviate the problem of traffic accidents. Instead, it has its own advantages and becomes an end in itself. Police officers benefit from the opportunity to stop, question, and search drivers. They make arrests, seize illegal guns and contraband, all of which gives them status in the department and law enforcement profession.

The allegory further explicates the deleterious effects of the law enforcement approach to disadvantaged groups. After decades of vigorous enforcement for minor traffic violations, the residents of Poor Neighbourhood hate the police. They do not trust them to do the right things, and so they administer their own form of justice, which is often violent. Pejorative references to "black on black" violence, is a benign form of prejudice. Instead of seeing the bigotry that causes poverty, unemployment, lack of education, and excessive interpersonal violence, the benign prejudice view explains inequality as the result of characteristics of the disadvantaged group itself (Levin & Nolan, 2017).

When Captain Hume finally sees the structured nature of the problem, he recognises how what appears as unbiased law enforcement can actually lead to discriminatory outcomes. In the allegory, there is no reason to believe that drivers from Poor Neighbourhood commit more traffic violations than those from Wealthy Neighbourhood. However, residents of Poor Neighbourhood end up in the court system at a much higher rate. This highlights how interactions may seem unbiased but within a system of inequality and structured disadvantage, they contribute to discriminatory outcomes. This is the nature of structural problems. They set in motion patterns of action that might seem unbiased at the individual transaction level, but overall they discriminate because of economic and social advantages or disadvantages, the structured way we meet each other and the police, and the habits of mind based on sacred beliefs that are never challenged.

The allegory of the dangerous intersection enables us to see what police reform could look like IF the focus would shift from law enforcement outputs to safe community outcomes (Chapter 5). Working with residents on the problems of most concern to the community will enable officers to know and understand the nature of local problems. It will also help them build trusting relationships in the community that will keep both the police and community safer.

References

Levenson, E., & Cooper, A. (2020, June 29). Ex-Minneapolis police officers charged in George Floyd's killing appear in court. CNN. Retrieved from https://www.cnn.com/2020/06/29/us/george-floyd-officers-chauvin-court/index.html.

Levin, J., & Nolan, J. (2017). *The violence of hate; understanding harmful forms of bias and bigotry* (4th ed.). New York: Rowman & Littlefield.

Vitale, A. S. (2017). *The end of policing*. New York: Verso.

16

Conclusions and Future Directions in Policing

James J. Nolan, Timothy Parsons, and Frank Crispino

Introduction

When we first talked about writing this book together, we believed that this LEOP group,[1] whose members were experienced law enforcement officials from Europe and North America, many of whom had since gone on to earn advanced academic degrees and were now teaching at major universities or at national police academies, would be well suited to write a book outlining a *consensus* way forward for police reform. Even though we were from different countries located in different regions of the world,

[1]LEOP is explained in the preface of this book. It was a programme of training for law enforcement officers on the topic of hate crime sponsored by the OSCE Office for Democratic Institutions and Human Rights (ODIHR). The editors and some of the chapter authors were part of the team that developed and delivered the training.

J. J. Nolan (✉)
Department of Sociology and Anthropology, West Virginia University, Morgantown, WV, USA
e-mail: jim.nolan@mail.wvu.edu

J. J. Nolan et al. (eds.), *Policing in an Age of Reform*,
Palgrave's Critical Policing Studies,
https://doi.org/10.1007/978-3-030-56765-1_16

we shared the common experience of police service, and our ideas seemed to coalesce around improving the police profession. However, as we have been collaborating on the book over the past year or so, both writing our own contributions and reading and editing the work of other chapter authors, we recognised more clearly the complexity of our task and the nuance in our perspectives. In fact, when we talked about the specifics of police reform it was not always clear that we were actually talking about the same thing.

This insight sparked a need to delineate two primary types of police reform, one which focuses on the *methods* and craft of policing, and the other which focuses on the law enforcement *mandate* itself. From these two types of reform, four perspectives emerge: maintaining, retrofitting, coopting, and transforming (Chapter 1).

Maintaining means to keep both the existing methods and mandate, as the standards of law enforcement are accepted and fixed, and police reform refers only to helping police departments meet them. Their aim at meeting professional standards often does not require changes to the methods or mandate of the profession. The Commission on Accreditation for Law Enforcement (CALEA) in the United States work from this perspective. CALEA (https://www.calea.org/) is a credentialing authority established through cooperation of major police organisations to help police departments meet established professional standards. *Retrofitting* means to change methods but keep the mandate. It fully accepts the long-established police mandate but recognises the need to add new methods and technologies, especially to deal with changing crime types in a rapidly evolving world. Evidence-based policing provides an example of this perspective, as it focuses on the testing of new strategies to

T. Parsons
School of Justice Studies, Liverpool John Moores University, Liverpool, UK
e-mail: t.f.parsons@ljmu.ac.uk

F. Crispino
Department of Chemistry, Biochemistry, Université Du Québec à Trois-Rivière, Québec, QC, Canada
e-mail: frank.crispino@uqtr.ca

see whether they work in an otherwise dependable law enforcement machine. *Coopting* and *transforming* go one step further challenging the basic assumptions about crime and criminality that underlie the law enforcement approach. They seek to change the police mandate while using some of the old methods while developing and testing new ones.

These four general perspectives on police reform—maintaining, retrofitting, coopting and transforming—were implied throughout this book. In Chapter 2, Nolan, Hinkle and Molnar applied a sociological perspective to explicate ways the *status quo* in policing is maintained and reproduced. Then, Parsons (Chapter 3) described the difficulties reformers have had in recent decades in overcoming these forces *against* change, whilst Olisa (Chapter 4) took a wide-ranging look at the style of policing in Britain. Lambert (Chapter 6) presented the thorny dilemmas created (and experienced) by police reformers who are trying to do the right things. He used hate crime policing in the UK as an example. Then Parsons (Chapter 7) used the contemporary problem of terrorism and radicalisation to show why the police, under a crime control mandate, must be able to adapt, i.e. *retrofitting* new strategies to the traditional police organisation. He explained how organisations and institutions exogenous to the police add complexity to this task. Petković (Chapter 10) also dealt with added complexities and new problems in contemporary policing through a strategy of partnership building with civil society organisations. She argued that these partnerships improve the ability of the police to fulfil its traditional crime control mandate using anti-discrimination laws as an example. Similarly, Crispino et al. (Chapter 8) explored how advances in forensic science can be *retrofitted* to improve the effectiveness of the police in fulfilling their mission (e.g. threat identification and resource allocations) but warns that this will require an improved understanding of forensic science by police managers. In addition, social networks could help identify criminal offenders (Chapter 13), offering new tools to reform policing within the professional law enforcement frame. Interestingly, Ribaux, et al. (Chapter 11) see forensic science as having the potential to *transform* policing. Where forensic scientists have traditionally been viewed as supporting the justice endeavour, these authors want to flip things. They claim the rapid and expansive developments in forensic science should drive police reforms in ways yet to be realised. Nolan and Hinkle (Chapters 5 and 12), also approached police reform from the *coopting* and *transforming* perspectives by offering a neighbourhood dynamics approach to policing.

Regardless of the perspective or approach to police reform, police administrators must plan for change. Brown (Chapter 9) explores the critical issues related to performance measures. He explains the steps in the process of planning for organisational change and measuring police performance along the way. Finally, Nolan, Parsons, Crispino (Chapter 14) explore the critical issues related to the ethics of policing in an era of reform. By asking the question "What does it mean to do the right thing?" it turns out that perspective matters!

Doxa prevents us from challenging the police mandate and therefore "maintaining" and "retrofitting" exist. Ideological thinking also explains why these two perspectives occur. Utopian thinking explains "coopting" and transforming. Self interest makes us want our truth to be *the* truth. This is why we don't agree and the sum of our insights don't equal the truth (Chapter 2).

At the time of writing (June 2020), the book's editors and co-authors observe new calls for major reform of the police in the United States following the death of George Floyd in Minnesota. These calls for reform are being echoed in the United Kingdom as well. The British Government with a secure parliamentary majority has proposed establishing a cross-government commission to examine a whole raft of issues affecting citizens from black and visible ethnic minority communities. These of course include treatment of people within and by the criminal justice system and the police. Critics have condemned this initiative pointing out that numerous working groups and inquiries have already examined these issues at length and their conclusions and recommendations have often been ignored by ministers. In the United States, with a presidential election in November, the future scope and appetite for police reform is at present, far from clear. In France too there have been protests and confrontations between the public and the police, even though the political structures and culture are quite different to that found in the Anglosphere. Although the sitting president often appears politically beleaguered presidential elections in France are not due for another two years.

As editors and authors of this book we continue to hope that a significant and sustained era of police reform in Britain, France and the USA may beckon. In this book, we have identified several paths along which such reforms could proceed. We have attempted to honestly examine the various possibilities and the many considerations—political, structural and social—that may affect a reform agenda. We sincerely hope that something different to the status quo emerges, but realise that serious reform requires strong and visionary political leadership, public support, public money and a willingness to accept short-term disruption and a possible drop in service provision whilst new structures and procedures become established. Ultimately, the impetus for any agenda for police reform must come from a range of different stakeholders that include citizens from across all communities and police officers themselves.

Index

J. J. Nolan et al. (eds.), *Policing in an Age of Reform*, Palgrave's Critical Policing Studies,
https://doi.org/10.1007/978-3-030-56765-1

The manufacturer's authorised representative in the EU is Springer Nature Customer Service Centre GmbH, Europaplatz 3, 69115 Heidelberg, Germany. If you have any concerns regarding our products, please contact ProductSafety@springernature.com

Printed and bound by CPI Group (UK) Ltd, Croydon, CR0 4YY
30/09/2026
02225451-0011